ALL SAINTS

THE HISTORY, PEOPLE, PLACES

ALL SAINTS

THE HISTORY, PEOPLE, PLACES

CLIVE HOLES DEREK MILLS

DEDICATIONS

Clive Holes:

To my mother, All Saints born and bred, and my father, All Saints by adoption, and to All Saints itself, for giving me a wonderful start in life.

Derek Mills:

To Mom and Dad, and all the gifted teachers at All Saints School, 1954-1960

CONTENTS

INTRODUCTION

In 2020, two ex-pupils of All Saints Primary School met up after a gap of 60 years. Between watching matches at Molineux and enjoying a few beers at hostelries like The Great Western, an idea to write a book in celebration of All Saints took root: for one of them his birthplace, for both the start of their educational odyssey.

Of course, there is often a lot of rose-tinted nostalgia on display, along with curiosity about what ever happened to so-and-so and tales of years gone by. That is how this book first took shape - as a set of reminiscences about All Saints School and what happened there: its teachers, its sports teams, its choir and dancing teams, as the authors remembered them from their own days at the school in the mid-1950s. But soon it broadened its scope to encompass All Saints Church, St Joseph's Secondary School, the Royal Hospital and the whole All Saints neighbourhood - its history, its industries, its society, the war years, immigration in the post war period - and its modern decline and (who knows) its future regeneration.

What had begun as a collection of very personal snippets relating to the authors' lives and families grew into a much broader account of the whole area based on the oral histories of people of different backgrounds who had lived in All Saints both before the authors were born and after they had left the neighbourhood, backed up by research in the City Archives, school log books, local and national newspapers and national census data.

Throughout the book, we have tried to present an honest picture of how All Saints was and is, as witnessed by those who lived there at various periods in its history. We have uncovered amusing and uplifting stories but also unpleasant and uncomfortable, even sordid facts. We have not hesitated to include these in the narrative. All Saints was never all maypole dancing and smiling children posing for the camera: poverty, unemployment and the social consequences that went with it - crime, prostitution and drug taking - have featured in its distant history, as well as the more recent past.

We have described it as we think it was, warts and all. That said, the authors were lucky to have grown up in the area at a time of full employment, social cohesion, and a properly funded educational and health service. Now in our early 70s, we both look back on growing up there as the firm foundation on which we built our subsequent lives.

Thanks for everything, All Saints! This is our tribute to you.

A MAP OF ALL SAINTS

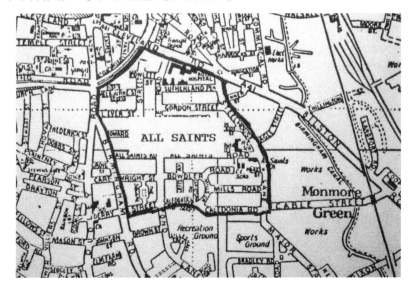

The black line on the 1980s map above shows the boundary of the All Saints neighbourhood, just south of the city centre. We acknowledge that some may disagree with the inclusion or exclusion of certain streets.

(Map courtesy of Barnardo's).

Clive Holes, Derek Mills

1

ALL SAINTS: 1775 -1842

Some sense of the early history of the All Saints area in Wolverhampton can be gained from looking at the series of maps published from 1577 onwards.

The 1750 map by Isaac Taylor focused on the township and provided no insight into its surrounding areas. In contrast, the 1775 map of the County of Stafford by William Yates provided far more detail beyond the town centre.

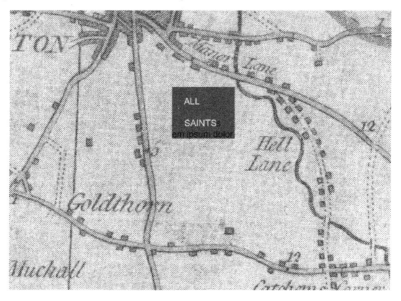

A Section of the 1775 map by William Yates showing the approximate location of All Saints. (W-ton Archives).

In the absence of roads and settlements, one can only estimate where the parish of All Saints would become established in the future.

Beyond the town centre, the countryside is underpopulated with few roads or buildings. What is now known as the

Dudley Road makes its way towards the settlement of Goldthorn. To the east an empty expanse of land extends across to the Birmingham Canal, snaking its way south, and Manor Lane, the present Bilston Road. Branching off is Hell Lane, now known as Ettingshall Road and surprisingly well populated.

Wolverhampton's Tithe map below, from 1842, reveals little change in the intervening years. (Cleveland) Road and Steelhouse Lane (barely legible) are two notable additions to the network of roads. The Union Poor House (Workhouse), with its distinctive shape, and the Eagle Foundry, alongside the canal, make up the two most prominent buildings.

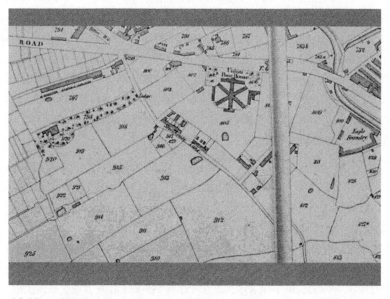

1842 Wolverhampton Tithe Map (courtesy of Wolverhampton Archives) with the individual plots of land numbered.

An advert from 1830 lists several of the items manufactured at the Eagle Foundry: light and heavy edge tools such as spades, shovels and plantation hoes. The business was established around 1824 by John Parsons and still described on the 1841 Census as 'Parsons Works'. Wolverhampton, at the time, was one of the centres of the edge tool trade.

Housing is restricted to a short section of Steelhouse Lane and the land around Sutherland Place and Portland Place. The 1841 Census listed 45 households in Steelhouse Lane. Mining was the dominant occupation among the population of 234 residents, with 35 miners living in Steelhouse Lane and 21 of the households occupied by at least one miner. In contrast, only one miner lived among the 160 residents in Portland Place.

Further to the west, Dudley Road and Green Lane (not labelled) go their separate ways. The map is probably more remarkable for the absence of the landmarks that we now associate with the area. The Royal Hospital is not to be seen (opened in 1849). Nor are All Saints Church and School, both completed by 1895. Some imagination is required to work out where Vicarage Road and All Saints Road would eventually be laid out.

The publication of Wolverhampton's 1842 Tithe map arose from an 1836 Act of Parliament. This survey of fields and buildings in a parish or township was carried out across the country to establish the rent payment due to the landowner by the tenant/occupier. The maps are particularly valuable for local historians as each plot of land was numbered. The Schedule document which accompanied the map revealed who owned each of the numbered plots, who occupied it and the nature of the property.

Using this information, we find that the land was almost completely owned by the Duke of Cleveland, e.g., Plot 915: Owner - Duke of Cleveland, Occupier - John Harding. Notable exceptions included the two plots, marked 805 and

806 to the east of Steelhouse Lane, owned by the Wolverhampton Poor Law Guardians. The site was occupied by the Union Poor House, designed by George Wilkinson in the uncommon 'St Andrew's Cross' plan. It was opened around 1837 at a cost of about £9,000 to accommodate 750 'inmates'. Workhouses were built across the country in response to the Poor Law Amendment Act of 1834. Their aim was to reduce the cost for ratepayers of looking after the poor people (paupers) in a parish. At the workhouses, paupers would be given accommodation, clothing and food in return for working. Described by some campaigners as 'prisons for the poor', workhouses were grim with basic facilities and manual labour intended to act as a deterrent to the able-bodied pauper. If an able-bodied man entered the workhouse, his whole family was expected to enter with him.

Another exception was Plot 798, the site of Cleveland House, to the west of Steelhouse Lane. The land, including a lodge and landscaped drive, was owned by the Perpetual Curate of Wolverhampton. The Cleveland House residence, described as a dignified late Georgian villa, was built for John Barker, a Justice of the Peace (J.P.) and a managing partner of Chillington Ironworks Company in Monmore Green.

The 1842 Tithe map also reveals the general layout. To the north-west, the land was agricultural. Below plots 910 and 912, south of what is now Caledonia Road, the area was industrial with coal pits, furnaces and brickworks.

The town itself had increased in population from just under 7,500 in 1750 to over 36,000 by 1841. The area we now know as the parish of All Saints had been little affected by this significant increase and remained a blank canvas for future development.

2

ALL SAINTS: 1842 - 1890

In 1849, there was a significant addition to the landscape around Steelhouse Lane and Cleveland Road. The first major hospital in Wolverhampton, the South Staffordshire General, opened in 1849 in Cleveland Road, replacing the dispensary in Queen Street in the town centre. It was designed by Edward Banks in the classical style and built between 1846 and 1849 on land acquired from Henry Vane, 2nd Duke of Cleveland.

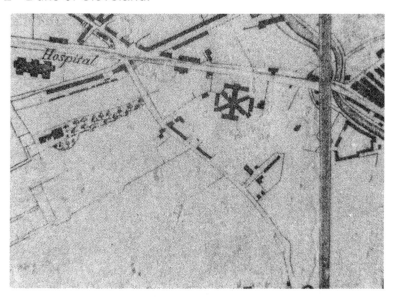

1850 Wolverhampton map (courtesy of Wolverhampton Archives) showing the landscape around All Saints.

Despite sporadic outbreaks of lethal diseases like cholera and smallpox, the hospital was unwilling to admit anyone with an infectious disease and reluctantly set up temporary smallpox accommodation in the basement of one of its wings. This was only on the understanding that the corporation would build a separate hospital for infectious diseases.

Following the construction of the hospital, a second lodge was constructed for Cleveland House on a newly created access track from Cleveland Road. The 1851 Census shows that the residence was still occupied by John Barker. He is now listed as married with four children. One can assume that the Chillington Ironworks Co. is flourishing as the household includes six servants. His social status has risen and as well as being described as an ironmaster, the census reveals he is High Sheriff of Staffordshire, Deputy Lieutenant of the County, a Borough magistrate and Alderman.

By 1851, the census records show that the town's population had continued to rise and had now reached 49,985.

To analyse the place of birth of residents in Steelhouse Lane, we looked at the data from that census for thirty adjoining households, randomly selected. 152 people were living in these thirty houses, or just over 5 per household. The figures are shown in Appendix 1.

So, whilst 84 (55%) had been born in Wolverhampton and the immediate vicinity, no less than 54 (35%) had been born in four neighbouring 'farming' counties, mainly Shropshire. There were only a handful of people who had moved from distant parts – Sheffield, West Wales and Stoke.

This strongly suggests that the huge increase in Wolverhampton's population was in large part fuelled by the migration of farm workers from nearby counties, seeking a better life as the industrialisation of Wolverhampton and the surrounding area took hold. This matched a national trend.

The type of work these migrants were doing fits this probable scenario. The jobs of most of the adult men living in these thirty households were manual and arduous, just like farm work: ten were 'coal miners', four were 'ironstone miners' and a large group described themselves as 'labourers' in various kinds of industrial settings: furnaces, brickworks, forges, ironworks, smithies. A number of their womenfolk had jobs as 'domestic servants'.

The housing which existed in and around Steelhouse Lane was privately owned, with the landlords providing rented accommodation to working class families. The Wolverhampton Chronicle and Staffordshire Advertiser of 30 November 1853 advertised the sale of two freehold dwelling houses and premises in Steelhouse Lane, near the junction with Cleveland Road. They were described as: "recently and substantially built, with good back premises and conveniences… The property produces a rental of £18 per annum and will prove a very eligible investment".

During the next decade, more private housing was built along the east side of Steelhouse Lane. An advert in the same paper in August 1868 describes the neighbourhood as consisting of 200 houses. It also mentions that "a great deal of small property was being erected near".

Wolverhampton, like many towns and cities, was severely affected by epidemics. In an eight-month period during 1863/64, over 1200 cases of smallpox were reported with 90 fatalities. Increasingly, the Union Workhouse between Jenner Street and Eagle Street took on the role of treating the physically ill. In response to these outbreaks, additional buildings including an infirmary and new infectious wards were added in 1867. Outbreaks of smallpox, cholera and scarlet fever followed in the early 1870s. Apart from sending paupers with smallpox to the Union Workhouse, Wolverhampton's provision for people with infectious diseases depended upon the limited goodwill of the South Staffordshire General Hospital.

During this period, the hospital was renamed the Wolverhampton and Staffordshire General Hospital. The 1871 Census shows it was staffed on the night of 2 April by one superintendent, one matron, just one surgeon and one physician, a team of four 'head' nurses and seven 'under' nurses with seven supporting staff including a cook and laundry maid. Ninety-seven patients were being treated.

The hospital and workhouse dominated the surroundings. To the west of Cleveland House, the area was occupied by allotment gardens (possibly commercial) while the rest of the area was a series of enclosed fields. Over the next thirty years, a major transformation would take place, changing the All Saints landscape for ever.

To the east, between Steelhouse Lane and the Birmingham Canal, pockets of industry appeared. The 1842 Tithe map showed only one factory in the vicinity, the Eagle Foundry. Adverts for the business in 1851 show it was now owned by William Wildsmith and Co. It continued to produce spades, hoes and other edge tools, and enjoyed a lucrative contract with Her Majesty's Navy.

By 1871, a line of factories, all involved in the iron industry, had also become established. Adjoining Eagle Street lay the Mitre Iron Works making metal roofing and galvanised fittings such as screws, nails, wire-netting and buckets. This was part of the Gospel Oak Iron Company run by Francis North Clerk, a civil engineer who had moved to Wolverhampton from London around 1862. It was a well-regarded business with a stand at London's International Exhibition in 1862. In 1869, F. N. Clerk became a member of the Institution of Mechanical Engineers. He died in 1874.

Further south, the Monmoor Iron Works was founded around 1850 by Mr E.T. Wright and Mr David North. Positioned alongside the canal by Cable Street, it produced high quality iron plates and sheets. On the opposite side of Cable Street, the Victoria Works of Bayliss, Jones and Bayliss was already well established, manufacturing a wide range of items including railings, gates, ornamental ironwork and chains for mining and shipping. The factory dated back to 1826 when William Bayliss, while still in his early twenties, had saved sufficient money from working at his father's blacksmith shop to buy a site on old colliery land.

Despite the developing industrialisation of the All Saints and Monmore Green neighbourhoods, the All Saints School logbook entry in 1866 refers to the presence of clean 'country' air which suggests that these establishments had not yet made a significant impact on the environment.

Close to the Wolverhampton and Staffordshire General Hospital in Cleveland Road, two prominent businesses became established. Baker's Boot and Shoe Manufactory, as it was formerly known, was positioned to the west of the hospital. The family business had been started in the town in 1850 by James Baker, manufacturing boots and footwear for the labouring classes. As the business grew, it expanded into producing stylish boots and shoes for ladies and gentlemen. The new premises which opened in 1868 comprised a traditional works layout with buildings set around a central courtyard. Unusually, the owner chose to live on the premises in the north-west corner. The 1871 Census records James Baker, originally from Princes End, Tipton, residing there with his wife, seven children, his grandmother and a domestic servant.

For over forty years the land on Cleveland Road, directly opposite the hospital, had been the site of the Tudor Works, a family-owned company, manufacturing coach and railway carriages. In 1880, the factory was acquired by Forder & Co's carriage making business, one of Wolverhampton's success stories. The firm was founded in 1864 by Frederick Forder and Mr Traves. In 1873, the company had won joint first prize in a competition run by the Society of Arts to find an improved design for the Hansom cab, a carriage which dominated the cobbled streets of Victorian Britain. By the end of the 1870s, the finest version is said to have been made by Forder's. The Prince of Wales, one of the patrons of the Society, granted Forder's his Royal Warrant, as did Queen Victoria. The company also built for the Duke of York.

Trading throughout the UK and abroad, they continued to win medals for their carriage designs. The success of their carriage-making business had put pressure on their town premises at the corner of Garrick Street and Bilston Street, hence the purchase of the Tudor Works. A purpose-built factory was constructed on the site to accommodate increased production of their carriages.

Further significant changes were taking place to the south of Cleveland House. In 1865, a school and a mission church were set up in Steelhouse Lane. They occupied two rooms side by side in a building, formerly used as a brickkiln, on land originally used as a pigsty. The mission church was replaced by a permanent building, consecrated in 1879. The school was not replaced until 1888 by a building, adjacent to the new church, for girls and infants. These two institutions were to become a focal point of the neighbourhood for generations of residents from All Saints and beyond. Further details about their history are provided in Chapter 5.

Up to the 1880s, most housing was restricted to the east side of Steelhouse Lane alongside the Union Workhouse. This was to change. Land between Cleveland House and All

Saints Church was sold off by the Duke of Cleveland, initially to Wolverhampton Borough Council. Housing plots in new roads such as Gordon Street were then sold to private developers like V. Stratton Esq and Mr J.H. Shepherd.

The plan below shows a series of parallel roads south of Sutherland Place: Gordon Street, Dartmouth Street, Granville Street, Adelaide Street, Gower Street and finally All Saints Road, adjacent to the church and school. Maxwell Road, for whatever reason, was not shown or named.

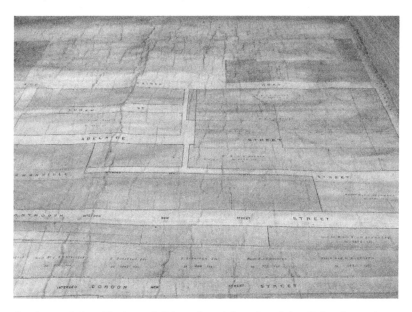

A plan of the Duke of Cleveland land sold off for housing in the 1880s with All Saints Road towards the top of the picture (courtesy of Wolverhampton Archives).

Progress with the All Saints housing development is revealed below by the Ordnance Survey map of Wolverhampton published in 1888. It shows the appearance of new roads and housing on the land sold off by the Duke of Cleveland. The first homes were built along Dartmouth

Street and Granville Street, extending westwards from Steelhouse Lane.

Between Sutherland Place and Dartmouth Street, Cleveland House continued to provide an oasis of rural calm with its landscaped gardens and private drive to Steelhouse Lane.

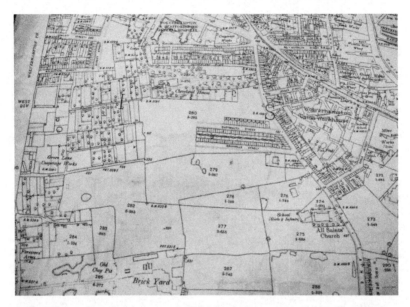

The new church and school buildings are adjacent to Steelhouse Lane, towards the bottom of the map (courtesy of Wolverhampton Archives).

Further south of All Saints Church, land belonging to the Duke of Cleveland was still unoccupied. This would remain the case for the next forty years.

3

EARLY INDUSTRY

The 1891 Census showed Wolverhampton's population had increased from 49,985 in 1851 to 81,620.

The global economic depression which started in 1873 afflicted Wolverhampton's industries for the next two decades. During this period, prominent factories like Chillington Ironworks and the Chubb Lock Works were forced to close.

By the early 1890s, the economy had recovered much of its vitality. There was a rapid growth in industries such as brass and tube trades, bicycle manufacture and electrical engineering. Monmore Iron Works, founded by Mr. E.T. Wright and Mr. David North, was purchased in 1896 by Bayliss, Jones and Bayliss. Following its amalgamation, the Monmore Iron Works expanded, occupying more space to the west and north alongside Steelhouse Lane.

Not all businesses were coping so well. The Engineer newspaper of 19 March 1897 announced: "The machinery, plant, etc, of the Mitre Galvanising Works, Wolverhampton, are to be brought under the hammer, by order of the receivers of Gospel Oak Iron Company, which will close what was once one of the most prosperous concerns in the trade."

In June 1897, the country celebrated the Golden Jubilee of the reign of Queen Victoria. In Wolverhampton, an illustrated review of businesses in the town was published. In terms of size and manufacturing importance, Wolverhampton was said to hold a premier position among the chief towns of Staffordshire. The review declared that business was booming and the town was flourishing. A wide range of factories and retailers was listed including several businesses operating in the All Saints neighbourhood. They included:

- John Barratt, Wulfruna Cycle Works, Melbourne Street;
- Beaumont Cycle Company, Cleveland Road and Vane Street;
- M. Bagnall, "Winona" Cycles and Cycle Fittings in Cable Street.

Cycling in the 1880s was based around the 'penny- farthing': expensive, dangerous and the preserve of wealthy young men. The invention of the 'safety bicycle' with smaller wheels, chain driven transmission and pneumatic tyres led to a bicycle boom. In 1891, 643 workers in the town were employed in the cycle trade, 5.6% of the total employment. The Wolverhampton Red Book of 1892 listed 33 cycle manufacturers with another 7 businesses involved in cycle accessories.

The Olympic Cycle Works opened in the early 1880s in Green Lane (the original name for the Birmingham Road) and in 1896 it moved to Granville Street. It was owned by a Cornishman, Frank Parkyn who introduced the latest machinery and manufacturing techniques at the works. By 1900, Frank had started to build motorised cycles and at the 1902 National Cycle Show he displayed a motorcycle with a 2hp engine. Future development focused on motorcycles carrying the Olympic brand name but by 1923 sales were low and the business disappeared. The name Parkyn lives on as the name of a street next to the church.

Other local businesses mentioned in the review were:

- J. Nicholls and Sons, Cleveland Wood Turning and Sawmills, All Saints Road;

- Blenkin and Ward, Cleveland Printing Works, Cleveland Road;
- George Cave and Son, Builders and Contractors, Raby Street and Powlett Street;
- T. J. Cooke and Son, Brassfounders, Cleveland Road, at the junction of Raby Street;
- Reade Brothers and Company, Limited, druggist and manufacturing chemists, Cleveland Road.

The street, behind All Saints Church, which carries the name of the gentleman who set up a successful cycle and motorcycle business in Granville Street.

For much of the 19th century, the two Reade brothers ran a successful business in the town centre producing varnishes and patent medicines. Following a split in the partnership in 1879, Thomas took on the business of wholesale and retail druggist and manufacturing chemist.

In 1894, he moved into premises in Cleveland Road purchased from Forder and Co. Ltd., the coachbuilders who were experiencing financial problems. In the same year,

Reade Brothers became a limited company. Over the next 40 years, it developed into a genuine family concern with sons and grandsons joining the business. During this period, the company continued to produce a wide range of patent medicines such as Indian Cerate, a skin ointment; Chest Balsam for coughs, colds and asthma and Egyptian Salve for sores and burns. In 1919, it was advertising an influenza powder to combat the Spanish flu pandemic that broke out in 1918 and killed millions worldwide.

The founder, Thomas Reade, retired in 1930, leaving the company in the capable hands of his son, Charles.

Baker's Shoe Factory in 2020, showing the 1900 extension at the back of the premises.

Nearby, James Baker & Sons Ltd, at the junction of Cleveland Road, Vicarage Road and Powlett Street, was another thriving business. By 1897 it was manufacturing 341,000 pairs of boots and shoes each year. Around 1900, to cope with the increased demand for their products, a major extension at the back of the factory was built.

Vicarage Road was the location for an eclectic mix of small businesses advertised in local and national newspapers:

- Mr Albert H. Clarke, available for dramas or sketches, 14, Vicarage Road, July 1906;
- The Midland Institute of Science, 51, Vicarage Road. Magnetism, Hypnotic healing, Correspondence lessons. February 1903;
- Robert Henry Lowe, MPS, Lowe's Pills, Chemist, 52, Vicarage Road. Sept. 1916.

R. H. Lowe, a Member of the Pharmaceutical Society (MPS), had moved his premises to 52, Vicarage Road from 330, Bilston Road in the early 1900s.

The Society was formed in 1841 'to increase the respectability of chemists and druggists'. Examinations were introduced after 1868: a major one leading to a qualification as a pharmaceutical chemist, a minor one to qualify as a druggist and chemist. By 1898 both groups of chemists were eligible to gain membership of the society.

Like Reade Brothers in Cleveland Road, Mr Lowe will have manufactured and sold his own patent medicines. Papers such as the Dudley Chronicle advertised the sale of Lowe's Pills, 'the noted family medicine', for afflictions including colds, rheumatism and lumbago.

By coincidence, 52, Vicarage Road had been the home in 1911 of another gentleman heavily involved, like Frank Parkyn, in Wolverhampton's blossoming motor industry.

On the day of the 1911 Census, John Thomas Ireland was living with his family at that house, the home of his wife's widowed mother. A motor and electrical engineer by trade, he had already set up his own garage business in Pipers Row. He relocated the business, now known as J.T. Ireland & Co. to Cleveland Road. Following financial difficulties, the business was purchased in 1914 by Wolverhampton Motor Services with John appointed as manager. The garage on the corner of Raby Street, was close to the new family home at 3, Raby Street.

As well as managing the car business, John pursued other motoring ventures producing, for example, a range of motorcycles in the early 1920s under the brand name of 'Bluebird'.

By the start of the 1930s, John Ireland was a well-respected member of Wolverhampton society: a Freemason, Rotarian and secretary to a Business and Sportsmen's Committee that organised the end of season dinner for Wolverhampton Wanderers F.C. in 1931.

John stayed with the firm until 1931 when he opened the 'John Ireland' car showroom and garage in Bilston Street. Following his death in 1932, John was described in his obituary in the Birmingham Gazette as "a well-known figure in Wolverhampton's motoring circles..." He had been vice-president of the Motor Traders Association and was often called by the police as a technical expert in motor cases.

His son, John Richard Ireland, born in 1907, attended the local school, All Saints Infants School, before being admitted to All Saints Boys School in 1915. John followed his father into the family business, eventually taking charge of the car showroom in Bilston Street, near to the Clifton cinema. Adjacent to the showroom, a die casting factory also carried the family name. Both were demolished in the early '80s as part of a major redevelopment to make way for the new police station and ring road.

If the name John (Richard) Ireland rings any bells, you are probably a knowledgeable fan of Wolverhampton Wanderers - John was the club's chairman during the '60s and '70s. He is remembered affectionately by players of that era both for his camera which he used endlessly on club tours and his cheeriness. Dave Wagstaffe, the gifted Wolves winger, is quoted as saying that on trips abroad: "He would not go to bed without a rendition of Molly Malone, to which we all sang along".

In contrast to his widespread popularity amongst the players, fans will have mixed memories. Best remembered by some for the new stand that was named after him in 1979, and never forgiven by many older ones for the brutal sacking in 1964 of Stan Cullis, acknowledged by most supporters as the club's greatest manager.

John died in 1984 in Spain. In 2003, the stand was renamed the Steve Bull Stand. While many felt it was a fitting tribute to the club's record goal scorer, it was a decision greeted with shock, disbelief and anger by John's family.

Opposite Baker's Shoe Factory in Cleveland Road, on land that had been part of the Duke of Cleveland's estate, the depot for Wolverhampton Corporation Transport opened in 1902. Horse-driven trams owned by Wolverhampton Tramways Company had provided transport around the town since 1878.

From 1902, Wolverhampton became one of four towns to use an electrification system for its trams, choosing to use a surface contact system instead of overhead wiring and poles. It was not until 1921 that routes were converted to overhead wires and trams began to be replaced by trolley buses. Services extended out of the town to Staffordshire villages like Pattingham and Cheslyn Hay.

Not all the businesses in the neighbourhood were thriving. The 1914 Ordnance Survey map indicated little change in the physical landscape but clear evidence that the industrial landscape was undergoing a transformation.

Many of the brickworks had disappeared from the map and several other manufacturing works such as Green Lane Cooperage, Mitre Iron Works, and Eagle Edge Tool Works were now labelled as 'disused'. Some sites became occupied by other businesses. By 1918, Gaunt and Hickman Ltd., the owners of British Oil Works, had moved to the Eagle Edge Tool Works site. Established in 1848, in the Horseley Fields area, it was one of the first companies in the country to produce oil and grease.

Even Bayliss, Jones and Bayliss (BJB) was unable to maintain its independence. In the early 1920s, sales were falling, particularly to the railway companies. In 1922 Guest, Keen and Nettlefolds (GKN) bought up the company. Although it was now a subsidiary, the company kept its name.

4

HOUSING: 1890 - 1930

PRE-THE GREAT WAR

We have seen in chapter 2 that the sale of land belonging to the 4th Duke of Cleveland was to bring about a major change in the landscape of All Saints.

The 1891 Census confirms that the first phase of housing between Cleveland Road and All Saints Church was almost complete. 64 dwellings, for example, made up the houses and courts of Gordon Street.

Living at No. 47 was Mr William Taylor, Derek Mills' 2nd great grandfather, with his wife, Mary, three children, one grandchild and two lodgers. A large household in what would have been a small dwelling. William worked as a baker, possibly as an assistant to someone like Mr. A. Pursehouse, a bakery owner in Steelhouse Lane. William's family will have been able to make use of other shops nearby with a butcher, fruiterer, grocer and a newsagent all listed in the trade directory. His neighbours were working in the shoemaking, edge tool, coach building and ironworks industries, reflecting the diverse range of factories on their doorstep.

The 1895 map below shows that a series of parallel roads north of All Saints Road were now complete. A new road, Vicarage Road, extended from Cleveland Road to All Saints Road. Also evident were the tramways on Cleveland Road and Bilston Street, represented by the thick dark lines.

Over the next 40 years, the expanse of open fields between Steelhouse Lane and Green Lane, to the west, would be replaced by three more waves of housing development that would change the landscape of the parish of All Saints.

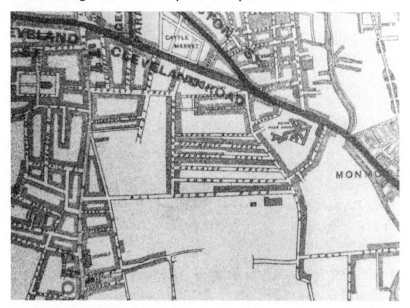

John Steen's 1895 map showing new roads laid out on the Duke of Cleveland's land. (Wolverhampton Archives).

WHAT DO WE KNOW ABOUT THE NEW RESIDENTS OF ALL SAINTS?

PLACE OF BIRTH

To give a snapshot of All Saints, we have examined the census data from 1891, 1901 and 1911. The data cannot be taken to be completely accurate. Mistakes were made by enumerators and residents completing the forms. Some residents may have absented themselves for political reasons, e.g., suffragettes or for other motives. However, despite these drawbacks, the census data give us a unique and invaluable picture of the basic social profile of the population of All Saints at the turn of the 20th century.

For the 'place of birth', information was obtained from only ten terraced houses, No. 78-87, on the north side of All Saints Road. A very small sample, but not, to judge from an examination of many pages of other census data, an unrepresentative one.

The raw data for our sample of ten houses are given in Appendix 2. The great majority were born in Wolverhampton: 76% of the 1901 Census, and 70% of the 1911 one. If those born within 15 miles of Wolverhampton are included, the figures for the 'locally born' rise to 84% and 93% respectively. The smaller group of 29 (5 houses) from the 1891 census is shown for comparison, and the pattern is similar: 55% born in Wolverhampton, and a whopping 96% born in or within 15 miles.

It looks as if the expansion of the population of All Saints during the late 19th/ early 20th century was being fed by incomers from other parts of Wolverhampton and its surrounding areas. A marked contrast with the situation in 1851 where significant numbers of families and individuals moved into Steelhouse Lane from farming villages in neighbouring counties.

FAMILY SIZE

At the time of the 1891 Census, when only five houses had been built in All Saints Road, twenty-nine people were living there, with one housing a family of nine. Considering the small size of these houses, one wonders what it must have been like for this family of eight adults, many of them doing hard manual work. Did they eat in shifts? And what were the sleeping arrangements?

The table below shows the average number of individuals per household, using the 1891, 1901 and 1911 Census data.

1891	5.8
1901	5.7
1911	4.4

By 1911, the average household size had fallen to 4.4 per house, and the average age to 41.7 years.

There seems to have been a rapid turnover in the population: in 1911, only three of the ten houses selected for this study were occupied by the same families as in 1901. Moreover, the ages of the 'heads' of the seven newly arrived families were in every case younger than those they replaced. This seems to suggest that younger families were moving into what was then a relatively newly developed area of Wolverhampton. Better housing and employment opportunities in the adjoining factories and the presence of a school were probably the main contributory factors.

EMPLOYMENT

Over the course of the 19th century, the industrialisation of Wolverhampton passed through several phases. During the first half of that century, mining, principally of coal and ironstone, attracted huge numbers to the east side of the town. But the raw materials of the area became depleted and the mining boom did not last.

In chapters 2 and 3 we have seen how mining was replaced by the mass production of metal products for both industrial and domestic use. The wealth and expertise produced by this eventually led to a third phase of specialist toolmaking, bicycle production and, eventually, precision automotive engineering. The production of fine quality consumer products was not far behind.

The data on employment from these ten houses (Appendix 3) provides a snapshot of some of these changes. Despite the small sample size, what is striking about the occupations in this chart is:

- the absence of mining as an occupation going back to the 1901 Census (also true for the 1891 Census);
- the continuing importance of heavy iron- and steel-based manufacturing (also true for the 1891 Census);
- the disappearance of bicycle manufacturing jobs in 1911, and the appearance of jobs in automotive engineering production;
- the increase in toolmaking jobs in 1911;
- the increase in boot-making/fitting in 1911.

The data reflected the employment opportunities on the doorstep of the residents. To the east of All Saints, around Bilston Road, factories were producing iron and steel and manufacturing all kinds of iron and steel products. The shift away from bicycle manufacture, for which Wolverhampton was renowned in the late 19th century, to the manufacture of motorcycles (AJS), cars (Sunbeam) and engines (Villiers) was also in full swing by 1913, when Sunbeam were already producing 650 cars per year. These automotive companies were all based no more than half a mile from All Saints, just the other side of Dudley Road in the industrial back streets of Graiseley and Blakenhall. Another major employer, especially of nimble-fingered young women, was James Baker's boot factory in Cleveland Road.

THE INTRODUCTION OF COUNCIL HOUSING

While businesses may have been booming in towns like Wolverhampton, the appalling sanitary conditions experienced by workers living in rented dwellings, particularly in town centres, grew into an important political and social issue. Several Acts of Parliament were introduced in the second half of the 19th century to address the problem. Towards the end of the century the government intervened again and the Housing of the Working Classes Act of 1890 gave local authorities more responsibility for improving housing conditions, encouraging them to buy up available land and build houses for rent.

The first 'council' housing in the country was built in 1896 by London City Council at Bethnal Green. Council housing in Wolverhampton was launched in 1902 and represented the second wave of housing. This development was on the edge of All Saints on Green Lane (now known as Birmingham Road), near its junction with Cartwright Street. This land was also part of the Duke of Cleveland's estate, but, following his death in 1891, there were no legitimate offspring. The title became 'extinct' and a distant relative, Henry de Vere Vane, was declared the rightful heir with the title of Lord Barnard.

4,000 sq. yards of this land, now belonging to Lord Barnard, was sold to Wolverhampton Corporation for £550 (£665 per acre) and the contract was eventually given to a local builder, G. Cave & Son at an enhanced price of £5,068. Twelve and a half housing units were erected with each unit made up of four dwellings: two on the ground floor and two on the upper floor, creating a total of 50 cottage tenements. The Committee responsible for preparing this scheme was made permanent in 1904 as the Housing of the Working-Classes Committee. Despite this impressive start by Wolverhampton Borough Council, the next ten years were marked by inactivity, despite periodic pressure from central government.

The General Election of 1906 had resulted in a Liberal Party landslide victory. This led to a period of significant social reform. In 1909 the first old age pensions were paid to people over the age of 70. Labour Exchanges were set up in 1910 to help the unemployed find work. The National Insurance Act was passed in 1911 to provide sickness and unemployment benefit for all wage earners between the ages of sixteen and seventy. It was based on contributions from the state, employer and worker. As well as their benefit payments, workers received free medical attention and medicine.

POST-THE GREAT WAR

It was not until 1914 that another housing scheme, the third wave of housing, was put forward. This was in Cartwright Street, adjacent to the 1902 development and referred to as the Green Lane scheme. However, the start of The Great War (First World War) in August 1914 ended all house-building activity.

In November 1918, when victory was in sight, the Council passed a resolution to proceed with the Green Lane scheme, but the necessary finance was not initially authorised by the government. The delay was temporary. Lloyd George's 'Coalition Coupon' Government, elected in December 1918, set about an ambitious programme of post-war social reform, including a programme of subsidised local authority house building.

By the start of The Great War in 1914, council housing still represented only 1% of the country's housing stock. The Great War was labelled as "The war fought to end all wars" and, when it finished, Lloyd George spoke at the Grand Theatre, Wolverhampton of "homes fit for heroes to live in".

Many motives have been suggested for this policy. Some have claimed that going back to the same poor, overcrowded conditions might have triggered a civil revolution by servicemen returning home. A more transparent reason was the government's concern about the nation's health, highlighted by the poor physical condition of many men who had joined the army. A housing poster of the period declared: "You cannot expect to get an A1 population out of C3 homes." One tenth of the volunteers and conscripts were barred from active service because of poor health, including Derek's grandfather, James Mills.

To carry out these ambitious promises, the Housing and Town Planning Act of 1919, better known as the 'Addison Act', required each town to make a survey of housing needs and submit schemes to the Minister of Health. The 'Addison Act' gave local authorities financial subsidies to build houses for working-class families. The costs for each house would be shared between tenants, local rate payers and the Government Treasury. The Act came into force on 31 July 1919 with its aim to provide, within a three-year period, 500,000 'homes for heroes' nationwide.

Wolverhampton Corporation lost no time in implementing the Act. Four suitable sites, including Green Lane, had already been selected and acquired. In October of that year the Council approved an ambitious scheme in which 5,659 houses would be built by 1927 at an approximate cost of £6M. Their impressive programme started on the edge of All Saints at Cartwright Street. This scheme dated back to 1914 when a 3¼ acre site, adjacent to the first council houses built in Green Lane in 1902, was purchased. In July 1919, a tender from Parkinson and Sons (Blackpool) Ltd of £33,848 was approved for 49 dwellings.

On 6 November 1919, the Mayor of Wolverhampton, Mr. Alfred G. Jeffs, unlocked the first pair of houses erected at the site. At the ceremony, Councillor Hughes, the Acting Chairman of the Housing Committee, proudly announced that these were the first 'Addison Act' houses to be completed in England.

During the 1920s, this ambitious council housing scheme progressed. More than 3,900 council houses were built across the borough but the ambitious target, set in 1919, of 5,659 new houses by 1927 was not achieved.

It was not until 1929 that the area south of All Saints Road reaped the benefits of this programme of council housing, The Ministry of Health requested that local authorities build houses which would meet the needs of lower paid workers. The Council bought up a 9¼ acre site near All Saints Church. This piece of land fronting All Saints Road, Vicarage Road and Steelhouse Lane was purchased for £2,800 from Lord Barnard. 268 houses were planned "in an area where the erection of working-class dwellings was desirable". The housing development would include a new road from Derry Street down to Cable Street, a road which was later to be named as Caledonia Road.

Mills Crescent looking towards Bowdler Road: part of the 1930s housing development. The photo was taken in 2021.

This finished around 1932 and marked the last of the three waves of council house building in the All Saints area, prior to the outbreak of the Second World War. Most are still standing today in streets like Bowdler Road, Jeffs Avenue and Mills Crescent, as are the houses in Cartwright Street.

Over a period of 50 years, the All Saints neighbourhood had undergone major changes. A landscape, once dominated by enclosed fields and the factories and shops of Steelhouse Lane, was transformed. Large swathes of private and council housing and an assorted range of industrial and retail businesses now extended beyond the primary school and parish church, the focal points of the area. A stable, working class community that was to alter little in the next twenty years.

5

ALL SAINTS CHURCH AND SCHOOL

HISTORY: 1860 - 1890

The Wolverhampton Chronicle from August 1863 advertised the sale of a plot of land in Steelhouse Lane, describing it as being situated in "the midst of a populous and improving neighbourhood".

This view of an 'improving neighbourhood' would not have been shared by the Reverend Henry Hampton, vicar of St John's Church. At the time, Steelhouse Lane lay within the parish of St John's. A man of forthright opinions, Hampton recalled when "it was not really decent for a woman with any sense of propriety to walk down Steelhouse Lane". The Lane used to be full of dog-fighters, pigeon flyers and other rough characters.

His opinion was backed up by a grim Birmingham Daily Gazette report from 24 September 1867 on a murder in Steelhouse Lane. It paints, in unappealing detail, a bleak image of the area. Steelhouse Lane is described as "a long lane which ends in a collection of 'spoil-banks' and 'cinder-heaps' which disfigure what are still called 'fields' on the 'Black Country' side of Wolverhampton. It has a row of about eighty small four roomed tenements. Every eight or ten of these houses has a common yard at the back which is entered by a passage or 'entry'. Flying pigeons, discussing their relative merits, and drinking and quarrelling over them, are the chief characteristics of Sundays thereabouts".

Undeterred, Hampton was instrumental in setting up both a school and a mission church in Steelhouse Lane. He described the mission church, built at a cost of £300 and capable of accommodating 300 worshippers, as "essentially a poor man's church to provide for the miners and grimy ironworkers of Steelhouse Lane, Monmore Green and parts of Rough Hills".

ALL SAINTS SCHOOL

Amid this social deprivation, All Saints Mixed Infant School opened as a Church of England (C of E) school on 4 February 1865. The school logbook reveals that the 73 pupils, boys and girls aged between two and twelve, who attended on that first day "were in a shocking state of ignorance, ten only being able to read".

Schooling was not free, and attendance was affected by the employment situation in the neighbourhood. Very soon after the school opened, there was a dramatic drop in attendance when workers in the iron trade came out on strike. In August of 1865, the school logbook reported: "three of the most regular scholars left this week, the Wainwrights; they gave as the reason: poverty".

The first few years were not without incident. The school was closed on 30 November 1866 for the visit of Queen Victoria to the town. In January 1869, "some boys opened the classroom door and turned a donkey in". In May of the same year, "a policeman took one of the boys during the dinner hour for going into adjoining field and running after sheep". These last two passages from the school logbook reflect more rural surroundings than one might have expected. This is confirmed by a report on the school in 1866. "The situation of this school is good; the children are supplied with country air and the playground is good."

Pupils followed a curriculum based on the 3 R's: reading, writing and arithmetic. Pupil numbers quickly increased, and an 1868 inspection report praised the achievements of the younger pupils. It was less complimentary about the performance of the older scholars. The presence of pupils above the age for which infant school teaching methods were appropriate was causing concern. The inspector questioned whether it should continue to be considered an infant school and the grant to the school was reduced by a tenth.

Successive reports also raised this issue, recommending that the older boys should go to one of the town's new Board schools and a separate department for infants and girls should be established. These proposals were slowly adopted. By 1875, a report announced that "several big boys left and had gone to the Board school at Monmore Green". By 1888 the school had moved from its original, modest premises to a new building, next to the church, designated for girls and infants only.

ALL SAINTS CHURCH

The church flourished. Before too long the congregation at the mission church had risen to around 120, while the day and Sunday School attendance averaged 250 youngsters. The church and school occupied two rooms side by side in a building, formerly used as a brickkiln, on land used as a pigsty. It was clearly unsuitable for church purposes and Reverend Hampton was calling for its replacement by a permanent building. A design in the early gothic style by London architects T. Taylor Smith & G. F. Roper was approved in 1876.

A bazaar was held in May 1877 at the skating rink in Darlington Street to raise funds for the erection of the church. The Midland Counties Evening News of 16 May 1877 described a splendid event held over four days. The venue was decked out in bunting and plants, with eight stalls devoted to an eclectic range of goods for sale. Music was provided by the band of the Royal Marines. The event raised over £400.

Building was carried out by Highams between 1877 and 1879. It was consecrated as a Church of England place of worship by the Bishop of Lichfield, Dr Maclagan, on All Saints Day, 1 November 1879. The church eventually gained its independence as a parish church in July 1881 when All Saints became a separate ecclesiastical parish. Sadly, the inspiration behind both the church and school, the Reverend Henry Hampton, had died a year earlier.

ALL SAINTS CHURCH: 1891 - 1979

1891 saw the arrival of a new vicar, the Reverend John Warner. He had resigned as the senior curate at St Michael's Church, Brereton, to take up his post, succeeding the Reverend Oliver James Dunn, M.A. On 2 February, a tea and social party was held in the school and a large gathering of his new parishioners were there to welcome him. Over the next ten years, he was to play a significant role in the parish, building on the achievements of the Reverend Henry Hampton.

Following his arrival, an appeal was made to raise £2000 to build a chancel and this was picked up by The Lichfield Mercury of 3 July 1891. The newspaper reported that "through the poverty of the congregation, the church has remained over 14 years in its present incomplete state". It described a large parish with around 6,000 parishioners. By 1892 new plans had been submitted by local architect Frederick Beck to add a chancel, vestry, sacristy and side chapel. These were approved and constructed during 1892-93 by Willcock & Co. of Wolverhampton.

The new additions were consecrated on All Saints' Day 1892 with the foundation stone being laid by the Bishop of Lichfield. He is reported to have said: "There was a time when it would have been difficult to walk through the neighbourhood without being insulted. But we have today witnessing the ceremony at least a good humoured and not irreverent crowd."

Work continued up to full completion in 1895. On 13 July of that year, the east window in the Lady Chapel was dedicated to the memory of the Reverend Henry Hampton, the inspiration behind the school and church buildings in All Saints parish.

The Reverend J. Warner was a strong advocate of the Temperance Movement. This organisation had grown during the 19th century to address the problems created by excessive drinking, primarily by workers. The clergy became increasingly involved and the Church of England Temperance Society (CETS) was founded in 1872. He held a resolute belief that no parish was complete without temperance. It is not clear whether he initiated the movement in the All Saints community or whether it was already well established. However, by June 1893, the Bridgnorth Journal and South Shropshire Advertiser reported a bicycle ride to Bridgnorth by All Saints (Temperance Guild Club) Cycle Club.

His view on poverty was equally evident. In later years, Warner spoke of the many lessons he had acquired during his time at All Saints Church, in the heart of "a great black town". One such lesson was, "the great need of compassion and sympathy for the poor of Christ's Church".

By the time the Reverend J. Warner left in 1901, he had made an enormous impact on both the church and school communities. The Wellington Journal reported on a ceremony on 7 December at All Saints schoolroom when the parishioners assembled to say farewell to the Reverend Warner and Mrs Warner. Presentations were made from the Friendly Society, All Saints choir, the All Saints and Powlett Street Mothers Meetings, as well as the Wolverhampton and Staffordshire General Hospital, resulting from his role as chaplain to the hospital. The churchwarden, Mr John Nokes, spoke in eloquent terms of their sorrow and regret at his resignation and highlighted the vicar's involvement in enlarging and beautifying the church, the institution of a young men's club, but above all the erection of the "large and excellent day church schools built mainly owing to his strenuous efforts".

In 1901, the Reverend Henry Hanson Jevons took over the parish duties, having moved from the post of senior curate at Christ Church, Wolverhampton.

In September 1904, members of the All Saints branch of the Girls Friendly Society were invited to visit Moreton in Staffordshire by the Vicar and Mrs Gentles, a curate at All Saints from 1897 to July 1901. The party, described in the Wellington Journal as their old friends from the 'grand old parish' of All Saints, were accompanied by Mrs Florence Jevons, wife of the vicar of All Saints Church, and Miss Perry, the headmistress. They travelled to the vicarage by a three-horse char-a-banc. Although Moreton was a beautiful spot, the party from All Saints felt they loved their "dear All Saints with all the smoke and hard work they had to face". After evensong had been attended, a tour of inspection made and a few games of croquet enjoyed, they made their way home.

The Reverend Jevons may well have been involved in the creation of the All Saints Old Boys' football team from 1910, featured in the photograph below. It is probable that the team was a member of the Wolverhampton and District Church and Chapel League, formed in 1903, to "meet the needs of young men in the Wolverhampton area". All clubs and players were required to show evidence of direct connection with a place of worship. In 1928 it was renamed The Wolverhampton & District Amateur Football League. (Photo: Mrs Roper.)

Over the years the parishioners of All Saints have often shown their appreciation of the work carried out by the vicars. Plaques, paid for by donations, can be seen on display in the chancel.

Those shown in the photo below recognise the contributions made by Reverend John Warner and Florence Jevons, the wife of the Rev. Henry Jevons, to the parish of All Saints.

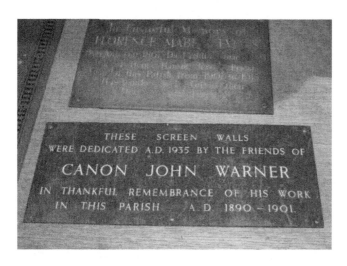

All Saints Church had a succession of vicars between 1879 and 1946.

J.W. Morison	1879-1882
Oliver James Dunn	1882-1891
John Warner	1891-1901
Henry H. Jevons	1901-1915
Henry C. A. Townsend	1915-1926
Graham W. Clitheroe	1926-1931
W.D. Boone	1931-1937
R.E. Smith	1939-1946

A glimpse into their backgrounds would sometimes reveal quite unexpected information. The Reverend Clitheroe, for example, was one of very few clergy to serve as a combatant in The Great War (First World War). He served with the Artists Rifles, a volunteer regiment which suffered one of the highest casualty rates.

When he arrived at All Saints in 1926, his six previous years had been spent, in total contrast, at a parish church in rural

Devon. Unruffled by these difficult circumstances, he devoted much of his time teaching the pupils at the All Saints schools. Mrs Clitheroe, in turn, organised a popular Women's Fellowship with a regular membership of over 80.

Indeed, the tenures of Father Townsend and Father Clitheroe are highlighted in the parish magazines as an especially happy time for the church community. A variety of activities were organised during this period, including tennis on the vicarage lawn, billiards in the vicarage cellars and annual trips in a lorry around the town to collect for the hospital.

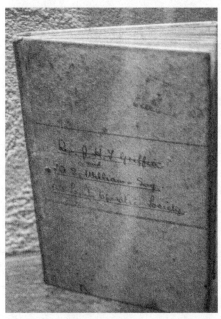

Several societies were well established. During Father Clitheroe's time, there was a popular Operatic Society. The book, shown above, with the minutes of the Society's meetings is on display in the chancel. Productions included 'The Dogs of Devon' and 'Pearl, the Fishermaiden', with no shortage of parishioners willing to fill the parts. The photo below (courtesy of Phil and Gill Collins) is believed to show the cast in costume for one of the Operatic Society's productions.

This rewarding time for everyone associated with the church was not to last. Inevitably, the fortunes of the church in the thirties reflected the major economic and social problems of the time. The Church Council was constantly worrying over money and debts, with the financial upkeep of the school creating particular concern. Fortunately, Father Boone's careful 'housekeeping' brought the annual deficit down to a manageable level. His diligence allowed his successor, Father Caiger, to focus on traditional ecclesiastical activities and an ambitious programme of parish visits and meetings. The workload, however, took its toll and the responsibility for looking after the parish during the war years was left to Father Smith when Father Caiger retired through ill-health in 1939.

Unfortunately, little is known about All Saints Church during World War 2. Following Father Caiger's resignation, Father

Smith arrived and remained during this period. According to Lyn Phillips' centenary pamphlet, the church "quietly went on being a great consolation to all during that long and difficult time". The men of All Saints were either serving in the armed forces, working in factories focused on the war effort or supporting the civil defence. Church activities consequently suffered. Services continued but a concession was eventually made for the black-out and Evensong was rescheduled for the afternoon!

Father Rundell took over in 1946 at a time of low attendances with an average number of 45 communicants. Despite his best efforts, worries about the future of the church escalated. Following his resignation, the Parochial Church Council (PCC) sent a letter to the Bishop expressing their deep concerns. It described a working-class parish increasingly reliant on "a small band of workers who organise such activities as the Mothers Union, Sunday School, Scouts and Cubs etc". It called for an "active, energetic priest who has had experience of the problems of a parish such as this …"

The appointment of Father Enser in 1952 proved to be a shrewd decision. He was a 'live wire' who set about addressing the low attendances and dwindling finances. He took advantage of the new vicarage built near the Dartmouth Arms in Vicarage Road to organise social events and meet parishioners. The financial position improved considerably when the local education authority took over control of the school. Money was made available to build a hall alongside the church and work began in 1954, with the bulk of the task being carried out by the parishioners. A close link was again being forged with the community, but tragedy befell the parish in November 1954 when Father Enser died during an Evensong service.

His successor was Father Shannon, a man with a warm, endearing personality, who maintained the 'catholic' tone of the church services. The new church hall was completed in 1956 and dedicated as the 'Enser Memorial Hall'. It became a major asset and Thursday and Saturday night dances at the venue proved successful for both social and financial reasons. Unfortunately, Father Shannon's tenure was short and he left in 1960.

Members of the All Saints Operatic Society at the Parish Carnival in 1952. In fancy dress we have, Left: Charlie Long, John Perry, Tom O'Connor. The two young ladies are Olive and Janet Pearce. (Photo: Phil and Gill Collins).

His successor, Father Morris, arrived at a watershed for the parish in terms of the significant social change that was taking place in the neighbourhood. He witnessed a series of house demolitions, a decline in the number of parishioners and a growing immigrant population. These factors resulted in a significant fall in the church's income. In 1964, it failed to pay its parish share to the diocese and in 1965 the parish was suspended and the post of vicar of All Saints was terminated. The retiring vicar, Father Morris, wrote: "Socially this is a dying or dead parish, there is no community spirit because the population is changing."

All Saints Church, fortunately, was not made redundant, a fate which befell other inner city churches in a similar situation. In 1970, it became part of the central parish of Wolverhampton with four other churches. A succession of talented curates from St Peter's and the support of the Rectors of Wolverhampton led to its recovery and the appointment of a new vicar.

It was a challenging time for the new vicar and his successors in the '70s. The arrival in Tilbury docks of the 'Empire Windrush' had brought the first wave of Caribbean immigrants. Many moved to towns like Wolverhampton where they met the prejudice and fear that would set the tone for the discrimination and struggles the Caribbean community would subsequently face. This discrimination was not restricted to housing and employment. There is evidence that Caribbean Christians had to endure a low level of acceptance. Dr Oliver Lyseight moved to Wolverhampton in 1953 and recalls when Caribbean Christians were "despised and made to feel unwelcome by some of the main-line churches". Immigrants responded by setting up 'Black Church' meeting places in schools and community centres.

Father Lyn Phillips in one of his 'Vicar's Letters' from 1978, remarks on 'Black Church' meetings which were taking place in All Saints School. A newcomer to Wolverhampton, he remarks that Father Barnett, his predecessor, "was very much concerned about our relation to these growing churches in Wolverhampton and did a great deal for the situation". Frustratingly, we are unaware of the details of the 'great deal' that he did. Attempts have been made to seek the views of the Black members of the New Testament Church of God, but no response has been forthcoming.

In the next article we have a photograph (courtesy of Dave Swift) taken around 1980 of the All Saints Church choir. The presence of five black youngsters suggests that some degree of integration had been successful. The number of choristers and the wide range of ages indicate that the church was once again enjoying close ties with the parish.

DAVE SWIFT AND THE ALL SAINTS CHURCH CHOIR, 1970s - '80s.

When the choir photograph was posted on Facebook, it led to over 200 responses. When a numbered photograph of the 32 members was re-posted, only one name remained incomplete. An astonishing response that clearly showed what a closely knit community it represented. Included in the list of choir members is a 15-year-old lad, Dave Swift, from Mills Road. Dave went on to become a professional musician, a bass guitarist with the Jools Holland Band. In the following article Dave describes his time with All Saints Church choir and his early musical development.

"I'd always sung in All Saints School choir, in both the Infant and Junior Schools. My two older brothers (Malcolm & Colin) had sung in the church choir but due to the big age gap between them and me, our paths never crossed.

1. Dawn Blood	2. Belinda ?	3. Joanne Galloway	4. Carl O'Shea	5. Maria Blood
6. Denise Perry	7. Michael Maye	8.Lyn Phillips (vicar)	9. Brian Chung	10. Conrad Brisset
11. Brian Williams	12. Richard Wells	13. Jennifer Wood	14. Everton Wood	15. Stan Morris (choir master and organist)
16. Helen Wells	17.Jo Morris	18. Dave Perry	19.Jacky Ray	20.Janine Perry

21. Stephanie Morris	22. Alison Churchill	23. George Paddock.	24. Margaret Gwilliam	25. Liz French
26. Angie Evans	27. Sue Bates	28. Selwyn Webb	29. Lance Morris	30. Dave Swift
31.Peter French	32. Bob Lee			

I remember the day when my life was about to change and put me on the path to a musical future even though I didn't know it at the time. It wasn't however the most auspicious start!

In 1974, when I was aged ten, I was playing with my friend and next door neighbour John Brindley who was a couple of years older than me. (I lived at No. 6 Mills Road, John and his family at No. 8). We must've been unusually bored that day because, for some reason, we found ourselves on the grass outside the front of the church throwing stones at it! I really don't know why, as, although we weren't angels, we weren't vandals either, and certainly had nothing against the church or any organised religion! I think we were simply exceptionally bored that day.

Very soon after the stone-throwing began, the vicar at the time, Father Jeffries, came striding out of the church and caught us red-handed! I can't remember if he frog-marched us into the church and the inner sanctum of his vestry, or if we were politely invited in, but once in the vestry, Father Jeffries stated that if we were so bored, why not join the church choir? And that was how it all began.

I was quite keen as I enjoyed singing and I was seemingly very good at it, so John and I went along to the next choir practice which was held every Friday evening.

We started singing treble which was always the melody line of the hymns and psalms and I was already familiar with many of those from the school choir. It turned out that John's forte was not singing so he didn't stay long, but I remained in All Saints Church choir for a good nine years, all because I had thrown a few stones!

I quickly made friends in the choir, and I was always more comfortable with and around the older members - I think I've always been a bit of an old soul myself - and I particularly enjoyed the company of choirmaster Stan Morris's son Lance, head chorister Selwyn Webb, and long-term chorister Bob Lee.

Our organist and choirmaster Stan Morris was a wonderful man and had a magnificent tenor voice as well as being a superb, accomplished organist and choirmaster. I can't 'sing' Stan's praises highly enough. It was under his tutelage and guidance that I learned so much about singing, harmony, performance, understanding and following written music, and developing and cultivating some much needed decorum and discipline to boot! Quite a feat for a young kid from All Saints! It was genuinely the best education and experience I'd ever known, and probably would ever know in those early formative years.

Bear in mind that at this early stage I wasn't playing a musical instrument, just singing. I'd fooled around at home on my brothers' guitars and the house piano, but nothing really captivated me. As time went on and my voice broke, I moved on to singing alto, and then began understanding even more about vocal harmony.

All Saints: The History, People, Places

At 14 I finally got around to playing a musical instrument, and at my secondary school (Colton Hills) I chose the trombone, an instrument I still play to this day. My trombone teacher Phil Johnson (who I'm pleased to say is still with us) went out on a limb for me as, technically and officially, at 14 I was too old for him to take on as a pupil, but thankfully he did, and that was another crucial and major turning point in my musical development.

I was still regularly singing in All Saints Church choir, and in the school choir, as well as playing trombone in the school band, and in numerous other bands and orchestras at Graiseley Music School. When I was 15, some school friends and I decided to form an offshoot of the school band, but we needed a bass player. I volunteered and began to teach myself bass guitar and then double bass. Even though at that stage, my life was absolutely replete with music and musical activities, I still hadn't even vaguely considered a future in the music industry. My parents were both factory workers and although my older brothers were big music fans and played guitar for their own amusement, no one in my immediate family had any connection to the arts, especially as a profession.

In All Saints choir as I got older, I stopped singing tenor completely and moved on to singing bass. All the time my ear was developing, and I was understanding harmony on a deeper level. I can't really say that being a member of All Saints Church choir was a religious experience, it really was all about my love of singing, singing with others, the friendship, fun, and camaraderie. But I most definitely had an appreciation for other aspects of the church itself including the beauty of its design and architecture, and the calmness and tranquillity I experienced whenever I was there. I enjoyed the 'sense of occasion' regarding the services and all the ensuing poignancy and solemnity.

Choir Group trip to London in 1980. Back Row: Angie Evans, Dave Swift, Selwyn Webb, Front Row: Alison Churchill, Stan Morris, ??, ??. (Photo: Dave Swift).

I remember being quite shy and not that confident as a young boy and teenager, and I believe singing in All Saints Church choir helped me get over that. Our head chorister Selwyn would also organise regular trips and outings for us, and we often visited the 'Silver Blades' ice rink in Birmingham to go ice skating and a ten pin bowling alley on Snow Hill (or it was in that area), and we'd also go to the speedway at Monmore Green Stadium. Not only were these regular outings lots of fun, but they were wonderful confidence building and boosting activities and very much early 'team building', way before the term became mainstream.

It never entered my mind that one day I would leave All Saints Church choir because to be honest, it was without question the happiest time of my early life. I loved it way more than my time at secondary school, and experienced and benefitted from my time as a chorister in so many ways, musically, spiritually, and socially, all of which were crucial to me ultimately becoming a professional musician. I even have particularly fond memories of the church hall. We used to attend barn dances, cheese and wine parties, jumble sales, all manner of social gatherings there. And the band that some of my secondary school friends and I formed (Taylor Mayd) used to rehearse there free of charge every Sunday afternoon in 1979/80, and, as a thank you, gave our musical services for free playing at some of those dances and parties.

I left school at 16 and after a brief stint working at a Wolverhampton music shop, I turned professional at 17. I was playing trombone, double bass and bass guitar and was singing in bands too. I was still in All Saints choir at 19, but things were changing very fast and dramatically for me at that time. I was getting invited to work abroad more and more, including working on various luxury cruise liners. And so that really did signal the end of my time in All Saints Church choir.

I don't remember exactly how I left, or if I made a thing of it and officially said goodbye and farewell to everyone, or I simply stopped going. I do hope it was the former as I made such good friends in the choir and shared so many happy experiences and memories with its members. I think I became quite overwhelmed, enamoured and infatuated with my new, somewhat glamorous life as a professional musician travelling all over the world at 19 and 20, and so I didn't think about my time in the choir for a long time after that. I suppose it was when I heard about the church being converted to a community centre, and then subsequently key people passing away, particularly Stan Morris, that made me reminisce about my time in the choir as much as I did and have ever since.

I finally (officially) left my hometown of Wolverhampton in 1988 as I wanted to move to London to see where my career could take me whilst living in the capital. I wanted to grow musically and play with better musicians than myself and to study and grow as a player.

I had already been a professional musician for ten years by the time I got the gig as full time bassist with Jools Holland in 1991. Ironically, even though I'd been singing all my life up until that point, when I joined Jools' band, one of the first things he asked me was: 'do you sing?' and I said: 'no!' In case you're wondering why, it's because I'd never been to music college or university at that time and I was focusing on my musicianship, the actual playing of my instruments and my private study of advanced harmony and improvisation. So, the singing didn't seem that important anymore and I almost felt it was a distraction and that for me it had 'had its time'.

Years later at a Jools Holland Band Christmas party, people started to sing carols and being in a festive mood and remembering the parts and harmonies I sang at All Saints, I joined in with the singing. Jools was VERY surprised and couldn't believe I'd said I didn't sing when he first asked me years before!

I look back at my time singing in All Saints choir with the warmest, fondest, most cherished memories imaginable. They really were halcyon days. What started out as a pastime to placate a disappointed and somewhat irate vicar changed my life. Joining All Saints Church choir helped me appreciate and gain a lot more respect for my elders. It also made me more confident, happy, outgoing, fulfilled, and part of a team. It gave me a sense of self-worth, tradition, and a true sense of belonging, more so than anything else I'd ever known.

Musically it was the best training I could've hoped for at that early age, and even though I was learning more organically and less academically, it was still an invaluable experience and guidance. But it was also fun! We all just loved singing! In fact, after some of the services, a few of us older choristers would stay behind and Stan would play the organ (and sing) and we would choose some of our favourite choral music/ hymns to sing purely for our own enjoyment. I remember never wanting to leave!

My time in the choir helped me a great deal socially, having to mix with people in vastly different age groups, and of course members of the opposite sex, which considering I came from a household of three brothers, was a big deal for me!

Of course, I didn't realise it at the time, but ALL of this was preparing me for a future as a professional touring and session musician and was absolutely a definitive and crucial time in my life which would ultimately change the course of everything. Part of me wishes I'd stayed in the choir for longer, but then I wouldn't have been able to do so many things and travel as extensively as I did. Even with all my achievements & accomplishments in later years, including playing with three of The Beatles, two of The Rolling Stones, Eric Clapton, Paul Simon, Smokey Robinson, Amy Winehouse etc... I honestly don't think I've experienced as much love, bliss and elation as when I spent those nine years in All Saints Church choir.

I always hoped that I would be able to visit the church again as it used to be before the conversion, and I most definitely wanted to see Stan Morris again so I could, as a more mature adult, show him my full gratitude and appreciation for all he'd done for me all those years. I thought I had plenty of time to do this but sadly it wasn't to be. In 1993, both Stan Morris and my own father Leslie Swift passed away suddenly without warning and within a few months of each other, so I never did get the chance to show my true gratitude and appreciation to either of these amazing, influential, nurturing men.

I really could wax lyrical about my time in All Saints Church choir till my dying day. It really did have that deep, far reaching, long lasting and emotional impact on me and the development of my musicality, and my character, personality, and pretty much every other aspect of my life. There have been periods of my adult life when I've felt quite lost and disconnected with everyone and everything, and I've often dreamt of being ten years old again and being able to go back to that sunny summer's day 'innocently' throwing stones at the church and being told by Father Jeffries that joining the choir might be a fun and enjoyable thing to do, and that I get to do it all over again…"

THE CHURCH CENTENARY

1 November 1979 marked the centenary of the church's consecration described in chapter 5. The Parish Newsletter in the months leading up to the centenary reveal that a wide range of activities were planned.

From the left: Fathers Vaughan, Jeffries, Barnett and Phillips cutting the Centenary Cake. (Photo: Phil and Gill Collins).

On the day itself, the event was first celebrated by a Mass in the church, presided over by the Bishop of Wolverhampton. In the December Parish Newsletter, Betty French describes that the church was "full to overflowing" with 500 people, including 300 communicants.

Following the church service, an after-Mass celebration took place in the Church Hall, which was absolutely rammed. The final highlight of the evening was the ceremonial cutting of the Centenary Cake to the accompaniment of "Happy Birthday All Saints". In the photo above, all four vicars with recent involvement in the church are seen preparing to cut the Centenary Cake as the church hall fills up.

… but this heyday for the church was not to last. In the 1980s four churches, including All Saints, in the Central Parish area of Wolverhampton faced challenges with declining congregations and the expense of maintaining large buildings. A difficult decision was made to 'reorder', a procedure whereby the church building was segmented to retain an area for church services and an area for secular activities.

The photograph above (courtesy of Dave Swift) shows the work under construction around 1989 with the pews already removed. The present churchwarden, Gill Collins, recalls their removal. "The oak pews were sold... The diocese sold them. They belonged to the church, those."

The chancel seen at the far end on the photo above still functions as a place of worship. It makes up about a quarter of the whole building. The nave was divided off from the chancel by a plastered wall and re-purposed as a community centre. Details about this 'reorder' and the events leading up to the opening of the community centre in 1990 are set out in chapter 11: All Saints in Transition.

The gentleman in the background is believed to be Stan Morris, choirmaster, and organist: an influential member of the church choir in the '70s and '80s and remembered with great affection by Dave Swift in his earlier article.

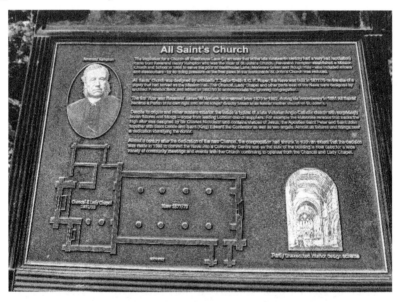

The plaque on the north wall describing the history of the church building and the role of Rev. Henry Hampton.

6

SCHOOLS

ALL SAINTS: 1888 -1939

The big advancements in state schooling which had taken place following the 1870 Education Act continued into the 1890s. In 1893, the minimum leaving age was raised to 11 and in 1899 to 12.

By the mid-1890s, the Anglican Church had a strong influence on education in the town. The Wolverhampton Chronicle of September 1893 reported that nearly 42% of the town's schools such as All Saints were church schools. Board schools such as Dudley Road represented 38.6%.

All Saints School was undergoing a significant change. The building, opened in 1888, for girls and infants was soon replaced by a detached pair of school buildings. The land for the school had been donated by Lord Barnard who laid the memorial stone in May 1894. The ceremony, described in the Wellington Journal, was attended by the Bishop of Lichfield and attracted many "inhabitants of the parish" who created a festive atmosphere with flags and bunting on display.

The two school buildings for up to 1014 pupils were constructed on the site. The new single storey building for boys was opened at 9 am on 7 January 1895. School life for the first intake of 108 pupils began with an address by the Reverend John Warner on manners, neatness and punctuality. Mr Andrew Tyler had been appointed as headmaster with George Wade as his assistant teacher. George Lawrence, a probationary teacher, was the other member of staff. The pupils were organised into six standards with most of the intake starting at i (58 boys) and ii (24 boys).

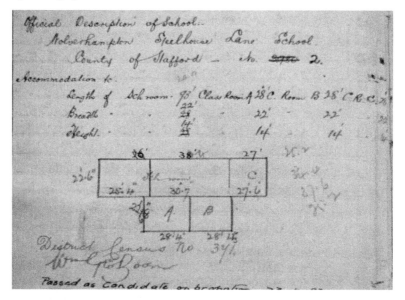

The plan of the new Boys School opened in 1895. (Wolverhampton Archives).

The headmistress of the Girls School was Miss Mary Perry who had worked at the school since 1879. Unfortunately, the corresponding plan for the Girls School has not yet been found.

The Wellington Journal of 31 August 1895 revealed that the entire cost of the new buildings and furnishings, £3,551, had been raised by subscriptions, grants from societies and money raised by a combination of bazaars, fairs, entertainments, box collections, etc. The same newspaper from 23 September listed the organisations which had provided grants towards the money required for the new buildings. The list of donors reveal that the church was heavily involved in all aspects of the fund raising. The vicar, the Reverend John Warner, is widely credited in that respect.

It was hoped that a further £200 could be raised to cover stationary, apparatus and incidental expenses for the Boys department.

Mr A. Tyler left in 1898 (or maybe earlier) to take up a post as headmaster of a Boys school in Hull. He was replaced by Mr William George Boon.

By 1901, a programme of night classes for men and youths were established. It is not clear whether Mr Boon was able to maintain the high standards set by his predecessor as the reports of Her Majesty's Inspectors (HMIs) became increasingly focused on the fabric of the school. Indeed, the 1908 report made no reference to academic progress, concentrating instead on its failings in the provision of heating, ventilation and hygiene.

Miss Perry's long service of 21 years was recognised and rewarded in 1900 when she was presented with an award of £3 at the annual distribution of prizes and certificates by the Staffordshire Board of Education.

In 1909, the infant school inaugurated its first May Queen festival, a tradition that was to continue right up to the 1960s. The school was flourishing under the leadership of Miss Perry. In December of that year, the school put on an operetta, 'A Bundle of Sticks'. The report in the Express and Star congratulated the children who had taken part and passed on "hearty congratulations to the headmistress and her staff for training the children so efficiently".

The raising of the school leaving age from 12 to 14, as required by the 1918 Education Act, had been postponed because of economic problems. The policy was reintroduced in the 1921 Act and finally came into force in October 1922. Local authorities began to reconsider what to do with these older pupils. Some set up 'higher tops' in their elementary schools. A minority reorganised their schools, creating separate junior and non-selective senior departments. In their 1926 report, the Hadow Committee recommended the division of schooling into primary and secondary stages with the break at age eleven.

At All Saints School, girls and boys were still taught in two separate buildings with contact discouraged by a sizeable wall, shown in the photograph below. Pupils stayed there beyond the age of 11. It will have been one of the schools which had set up 'higher tops' classes to accommodate the older pupils. The netball team of 1929 below represents one of the final year groups in the Girls School before the Hadow Committee recommendations were implemented.

The young girl in the centre of the photo is Kate 'Kitty' Grafton, the mother of Clive Holes. Kate spent nine years at All Saints School and below is a copy of the outstanding school report she received when she left at the age of 14.

All Saints' School,
Wolverhampton.
20. Dec. 1929.

Kitty Grafton has been a Scholar at the above School for 9 years & is now leaving after successfully passing Standard 8.

Her attendance has been excellent.

Her punctuality has been excellent.

Her general standard of work is excellent. She always does neat, careful & thorough work, being especially good at Needlework, Art, Music, Drama & all forms of Physical Work. She has been Games Captain, & for the last three terms has been elected Head Prefect of the School by her School fellows.

She is very alert, intelligent, reliable, & thoroughly capable. She has an unselfish & happy disposition & is very popular.

E. D. Jemmett.
Hd Mistress.

Sport, for both girls and boys, was evidently well organised at All Saints. Below is a photograph of the highly successful school football team from 1930.

The photo is of great interest for two reasons. One is the very splendid cup which the team won that season. The second is the presence of Ben Owen in the team. Ben makes two additional appearances in this book across two world wars; the baby son of a soldier who fought and was injured in The Great War and in an account of his own impressive and fascinating military life during World War Two.

The two men at the back are the teacher, Mr Nicholls and Mr J.J. Dean, the Wolverhampton Boys Manager.

Back Row, left to right: Ben Owen, Albert Holmes, George Jeavons, Victor Fieldhouse, Fred Fisher, David Ratcliffe.

Front Row, left to right: Doug Martin, Billy Foster, Billy Lane, Charlie Pinches, Leslie Law.

(Photo: Alex Brew).

In 1931, the Committee published a report, 'The Primary School'. Its proposals for both its organisation and curriculum were progressive for the time. Primary education, said the Committee, should comprise two stages - infants (up to seven) and juniors (from seven to eleven); there should be separate infant schools where possible, and close cooperation between infant and junior schools. Primary schools should be coeducational but should cater for the differing needs of boys and girls in games and physical exercises.

Whether it was this report which led to the All Saints schools becoming so quickly reorganised in 1931 is not clear, Nevertheless, when the school closed on 27 March. the Headmistress wrote: "This School ceased as All Saints Girls School."

When the pupils returned to school at 9 am on 13 April, all pupils over 7 years of age transferred to two Boys and Girls Junior departments for pupils aged 7 to 11. 110 boys, aged 7 to 11, arrived from other schools. Amongst them was Roland Mills, the father of Derek, who transferred from Dudley Road School while it was being set up as a Senior School. 22 Boys, aged 11+, left for Senior Schools. No details have been found for the girls.

One teacher who was not present for this important changeover was Miss Mary Perry, the headmistress of All Saints Girls School for 33 years who had retired in 1922 due to ill-health. A window in the chancel, shown above, was dedicated, years later, to both Mary Perry and her sister Sarah Jane Perry.

Another major reorganisation took place in 1934. Mr Boon, who had been headmaster of the Boys School for 36 years provided the following information on 31 July in the school logbook: "Today, this [Boys] school ceases to exist and will in future be amalgamated with the Girls Dept. to form a mixed school."

The building for boys became the infant school while the building for girls became the mixed junior school. The day of the reorganisation coincided with the announcement of his retirement. Unfortunately, a year later the Staffordshire Advertiser of 27 July 1935 announced his death.

In the same year, St Joseph's became a senior boys' school. It is not clear where the girls and infants went.

One further Education Act was passed in February 1936. This Bill raised the school leaving age to 15 with exemptions for 'beneficial employment', e.g., where a family would suffer 'exceptional hardship' if the child did not work.

Margaret Carroll (nee Williams) attended the infant school from 1937 to 1940 and recalls Miss Lucy Smith, the headmistress and four teachers: 'little' Miss Brown, 'big' Miss Brown, Miss Overton and Miss Ford.

"I seem to remember", says Margaret, "there were around 40 children in each class. The Reception class was overseen by 'little' Miss Brown, and after a while we went into Miss Overton's class, then we were divided into 'big' Miss Brown's class and the top (6-7 yrs.) were in Miss Ford's class. I remember in Miss Ford's class we were taught to knit, and I learned with two meat skewers and some string! I am not sure whether the Misses Brown were sisters, one was short and chubby and the other taller and slimmer. The area at the front of the infant school was for the infants. As Miss Smith's office overlooked this area, she was able to keep an eye on us."

The All Saints logbook reveals that the two Miss Browns were sisters. They made a big impression on John Neave when he started school in 1942. His own recollections of the school are found in an article in chapter 7.

Margaret remembers two celebrations taking place each May. On 24 May, the school celebrated Empire Day and girls could wear their Brownie uniforms which "made us feel very important". Far more important, however, was the May Day event, celebrated annually since 1909.

A May Day celebration from around 1929. The May Queen is Kate 'Kitty' Grafton, the mother of Clive Holes. She would have been about 13 or 14 at the time. (Photo: Wolverhampton Archives).

Margaret believes the photograph below (courtesy of Margaret Williams) of the event was taken in May 1939. The young lad, Stanley Bryan, standing next to Margaret, is the father of Roger, the goalkeeper in the school's 1959/60 football team featured in a later section of this chapter.

Top row: Sidney Dear, Rita Pittaway, Tommy Taggart, Joan Walton, Roy Hammond, Beryl Davies, Donald Davies.

Bottom Row: Olive Round, Reg Turner, Doreen Welsby, Stanley Bryan, Margaret Williams, Alan Griffiths, ? , ?, Rita Anderson.

The outbreak of the Second World War meant the raising of the school leaving age, due to come into effect on 1 September 1939, was postponed.

ALL SAINTS: 1954 -1965

Just prior to Derek and Clive's arrival in 1954, the Infant School had been visited by Her Majesty's Inspectors (HMIs). Their inspection would have taken place over several days and covered an assessment of the school building, the quality of the teaching and the achievements of the pupils.

In their report, it was described as a school which "serves an area of industrial housing in the south east of the town centre… and consists of a room for the Headmistress, two cloakrooms and six classrooms; one of the last-named is used as a hall and for dining purposes… Heating is by open fires, is reasonably satisfactory in the two rooms where it is augmented by gas fires, but inefficient elsewhere".

It made disheartening references to the neighbourhood and the perceived shortcomings of the school's pupil intake. "These deficiencies in the lavatory and sanitary facilities are the more regrettable in view of the overwhelming need for good social training in the area from which the pupils are drawn." It went on to state: "Standards of work in the school have to be assessed against this background and against the problem presented to the school by the poor home background and lack of ability of many of the children."

Despite these somewhat dispiriting comments put forward by the HMIs, we were to be exposed to a series of educational, sporting and musical experiences that challenged us academically and socially and successfully prepared us for the next stage of our school career.

The following articles which cover the period from 1954 to 1960 describe a diverse range of experiences by the two authors at the school.

SONG AND DANCE

MAY DAY CELEBRATIONS

May Day celebrations were first held at All Saints School in 1909. They continued every year without a break for over fifty years, ending in the 1960s.

Maypole dancing is a very old, and an originally pagan tradition, first recorded in Britain at Llanidloes, central Wales, in the 14th century. It was once (in 1644) banned by the Puritans in England as 'a heathenish vanity'. In a school like All Saints, which in 1909 was already surrounded by industrial wastelands, it might have seemed a little out of place. However, by the end of the 19th century, increased urbanisation was encouraging people to take a greater interest in the country's rural traditions. Education authorities were being influenced by individuals, particularly Cecil Sharp, to introduce folk music and dance into schools. In 1909, the Board of Education bowed to pressure and folk dancing became a part of the school curriculum. Although All Saints was not a Board School, it appears to have made the same decision. The performance of an operetta, mentioned earlier in this chapter, indicates that music and dance had already become a prominent part of the school's curriculum.

There were two main aspects to the May Day celebrations: the crowning of the May Queen, usually a girl aged around 7 from All Saints School, and dancing around the maypole in the school playground, together with traditional Morris dancing.

At the time when Derek and Clive attended All Saints (1954-60), the May Queen was usually chosen from the 2nd year of the infant school or 1st year of the junior school. She always had a retinue of maids of honour and page-boys. The whole occasion was basically an excuse for elaborate dressing-up, as can be seen from the photograph below, taken in May 1957, where bows, frilly dresses, bouquets and velvet capes are much in evidence.

The May Queen, Mary Anslow, and her court in 1957.

How the May Queen was chosen was something of a mystery. There was certainly no pupils' vote. Every year the May Queen simply 'emerged', probably chosen by the teachers, and (who knows) with the influence of a few well-placed parents. It was once said that girls from the All Saints parish tended to be preferred, and, very plausibly, that the choice needed to take account of the ability of the May Queen's parents to pay for the cost of making her frilly dress and all her accoutrements.

In 1957, the choice had fallen on Mary Anslow who lived on the Rough Hills Estate. Mary had a Greek mother and an English father and was for that reason thought of as somewhat exotic. She had jet-black hair and a dark complexion, inherited from her Mom. Many of the boys in her class (including Clive) were in love with her, if you can be in love when you are 7 or 8.

The choice the previous year was Gillian Selvey, whose Dad ran the Dartmouth Arms. Did the teachers perhaps drink there? Certainly, some parents did. She was the opposite of Mary in looks, with flaxen hair and an 'English rose' complexion.

Derek and Clive don't remember what the May Queen had to do other than pose for photographs with her 'court' and grace the maypole dancing with her noble presence.

Practice sessions in the playground at All Saints School in the 1950s. (Photo: Alan Fisher).

Maypole dancing at All Saints was performed to music and was a very elaborate affair. Multi-coloured bands of ribbon were slowly, carefully and tightly intertwined by the dancers as they moved round the maypole again and again to create symmetrical patterns. It took at least a couple of weeks to train the maypole dancing team, composed of equal numbers of boys and girls, in the skills required, with regular practices in the playground. Then the day finally came when parents and local bigwigs were invited to witness the May Queen being crowned and the maypole dances performed. If the weather was wet, as it often was, St Joseph's school opposite lent All Saints its large hall, and the dancing was held indoors.

In 1957, the Express & Star reported that the Mayoress of Wolverhampton, Mrs G Rastall, came to crown the May Queen, and Clive Holes (above) presented her with a bouquet of flowers.

Change was on its way. South Asian families had started to arrive in All Saints in the late 1950s (Clive believes his own family was one of the first in All Saints Road to sell their house to an Indian family in 1958). By 1961, the school governors were discussing the issue of Asian children who arrived at the school with little or no English. All Saints was beginning its gradual shift, a small part of the same shift that was happening all over the West Midlands, to the multicultural society we know today.

Whatever the reasons were, and we have not yet found a definitive explanation, the May Day celebrations at All Saints School came to an end in the mid-1960s. It may well have been the departure in 1964 of Mr Lancaster, the headmaster, a passionate advocate of folk music and dance during his tenure at the school. Maybe a decision was made by his successor that the May Day event was not appropriate in a multicultural school. One parent recalls a teacher saying that the pupils of Indian heritage wouldn't understand or be much interested in such quintessentially English pursuits.

SCHOOL CHOIR AND DANCING TEAMS

All Saints was a Church of England controlled school, so there was always a close relationship with the church of the same name next door.

From a pupil's point of view, one of the main benefits of this was that we got quite a few extra half days off in term time for religious festivals. All Saints Day, Ascension Day, Harvest Festival, and more obscure occasions like Corpus Christi involved a set pattern: the whole school went to church in the morning and the rest of the day was a holiday.

The morning service involved singing hymns, and lots of them. On All Saints Day, without fail, we finished with 'For All the Saints', words by William Walsham How, put to music by the great English composer Ralph Vaughan-Williams. It has the stirring opening verse:

'For all the saints, who from their labours rest;
who to the world by faith their Lord confessed,

your name, O Jesus, be for ever blessed:
Alleluia, alleluia!'

At Harvest Festival, when the church was always overflowing with donated produce – in particular, Clive remembers large loaves baked into elaborate plaits – it was 'We plough the fields and scatter':

'We plough the fields and scatter
the good seed on the land,
but it is fed and watered
by God's almighty hand;

These church services were conducted by the vicar of All Saints Church, Father Shannon, aided by the headmaster of the school, Mr Alf 'Lanky' Lancaster, immaculately turned out in his red lay preacher's cassock, patrolling the aisle between the rows of pews filled with his charges.

'Lanky' was a lover of classical music, especially choral religious music by the greats of the genre such as Johann Sebastian Bach, but he also loved the English folk song tradition. One of his main passions was the school choir, which he ran more or less single-handedly for the whole of his tenure as headmaster. It had around three dozen members covering the age-range 7 to 11 and performed regularly at concerts in Wolverhampton, including the Civic Hall.

However, the festival of singing and country dancing held every summer at Leamington, attracting competitors from all over the West Midlands, and as far afield as Leicester, Northampton and High Wycombe, was without doubt the highlight of the year. More of that below.

Entry to the school choir was by a rather brutal voice test. Groups of pupils would be asked to sing verses of well-known songs or hymns all together while 'Lanky' walked around them listening to the individual voices. Those who were tone-deaf, sang flat or couldn't project their voices were side-lined, and the worst were labelled 'growlers' and of no further use. The ones who passed the test were offered the chance to join the choir, and the best of them were eventually given the opportunity, after further training, to perform solo or in duets at concerts.

Clive recalls he was one with a decent voice, and remembers singing a duet with another choir member, David Morgan, in which they performed Franz Schubert's song 'The Wild Rose' at a concert given in St Joseph's school across the road from All Saints. Our school didn't have a hall big enough to accommodate the choir and an audience.

Choir practice was held regularly in the music room at All Saints, with 'Lanky' conducting and one of the teachers playing the piano. The selection of pieces was eclectic and challenging. "I remember", says Clive, "my first encounter with Latin at the age of 9 in the song 'In Dulci Jubilo', (later made popular in the 1970s by Mike Oldfield of 'Tubular Bells' fame) which had a descant that began 'Ubi sunt gaudia' (Where are the joys?). There was also the perennial favourite 'Linden Lea', a traditional Dorset folk song with music arranged, again, by Ralph Vaughan Williams, which I clearly remember singing at Leamington. This song is an evocation of an idyllic late 19th century rural England and has the lines:

'For I be free to go abroad
Or take again my homeward road
To where, for me, the apple tree
Do lean down low, in Linden Lea.'

But our choir wasn't from Dorset and had its own unofficial version, which we sang for a laugh in Black Country English:

'For I yam free to gew abrow-ud
Or tek agen me 'omewud row-ud
Beneath the chimbleys where the air
Is full of soot, by Tipton Cut.'

Choir practice was a serious business, and woe betide anyone who didn't pay attention. On one occasion a girl member of the choir carried on chattering after we had all been told to shut up. Two strides from the front of the music room and 'Lanky' was in front of her and… smack!... with his open hand he almost knocked her block off. Different times!

Throughout the 1950s, Leamington was the annual highlight for both the dancers and the singers of All Saints.

The Morris Dance team with their certificate from the Leamington Festival in 1953 (?): ??, Frank Edwards, ??, ??, ??, ??. (Photo: Wolverhampton Archives).

There is a long report in the Express and Star of 25 June 1956 listing the results in various categories of dance (country, square, Morris), singing (madrigals, folk songs) by various types of choirs (male, female, mixed) and across various age groups. The winners and runners up listed include All Saints and other Wolverhampton schools such as Elston Hall.

Everybody got dressed up for Leamington: boys in white shirts, grey flannel shorts and open sandals; girls in identical, invariably floral-patterned dresses. It was a long day. We left early from the school gates in a Don Everall coach, clutching our packed lunches and accompanied by several teachers and volunteer parents.

The hall at Leamington was huge and tiered, like a theatre, in which we sat and watched our rivals perform before going up on the stage when it was our turn.

All Saints Senior Dance team, Winners of First Prize, with their Certificate and Cup, Leamington, June 1958.

At the end of each competition the judges announced their marks: sometimes it was triumph, only rarely disaster. I went to Leamington on at least two occasions and the photographic evidence of the framed certificates we are clutching (my memory isn't great) suggests that we usually did well.

The day always ended with a stop for tea on the way back at Kenilworth. We piled out of the coach onto a grassy hillock overlooking the castle. After the discipline of having to sit silently for hours in the theatre, and then the concentration of public performance on stage, we were ready to let off steam. For some the games of 'tick' and hide and seek were the highlight of the day. For others it was all a bit too much, and there were complaints of headaches and nausea from the bumpy coach ride. For yet others, the older ones, it was a chance for the boys to chase the girls, and the girls to chase the boys... all the while pretending not to, of course. 'Twas ever thus ..."

SPORT

A FOOTBALL CELEBRITY AT ALL SAINTS

The 1950s was a great time for local kids mad on sport, and football, especially. We were lucky that our local team were the mighty Wolverhampton Wanderers. The 1959-60 season saw them win the FA Cup for only the fourth time in their history, beating Blackburn Rovers 3-0 at Wembley, and miss out by just one point on both an FA Cup and League Double, and a third successive League Championship

In 1957, the school enjoyed a short period of football glamour with the arrival in October 1956 of a new teacher, Mrs Margaret (Meg) Hooper, the wife of Harry Hooper, a recent signing by Wolves from West Ham United in March 1956 for the (then) huge sum of £25,000.

At Wolves, he played right-wing in the No 7 shirt and was an instant hit, scoring on the opening day of the 1956-7 season in a 5-1 defeat of Manchester City. He went on to be Wolves top scorer that season, with 19 goals in 39 appearances, including a hat-trick against Preston in a 4-3 win.

Harry had married Margaret in 1955, and when she turned up as a teacher at All Saints Infants School in the autumn of 1956, the name 'Hooper' caused a frisson of excitement among the many young Wolves fans who attended the school. Could she really be the wife of the Wolves 1st team right-winger? Confirmation of the rumour came when the great man himself began turning up at the school gates to pick Meg up when the school day was over. If memory serves, this was in a brand-new sports car, something not often seen in All Saints Road at the time. Harry, in a photo below, is seen in the car.

The All Saints teachers of those days came to work in a variety of vehicles, but none of them was in that price range: Mr Henning came in one of the new-fangled 'bubble-cars', Mr Tod drove a 'sit-up-and-beg' Ford Anglia, and most of the others arrived by bus.

(Photo: 'Wolves Heroes' website).

But Harry, though a well-paid footballer who originally came from a pit village in County Durham, was very approachable. He happily signed his name in the autograph books of the All Saints school kids, including that owned by one of the authors of this book! But Harry didn't stay at Wolves very long. After his one season, highly successful though it was, he was replaced by the returning Norman Deeley, who had been away doing his National Service in the Suez Canal Zone.

Harry was sold to Birmingham City, and then, in 1960, he moved to Sunderland. But for the many Wolves fans at All Saints School in the mid-1950s, their brush with a Wolves hero, however transient, is something they will never forget.

Harry died peacefully at his home in Hunstanton, Norfolk on August 20, 2020, at the age of 87.

SPORTING SUCCESSES

Derek's growling voice and his two left feet meant he would not become a member of those highly successful school choir and dancing teams. He did, however, show enough sporting talent to gain selection for the school's football and cricket teams and recalls their achievements.

FOOTBALL

"Like most lads in Wolverhampton, I was football mad. During the school holidays, our 'gang' of six devoted Wolves fans from Rough Hills Estate would assemble in Cheviot Road, check the condition of the red vinyl Frido football and make our way to the Dixon Street playing fields. Footballing skills: heading, ball-control and goalkeeping were perfected and daily checks on the keepy-uppy tally were made. After returning home for midday dinner, the same routine would be repeated in the afternoon. Time would also be put aside for a session of trainspotting, but our priority was football.

At school, I was more than happy to join in with the impromptu games of football that were held in the playground at break. I had always followed my Dad's army advice: keep a low profile and do not volunteer for anything. Playing for the school team was not on my wish list.

That philosophy had worked well for me in my first three years at the Junior School. I expected it to continue as year 4 began in September 1959. The annual pre-season friendly had taken place without my name on the team sheet. No problem – plenty of games to be had with my mates from Rough Hills. I was aware that one member of the team, John Disley, felt that I was good enough to be selected. I had resisted attempts in year 3 to play and would do the same. It was not to be. Mr Henning (teacher and coach) and Mr Lancaster (headmaster) became involved and my resistance was broken.

The school's approach to sport was inconsistent. We rarely had games or PE lessons. The slightest shower seemed sufficient to deter the teachers from organising rounders on the playground or football, initially on Pond Lane Recreation Ground ('The Rec.') and, later, the Dixon Street playing fields. Despite its complacent attitude towards providing exercise for its pupils, the school took the fortunes of its football and cricket teams very seriously.

Our first match of the 1959/60 season was an away fixture against Elston Hall, a school in Fordhouses on the edge of town. My Dad came along. He was probably thrilled; I was terrified. The routine for away games was to meet up outside the Gaumont cinema at the bottom of Snow Hill. Mr Henning would be there to escort us to the appropriate bus stop for our destination. No coach with tinted windows, TV screens and a drinks cabinet for the All Saints School football team.

To use that sporting cliché, the next couple of hours passed in a blur. We arrived at the school, were directed to the changing room and I put on the All Saints shirt and shorts, taking care that I did not leave my vest on. If I felt any pride in representing my school, I was not aware of it; I was a bag of nerves. I wore my favourite white socks with two red rings and my made-to-last boots, heavily coated with dubbin applied by Dad the night before. We walked onto the pitch, my Dad said: "Get stuck in", the whistle blew and one hour later, we walked off. In the interim, we had lost 3-0, outplayed if not humiliated; it could have been worse. I glanced up at Dad standing on the touchline. "You didn't get stuck in." He was right.

The coach with the tinted windows, etc had once again been double booked and we waited with our red faces and muddy knees on Stafford Road for the town bus to arrive. A couple of the lads who had played for the school team in year 3 tried to put the result into perspective by emphasising that we never beat Elston Hall, and for further reassurance, neither did we ever defeat Bushbury County. That would be another game to look forward to, I thought, picturing the scene of disappointment from earlier that day. Little did I know.

I heard nothing from the other lads in the team to suggest that the season would be anything other than mediocre. To be fair, All Saints were in Division One of the primary school leagues; nine teams in each division. The school, however, had a better reputation it seems for cricket. More of that later. As far as football was concerned, we would be expected to drift through the league season and make an early exit from the cup competition when both divisions were involved. Despite the shambles against Elston Hall, I was a bit mystified by this negativity. The team had a strong core of players who had already played regular school team football: John Disley, centre forward; Alan Fisher, half back; Richard Gullick, captain and centre half. These three talented youngsters formed the spine of the team.

Fortunately for team morale, our next game the following Saturday was at home against Warstones. Although the Dixon Street playing fields were about half a mile from the school, they were close to Rough Hills Estate and the dense housing around Kent Road and Pond Lane. This meant all our home games would attract a healthy number of spectators: children and adults looking to support the local school.

We put last week's trouncing behind us, settled quickly and with the vocal support from the crowd and the brooding presence of Mr Lancaster, the headmaster, we thrashed the team from the Penn area of town by 6-1. We were happy, the crowd were happy and our prospects for the rest of the season suddenly took an upward turn.

The advantage from this regular home support was supplemented by the pitch itself. It was set up for Works League football with full size goals and pitch dimensions. Schools used to their small pitches were in for a shock. We used a full back, a tall lad called Terry Pugh, to take the corners as only he could reach the penalty area. We soon learnt that rather than shooting to one side of the goalkeeper, it was easier to score by lobbing it over his head. With this strong home advantage, we prospered. We played four home games; we won them all.

A view, taken in 2020, of the Dixon Street Playing Fields.

The Warstones match set the standard for the rest of the season. Mr Henning kept to a settled team with Clive Holes making occasional appearances in defence. This stability and confidence was reflected in our impressive results.

TEAM	VENUE	RESULT
Elston Hall	A	0-3
Warstones	H	6-1
Eastfield	H	1-0
Christ Church	A	0-0
Whitgreave	H	2-0
Rake Gate	A	4-1
Bushbury Hill	H	3-0

Apart from a disappointing draw against Christ Church, our winning streak continued. However, our league season was not to finish on a high. In the final league match, we played Bushbury County. It proved to be an anti-climax. The early season prediction that we would lose to Bushbury County came to pass. In a game that resembled our opening game of the season, we put in a dismal performance and deservedly lost 4-0, missing the chance to leapfrog Elston Hall into second place.

Bushbury County completed the league season unbeaten on 16 points. Third place in Division One meant it was already a football season to be proud of - and there was more to come."

GIANT KILLERS

Season 1959-60 was a momentous one for Wolverhampton Wanderers FC. In its own way, All Saints School's football team, filled with avid Wolves fans, also had a season to remember, coached by the unflappable Mr Henning and roared on from the touchline by the fearsome headmaster, Mr Lancaster. 'Come on the Saints!' he would bawl on those freezing Saturday mornings at the Dixon Street playing fields.

A superb league campaign was topped off by a thrilling run in the Bird Cup. There were routine victories against lesser teams in the early rounds, and then the draw was made for the semi-finals: All Saints v. Bushbury County.

This looked like the end of the road. Nobody could remember when we had ever beaten them, or come to that, their near neighbours Elston Hall. These two dominated the league and thrashed everybody they played. There must have been something in the north Wolverhampton air!

This is Clive and Derek's account of a memorable Cup match.

"The semi-final was played on a dank Wednesday afternoon at Dunstall Park, the town's racecourse. Inside the main gates was a line of changing rooms: cold, corrugated iron sheds with a bench and hooks on which to hang your clothes - it was not Wembley with the sunken bath we saw on TV! The football pitches were spread across a green expanse inside the rails of the racecourse. We left the changing room to walk to a distant pitch and face what we all thought would be an inevitable drubbing.

We lined up in our blue and yellow tops and white 'knicks' (as they called them back then), County in their white shirts and black shorts, and off we went…

Were we brilliant that day or did they underestimate us? Sixty years later it's hard to be sure, but flashbacks from the match suggest a bit of both. Our centre-half and captain, Richard Gullick, played an absolute blinder as we battled to keep them out in the first half. We were still holding our own as the half-time whistle sounded: 0-0... and all to play for!

By the time the second half started, the drizzle had turned into rain. It was all a bit of a blur in our memories, but we remember them getting more and more rattled - they would have expected to be winning by now. County's tall, dangerous centre forward was playing in goal for some reason and their attacks carried little of their usual potency. Our defence was comfortable and gaining confidence. Clive was playing at right-back that day and remembers finding himself half-way into the County's half - a rare event in any game, let alone in one against them!

As the weather deteriorated, the game was calling out for a goal to break the stalemate. But when it came, it was All Saints, not Bushbury County, who ended the deadlock. And it was not our talisman, John Disley, but an unsung hero, Maurice Price. In quick succession, Maurice conjured up not one but two outstanding goals. The second one seemed to knock the stuffing out of Bushbury and we held on, with Mr Henning watching nervously as the minutes ticked away. The final whistle... and we could hardly believe it: All Saints 2 - Bushbury County 0, and into the Final!

We walked into school the next day on cloud nine. The team were singled out in assembly for special praise by Mr Lancaster - a proud day for everyone."

Clive was not so proud about an unfortunate footnote to that memorable match.

"One afternoon about a week after that semi-final victory, we were all quietly working away in Class 4A when a kid came in carrying a brown paper bag with a message for our class teacher, Mr Tod. The kid went out as Mr Tod read the note and opened the bag. After a few seconds, he startled us by asking in a loud voice: 'Do these belong to anybody?' As it gradually dawned on the class what 'these' were, a ripple of laughter started, quiet at first but getting louder. 'These' were a pair of boys' underpants. I joined in the laughter like everybody else until I suddenly realised whose underpants they were. Mine.

After the semi-final at Dunstall Park, the changing rooms were a chaos of dirty towels, football boots and clothes scattered everywhere. I was in a tearing hurry to leave after the match, as my parents were taking me and my sisters to see a film, 'A Nun's Story', starring Audrey Hepburn, at the Odeon in Wolverhampton town centre. But I couldn't find my underpants anywhere. In the end, I just gave up and put my trousers on without them. Needless to say, later on that evening there was an inquest and I got a telling off from my Mom, but, still in the euphoria of victory, I couldn't have cared less. 'They're just an old pair of underpants with holes in, so what?' I told her.

Now here they were being held aloft like a victory banner by Mr Tod for the gleeful inspection of my classmates. Wishing that the ground would open up and swallow me, I raised my hand and answered him: 'They're mine, sir!' As I blundered to the front of the class, tripping over satchels and chair-legs in confusion, the guffaws reached a crescendo - and especially from the girls! I was 11 then and I'm 74 now, and in the intervening sixty years I can't think of an occasion when I have felt more embarrassed!"

And onto the final. It is fair to say that we went into the final expecting to win. The other favourites, Elston Hall, had been beaten unexpectedly by Bushbury Hill. Having already beaten Bushbury Hill comfortably in a league match, we were very confident, maybe too confident?

Unfortunately, the football part of the story ended in a bit of an anti-climax. Maybe it was cup final nerves? We didn't win the Cup, but we didn't lose it either - we shared it with Bushbury Hill for 6 months each after a boring 0-0 draw. No replays back then. Ah well.

Back: Derek Mills, John Disley, Roger Bryan, Terry Pugh, Clive Holes.

Middle: Michael Hartland, Melvyn Hartland, Mr Lancaster (headmaster), Richard Gullick (holding the Bird Cup we shared with Bushbury Hill), Mr Henning (teacher and coach), Malcolm Evans, Maurice Price.

Front: Alan Fisher, Tony Howells.

It should have been one of those special occasions locked into our memory banks for ever. However, despite the importance of the event, the first cup final experience for us all, no one has any significant recollection of the day! It beggars belief - the date, the ground, the match itself: all details lost in the mist of time. Derek vaguely remembers it was 'all ticket' and drew a good crowd, as one would expect, with many parents and teachers watching us play for the first time. This only added to the dreadful disappointment of failing to win such a crucial match. Well, if anyone reading this book can remember that match, please come to our rescue.

CRICKET

It had been an exceptional season and a wonderful experience for the school football team. More was to come on the sporting front, as Derek recalls:

"The school was more noted for its cricketing performances. The season before the team had beaten all-comers, thanks in part to the outstanding performances of Sid McDonald, a close neighbour from Cheviot Road. A sturdy lad, not made for football, but tailor-made for bat and ball.

It was to our advantage that the cricket league was made up of fewer schools. Dominant footballing schools like Elston Hall and Bushbury County did not organise cricket teams. Maybe they felt the pitches required too much care and maintenance. This evidently did not deter Mr Lancaster and Mr Tod, teacher and coach, who decided the Dixon Street playing fields would be adequate. On our way, we would pass the sports ground of Bayliss, Jones and Bayliss and glance across enviously at their pristine cricket square, roped off in preparation for their next home match, the immaculate outfield and the steps leading up to a pavilion: small but perfectly formed. We did not believe Lord's Cricket Ground could be any more impressive.

Dixon Street playing field did not have a cricket pitch. Once the football season was over, the council would mow the grass on a regular basis but otherwise it was left alone. No finely mowed square, lush outfield or pavilion. To recreate a cricket environment, we took along a strip of coarse matting and a pair of wickets in a support stand. Bats, gloves and pads were provided by the school and our kit consisted of white shirts, grey shorts and pumps. Mr Tod would find one of the flatter sections on the field, matting and wickets were put in place and we were ready to start.

All matches were played midweek immediately after school. We never enjoyed the same level of interest from the residents, but welcome support was provided by some of our mothers.

Eight of the successful football team made up the bulk of the cricket team. Laurie Light, David Morgan and Derek Lawrance came in to complete the rest of the places. Clive Holes and Melvyn Hartland provided invaluable support as the scorers. The 'Holy Trinity' of John Disley, Alan Fisher and Richard Gullick who had been so effective in the football season carried on from where they left off. My own role in the team was as part-time bowler, number 6 batsman and fielder in the gully position. This role was more in theory than practice and for most games I was little more than a spectator and may just as well have sat down alongside the mothers. I was never required to bowl and only on two occasions can I recall being called on to bat.

Two contrasting matches come to mind, both against Warstones School. In one of our earlier games of the season, we made the journey on a sunny afternoon to Penn. The pitch was set up on their playing field just beyond the school buildings. Our bowlers ripped through their batting and yours truly took his one and only catch at gully. The All Saints opening pair came out and picked off the required runs without any problems – an extremely comfortable 10 wicket victory. An early bus back to town and home for tea.

A few weeks later, we faced them again. This time we were playing at Dixon Street in the Cup competition. Our unbeaten run had continued and an easy victory was on the cards. It did not work to plan. The beneficiary of a footballing upset against Bushbury County; we were now the victim of a cricketing one. The slow, despondent walk back to school was a painful experience. The defeat took some of the shine off our season, but we could still be proud of finishing as unbeaten league champions."

Back: Clive Holes, John Disley, Roger Bryan, Melvyn Hartland, Terry Pugh, Michael Hartland, Derek Lawrance.

Middle: Laurie Light, Mr Lancaster (headmaster), Richard Gullick, Mr Tod (teacher and coach), David Morgan.

Front: Alan Fisher, Tony Howells (holding the League Cup), Derek Mills. (Photo: Alan Fisher).

NETBALL

It would be incorrect to imply that sport at All Saints was the sole preserve of boys. The tradition of girls playing netball for the school, seen in an earlier 1929 photograph, extended into the 1950s. (Photo below: Wolverhampton Archives).

Back: Mr Lancaster, Miss Kirby (teacher and coach).

Middle: Lilian Mason, ??, ??, ??,??.

Front: Sylvia Enefer, ??, Carol Plimmer.

Unlike the boys, the girls did not have to make that long trek to 'The Rec' on Caledonia Road or the Dixon Street playing fields. The netball pitch was laid out on the tarmac of the school playground.

The photograph above shows the team from the 1952/53 season with smart jumpers incorporating a school badge. Mr Lancaster makes his customary appearance. Standing to his left is Miss Kirby, our much loved class teacher when Clive and Derek were in 3A during the 1958/59 school year.

Little is known about the team or its achievements and we welcome feedback from readers of the book.

THE 11 PLUS EXAMS

While not wishing to underestimate the stress of those sport, music and dance competitions, our biggest challenge in Year 4, by far, was the 11 Plus (11+) examination.

The 11 Plus exam had been introduced in 1944 to determine whether you went onto a grammar, technical or secondary modern education. The consequences of passing or failing were potentially critical to the rest of your life. Although Derek was far too young to appreciate fully their significance, this did not stop him facing up to the exam with great apprehension. He recounts that ordeal.

"I had hoped this challenge would never have to materialise. My parents had suggested a year earlier that if the Labour Party won the General Election in 1959, they would abolish the exam, bring in comprehensive schools and we would all go off to our local secondary school. Easy. For the first time, I took a passing interest in politics and in the morning after the election, rushed into my parent's bedroom hoping for good news. It was not to be, and I knew this forthcoming academic challenge could not be avoided.

At All Saints we were part of a school with large class sizes and relatively few resources. It did not have as strong an academic record as schools on the west side of the town and followed an eclectic curriculum which was probably less focused on passing the 11 Plus. Music and dance played a particularly important and successful role in school life, as described by Clive Holes in an earlier article. Art and Craft also took up a significant portion of the school week and the display for the annual Open Day was put together over several days with considerable skill, effort and imagination.

An Open Day display in progress. Standing: ??, Diane Saunders. Kneeling: Derek Lawrance, Clive Holes, Joan Maullin.

The first set of 11 Plus exams took place over two days in November. To rub salt into the wound, in the evening before the first test, Wolves were playing Red Star Belgrade in the first round of the European Cup, the elite competition only open to the Championship winning teams of Europe's major leagues. Understandably, Dad said it was more important to get a good night's sleep and my first chance to watch a foreign club at Molineux was regrettably missed.

The Intelligence Test was followed a day later by the Space Test. I am still none the wiser as to what those questions consisted of. The anticipation and the strain of sitting the exam produced so much distress my Mom said I returned home as 'white as a ghost'.

The second part took place the following year in March. This consisted of four separate exams held over four days. It started with a Composition Test, followed a few days later by another Intelligence Test, and finally the Arithmetic and English Tests. I was much more confident about these subjects and faced the experience without the previous consequences. Within a couple of days, the exams were forgotten.

Towards the end of the summer term, the school announced the 11 Plus results would be posted to homes the following Saturday. Nerves kicked in. My parents were incredibly good and at no point did I feel any pressure from them. If there was any pressure, it was self-inflicted.

In Wolverhampton, parents were given a choice of three schools if their child passed and three secondary modern schools if they failed. Most would put the Technical High School in the town centre in third place, the Municipal Grammar School in Newhampton Road, Whitmore Reans, in second position and Wolverhampton Grammar School, founded in 1512 and situated in a leafy suburb of the town, at the top.

At the back of my mind was the prospect of four gruesome years at the local secondary modern school, Graiseley. New lads, it was said, could expect their heads to end up in the toilet bowl and the chain pulled. Some of the teachers were legendary, but not necessarily for appropriate reasons. Mr (Killer) Morris would demonstrate his prowess at hurling the chisel. Mr (Froggy) Martin would fall asleep in lessons, but God help anyone who was misbehaving when he woke up.

On the Friday afternoon, I remember Mr Tod came round to each of us, asking which secondary school we hoped to go to. I said the Technical High School, my third choice if I passed. I felt I had made better progress in years 3 and 4 after a slow start in the first two years and was reasonably confident. I remember his 'hmm' which worried me somewhat. I tried not to read too much into it, but I was concerned in case he felt I had overestimated my academic abilities. The teachers by now would have known the results.

The nerves built up during the remainder of the day. I went to bed reassured by my parents that I had done as well as I could in the exams and there was no reason to worry. The following morning, I awoke and immediately thought about the 11 Plus letter. The postman had started at the top of Cheviot Road. As he made his way down to No. 48, I looked up the road to see parents and classmates celebrating or consoling.

While neither of my parents could be described as scholarly, they strongly believed in the importance of education, expressed confidence in Mr Lancaster and his staff and showed restrained interest and encouragement for me during my time at the school. Even so, I suspect they were as surprised as I was when with great apprehension the letter was opened to reveal that not only had I passed the fearsome 11 Plus but I had won a place at the prestigious Wolverhampton Grammar School. I was one of five (Derek Lawrance, David Brown, John Disley, Laurie Light were the others) who would be going there. In previous years no more than one or two had been successful. Melvyn Hartland and Mary Anslow had gained entry to the Municipal Grammar School and others, including Michael Hartland, would be going to the Technical High School. Moreover, three pupils who were leaving the Wolverhampton area had gained places at the grammar schools in Wednesfield (Alan Fisher) and Sedgley (Clive Holes and Jacqueline Eyre).

We would not have been aware at the time, but these results would have been celebrated with similar joy in the staffroom."

WE MEET A WOLVES' LEGEND

Quite soon after the 11 Plus announcements, we were given details of the presentation evening for the sports awards. Derek remembers the event with great pride.

"The award evening took place in July at the Wolverhampton Technical College, later to become the University, in Wulfruna Street. As if the year could not get any better, our two trophies were to be presented by none other than the legendary manager of Wolverhampton Wanderers, Stan Cullis. It had been another highly successful season for Wolves. The hall was packed for the event. Parents were invited and I suspect many Dads (and a few Moms) were there for a chance to see Stan.

An opportunity to shake hands just once with Stan at this glorious point in the club's history was marvellous; to shake hands with him twice, as a member of both the football and cricket teams, was beyond my wildest dreams.

This was a fitting end to a memorable final year. Our sporting triumphs had been mirrored by examination success. We did not know it at the time, but we were probably the school's 'golden generation', its most successful in terms of academic, music and sporting achievements.

A great debt of gratitude would always be owed to Mr Lancaster and his devoted staff at All Saints Junior School. However,..."

'LANKY': A BRILLIANT HEADMASTER… OR A 'SICK MAN'?

Clive gives an assessment based on his and others' personal experiences and on Derek's archival research.

"All Saints in my time (late 1950s) was a good school. Though in a neighbourhood which was economically underprivileged, it did well if we judge by examination results. A few pupils every year passed the 11 Plus for the most academically demanding secondary institutions, Wolverhampton Girls' High School and Wolverhampton Grammar School, along with others who went to the Municipal Grammar or the Technical High School.

This academic success can be put down to the quality of the teaching staff and the exacting standards of one dominant personality: the headmaster, Mr Alf 'Lanky' Lancaster.

Alfred William Lancaster was born on 4 July 1916 in Cullercoats, a small village to the north of Newcastle-on-Tyne. After completing secondary school, he attended St John's Teachers' College, York from 1936 to 1938, and began his teaching career shortly before the outbreak of the Second World War. Like millions of other young men, he was called up, becoming a commissioned officer in the Royal Artillery, and fighting for king and country in France, Belgium and Holland.

When the war ended, his rise through the teaching profession was meteoric. First, after a couple of years, he was appointed to a deputy headship and then, on 10 January 1949, at the age of only 32, he took up the position of headmaster of All Saints Junior School, Wolverhampton.

He remained at All Saints for almost sixteen years until he was appointed headmaster of Christ Church C of E Junior

School, North Shields, Northumberland, a few miles from where he was born, taking up his new duties on 1 January 1965. He was a great loss to All Saints - or so it seemed at the time.

Mr Lancaster, or 'Lanky' as he was universally known to All Saints schoolchildren, stamped his authority and style on All Saints School from the start. He fitted the bill perfectly. He was a lay preacher in a C of E controlled school and his relations with the church next door were close and cordial. It is fair to say that throughout his career at All Saints, Mr Lancaster was viewed with a mixture of respect and fear by many, perhaps most, of its pupils.

He was an intimidating figure: tall, with a clipped moustache, a loud voice revealing a slight Geordie accent, and a sergeant-majorly presence both in and out of the classroom. He was also, by today's standards, an elitist. Many of the same pupils appear again and again in school photographs of his time: the academically gifted, the singers, the dancers, the sporty types: 'Lanky's' 'golden' boys and girls. Not many from the 'B' stream, and certainly none from the 'R' stream, the remedial class. But in all the photographs there is one constant: Mr Lancaster sitting front and centre, smiling at the camera.

No harm, perhaps, in blowing your own trumpet, but there was a darker side to 'Lanky's' personality: a fondness for administering corporal punishment. To be sure, back in the 1950s, there was nothing unusual about schoolchildren being beaten with a cane or hit with a ruler when they misbehaved. That was how it was back then. 'Lanky', however, tended to resort to these punishments for even the most minor misdemeanours.

I and my elder sister Jennifer counted ourselves lucky to be among Lanky's favourites. That being the case, one of the most unexpected and traumatic episodes of my time at All Saints was getting caned by 'Lanky'."

ON GETTING THE CANE

Clive recalls a painful memory.

"It was when we were in Mr Tod's class, 4A. A rainy playtime meant we were kept in, unsupervised. Things got a bit boisterous and I collided with a kid called John Bates, knocking a large loudspeaker off the top of a cupboard onto the floor. We managed to put it back. It wasn't broken, and we forgot about it as we continued gaming about.

About half an hour later, in an art and craft class held in a different room to 4A, a kid came in with a note. The teacher, can't think who it was, said: 'Mr Lancaster wants to see you two in his office.' I had no idea why.

We both went down to his office and knocked on the door. I can't remember what he said, but we were lined up and told to hold out our hand. He then produced a bamboo cane from behind his desk and we realised what was about to happen.

Clive Holes, Derek Mills

The cane stung like hell. I've never forgotten it. Three strokes each - but the shock was worse. I was not used to being hit, apart from odd punches in the playground and the occasional clip round the ear from my Mom, and certainly not in the controlled, ritualistic manner 'Lanky' employed.

We were sent back to class and I spent the rest of the morning feeling mortally embarrassed, confused and sorry for myself. I went to my Aunty Lal's in Gordon Street for lunch as normal, but nothing was normal. I couldn't eat anything and simply burst into tears when she asked me what the matter was. Of course, I got over it, but I have never forgotten that day. I bitterly regret that I never saw 'Lanky' after I left the school as I would have liked to ask him why we deserved a caning for such a minor misdemeanour. Did he enjoy it perhaps? To judge from what came to light a few years later, he very probably did.

In the course of research for this book, I was startled to discover how frequent 'Lanky's' use of the cane was, and on girls as well as boys. Around ten ex-pupils independently commented to me on it. One reported he caned her "for not knowing what an adjective was"; another because she was caught "running in the corridor". A girl in my class was "rulered" by him "for nothing", which caused her mild-mannered father to pay Mr Lancaster a home visit to warn him about what would happen if he did it again - he didn't. Another parent remarked that her son was caned by him often and seemingly deliberately in cold weather when the cane hurt more. All these ex-pupils are now in their 70s but, like me, they have never forgotten being beaten by 'Lanky' more than sixty years ago, and often for next to nothing.

I found out that a girl in my class who shall remain nameless had snitched on us. I bided my time and got my own back a few days later in an art and craft class. The class was busy making papier mâché models which we sealed with 'Gloy' - a thick grey glue in large conical pots. The girl who grassed me up had long blonde hair trailing down her back.

She was engrossed in what she was doing like everyone else. As I passed behind her on the way back from fetching some Gloy, I casually deposited a large blob in her golden tresses so they wouldn't flow quite as freely as her tell-tale tongue had. She never batted an eyelid, and nor did anyone else. I moved swiftly to my desk and resumed modelling a policeman on point duty.

Revenge, as they say, is a dish best served cold."

POSTSCRIPT

Mr Lancaster left All Saints School for his new job in the North-East at Christmas 1964. After sixteen years at All Saints, a fresh challenge in another Church of England school full of pupils with whose language, culture and outlook he had more empathy, and in the area he himself had grown up, must surely have looked attractive to an English traditionalist like him.

This career move seems not to have been a spur of the moment decision. The All Saints School logbooks kept at Wolverhampton City Archives show that, as early as 1961, he had expressed his concern at governors' meetings about the problems caused by the increasing numbers of migrant children who were arriving at the school with poor to non-existent English. The logbooks show that he had been given the day off on 24 July 1964 to attend an interview for what must have been this new position.

So, on 14 December 1964, he was given a lavish and well-attended send off. The then Director of Education for Wolverhampton, Mr G.W.R. Lines, gave a speech and presented him with a gold watch and a cheque. Many tributes were paid to him by present and former staff, school governors, Father Shannon, the ex-vicar of All Saints (1955-60), and several other local worthies before all those present adjourned to All Saints Church Hall for a farewell tea party. His last day at All Saints School was 18 December 1964, and off he went to take up a new headship on New Year's Day 1965.

Nothing more was heard of Mr Lancaster until almost exactly four years later, when an extraordinary series of articles began appearing in the Newcastle-on-Tyne press. The Newcastle Evening Chronicle reported on 11 December 1968 that Mr Alfred William Lancaster, aged 52, appeared before Tynemouth Magistrates on charges of indecent assault against eight of his male pupils: two 10-year-olds and six 11-year-olds. The assaults were alleged to have taken place in his office at Christ Church Junior School, North Shields. Following a complaint from a parent with a child at the school (not a parent of one of the alleged victims), the School Managers had referred the allegations to the police who had confronted Mr Lancaster. He had immediately admitted the assaults and resigned his headship forthwith.

Because of its seriousness, the case was referred by the Tynemouth Magistrates to Newcastle Quarter Sessions for trial, which took place in early January 1969. In its edition of 16 January 1969, the Newcastle Evening Chronicle reported that Mr Lancaster, now described as "an unemployed schoolmaster", pleaded guilty to all the charges and was sentenced to 18 months in prison. Passing sentence, Mr Grierson, the judge, described the case as the "most tragic that had ever come before him in his nine years on the bench". Mr Lancaster's career had been outstanding, he said. Medical reports had described Mr Lancaster as a "sick man" but "not a wicked man", and his admission of guilt was to his credit, continued the judge, as this meant the boys he had assaulted would not have to appear in court to testify against him. Further to his credit, the judge noted, was that following his resignation as headmaster, in the period between his arrest and trial, he had worked as a voluntary clerical assistant in a religious sanctuary. Despite all these mitigating circumstances, Mr Grierson declared that he had a public duty to impose a custodial sentence for such serious offences. It is not known in which prison Mr Lancaster served his sentence, or for how long.

News of Mr Lancaster's trial and conviction reached some homes in All Saints. People were understandably shocked, asking whether this kind of offending had been going on whilst Mr Lancaster had been headmaster of All Saints School. At the time, no one (to our knowledge) came forward to say that it had, but it must be remembered that the world of sixty years ago was a different place to now.

In the course of research for this book, Clive heard one specific allegation, but, as far as we know, it was never referred to the police.

Mr Lancaster died in a North Tyneside care home aged 85, in January 2002.

ST JOSEPH'S SECONDARY MODERN SCHOOL FOR BOYS

Directly opposite All Saints School was St Joseph's School. The contrast in the two schools could not have been greater. St Joseph's, popularly known as 'Joey's', was a Roman Catholic Secondary Modern School for boys aged 11 to 16.

The original St Joseph's School was built in 1868 on a piece of land in East Street, Horseley Fields, purchased for £350 by John Hawksford. This gentleman, incidentally, became the first Catholic Mayor of Wolverhampton. The school was opened on 2 November 1868 and was put in the charge of the Sisters of Mercy. They soon ran into financial difficulties with the result that it became a charge on S.S. Mary & John's parish. Almost immediately the school had to be enlarged to meet the demands of a growing population and the demands of Her Majesty's Inspectors.

St Joseph's School. (Photo: Wolverhampton Archives).

In 1914 the school, serving boys, girls and infants, moved from East Street to a new site on All Saints Road, opposite the school and church. Separated only by a narrow road, the temptation to antagonise each other was too much for both sets of pupils. As early as 1918, the All Saints logbook recorded that the headmaster of the Boys School complained to the "Mistress of St Joseph's R.C. School about the children throwing stones at our children whilst they were playing". It went on to say that: "one boy deliberately took aim at me, but fortunately he missed his objective".

Following school reorganisation in the borough, it became a school for senior boys in September 1934. Archbishop Williams laid the foundation stone for the school, built to provide space for 250 pupils. At the time of the reorganisation the infants were transferred to Holy Rosary School in Hickman Avenue.

Carol Bucknall recalls that her husband, his brothers and many of his friends were there in the 1940s. During the war years, most of the male teachers were in the army and some of the time they were taught by nuns who he said could be cruel.

In 1944/45 it became a Secondary Modern school, the only one just for boys in the town. The girls went to St Patrick's Secondary School.

WHERE EDUCATION WAS HAMMERED INTO YOU IN THE DAYS JUST AFTER THE WAR.

Billy Howe attended the senior school from 1948-52 and in his 'Lost Wolverhampton' website he has shared his memories, good and sad, with other ex-pupils. Some of his memories are recorded below. All photos are courtesy of Billy Howe and the 'Lost Wolverhampton' website.

"The photo above is Mr McVeigh's class of 1949. I am the tall chap at the back. As you can see, not many of the pupils could afford the school blazer then and, a little later, caps would become compulsory. Uniforms were bought from our school tailors Albert Williams, then on Snow Hill.

The school day would start with a bus journey from the bus stop outside the large Co-op store in Lichfield Street. This was the cross-town route from Claregate to Thompson Avenue via Vicarage Road, the nearest spot to the school. I would catch the returning bus from the stop in Vicarage Road opposite Maxwell Road.

Like most schools, we had a school song that was sung with great gusto on special occasions.

'The battle for life is the sternest strife.
The boy becomes the man.
Here we are learning the lessons of life,
Just do the best you can.

Sing, boys, sing, with a lilt and a swing,
The fame of Saint Joseph's School.
In chorus clear let your voices ring,
God Bless the dear old School.'

Life was strict at Joey's. I had the stick on numerous occasions for various misdemeanours but most of us were taught very well by some very good teachers, I certainly came away from there being numerate, literate, knew right from wrong and had respect for others.

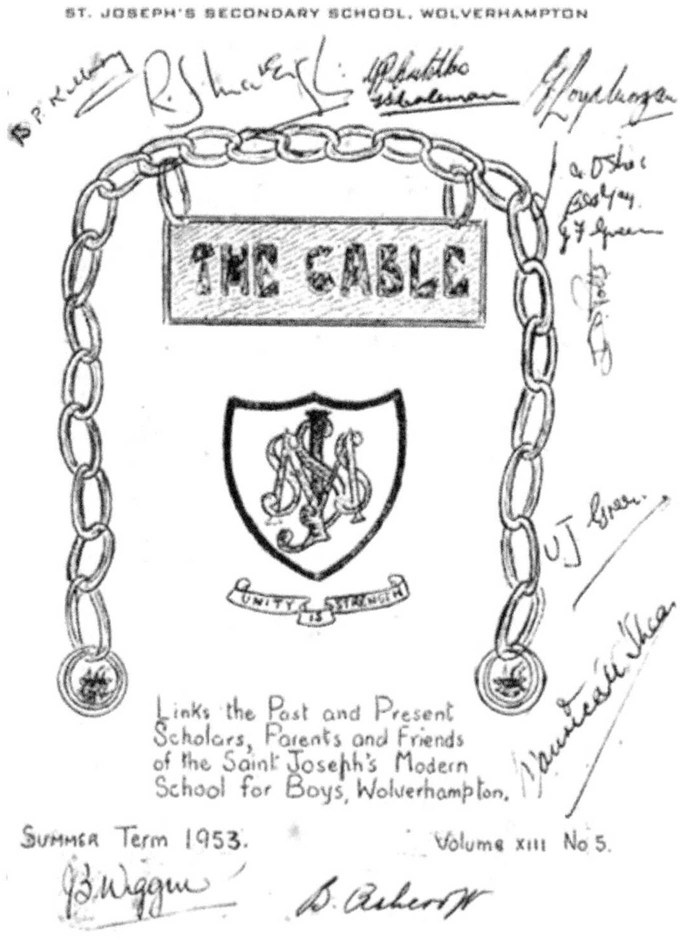

ST. JOSEPH'S SECONDARY SCHOOL, WOLVERHAMPTON

THE CABLE

UNITY IS STRENGTH

Links the Past and Present
Scholars, Parents and Friends
of the Saint Joseph's Modern
School for Boys, Wolverhampton.

Summer Term 1953.   Volume XIII No 5.

I can recall many of the teachers from the early 1950s: Mr Morgan (headmaster), Mr McVeigh, Mr Kilboy, Mr Critchlow, Mr Gorman, Mr McDonaugh, Mr Ashcroft, Mr Coleman, Mr Green and Mr Potts who all signed the school newsletter, 'The Cable', published by the students.

Mr Ashcroft doubled up as Woodwork teacher and Music teacher. He put on Gilbert & Sullivan shows every other year. The lads did HMS Pinafore, Pirates of Penzance, and Patience while I was there. Can you imagine that with not a girl in sight? What do you think that did to our street cred?

It was customary for teachers like Mr Ashcroft, to help with extra–curricular activities, especially sport. Mr Coleman, for example, combined his metalwork teaching with coaching the boxing team. He is remembered as a tough guy with his trusted ally, Lucifer – his cane."

Boxing seems to have been a major part of the sporting culture at the school. Colin James' late father went to St

Joseph's in the early 1950s and talked fondly of his days there.

"When he started, he had an ear problem which resulted in an operation to remove a mastoid. So, he was remembered as 'the kid with the bandage on his head'. However, this did not stop him from becoming the captain of the boxing team, taking over from John McLaughlin. These days were amongst his most cherished memories. The photo above is of the boxing team from 1954 and my Dad is the captain in the centre holding the cup."

Chris Collins, whose Dad taught at the school, remembers that "boxing nights were great and nearly always a win for Joey's. Nobody messed with Joey's lads".

Billy Howe has found a letter written in 1953 by the headmaster, G. Lloyd Morgan, which gives a fascinating insight into his beliefs and his deep respect for the teaching profession.

"Today we live in a world, where the air is fraught with change; old values have gone; old ideas and customs are in the melting pot, and new ones are challenging their places...

... This age presents a challenge to us as teachers, for never let it be forgotten, that it is upon the Teachers, that the main burden of building the new world will fall, for it is upon the education of the children the whole life of the community depends...

... Magna est veritas et prevalebit (truth is mighty and will prevail), that is the motto inscribed in secret on the heart of every true member of the teaching profession; it is certainly the spirit of St Joseph's."

Eric Gittins attended the school from 1959 to 1963 and remembers Mr Morgan. "He used to love giving the cane, but never hurt anyone. Abhorred swearing and used silly names instead of swearing words. Mr Critchlow oversaw the first year intake. Pupils were placed in classes A, B and C based on their 11+ exam results."

Mr Morgan with the school prefects.

Many of the teachers that Billy remembers from the early '50s were still there and Eric and a friend, Michael Sallis, reveal another side to their lives outside St Joseph's.

Mr Coleman of 'Lucifer' fame, for example, had an interest in model railways and bought all of Eric's Hornby railway gear. Mr Collins, as well as being a member of the Territorial Army, was a photography enthusiast and taught Eric how to develop films. He also ran a printing business in Lea Road, Penn Fields. Mr Peter Evans, the music teacher, played the organ at St Mary and St John's Church for school Masses, sometimes needing Eric's help with the stops. Peter played at Eric's wedding in 1969.

The school's curriculum was undergoing changes by the time Eric and Michael were about to leave. GCE (General

Certificate of Education) 'O' Level courses were introduced at the school in 1962. As the school leaving age was still 15, pupils wishing to finish the courses and take the exams would have had to stay on for one extra year. This would have required considerable changes to staffing, timetables and classrooms. Whether this influenced the thoughts of Mr Morgan is unknown, but he retired as headmaster in 1963.

Joey's by now was known to all as 'Joey's Jailhouse'. Whiffa Smith asks: "Was it because of the bars up the windows? I was never sure if it was to keep people out or to keep the kids in."

When Terry Barlow started in 1963, the headmaster was Mr O.D. Pass. It was rumoured that he was transferred from an approved school to sort out Joey's. Terry remembers him as a good head, very strict but fair. Terry recalls his five years at the school.

"There were all sorts of stories that were told to me about what to expect when I started; initiation ceremonies and such which, of course, never happened. There was strict discipline in force, and we had some tough characters as schoolmates, but on the whole, we were taught right from wrong, manners and respect. Woe betides anyone who strayed from good manners and a lack of respect.

We had very few facilities but there were some excellent teachers there and also some pretty ropey ones. The good ones made up for the bad ones; amongst others we had Maurice ('The Weed') O'Shea for Maths, Mr J. O'Shea (no relation) for English. He was a temperamental and, at times, a hilarious Irishman, very easily wound up. Mr McDonagh was deputy head. Another legendary teacher was Mr Coleman (Metalwork) with his famous weapon of torture - Lucifer, his cane. The Woodwork teacher during my time was

Clive Holes, Derek Mills

Mr 'Whistling Willy' Wiggett. A Londoner and Fulham fan. He had an unfortunate whistling lisp and a bad temper. He was also known to throw blocks of wood around. He ran the school Stamp Society or 'Starmp' Club as he called it. Think I remember 'Whistling Willy' throwing a jack plane!!

Geoff Pope was an excellent Art teacher, a sort of bohemian type character. He was also fond of golf and cricket. I can remember him practising his golf swing, with a piece of chalk on a kid's head. During cricket practice in the playground there would be 'The Weed' bowling to Geoff Pope and us kids fielding. Geoff would take great delight in padding-up to The Weed's leg-breaks with his false leg, thereby creating a superb 'clonking' sound. Can you imagine this happening today?"

Mr Pope is remembered by others like Michael O'Connor. "He designed the abstract Christmas Crib in St Peter's Gardens Wolverhampton. He also arranged a painting competition with the Gaumont cinema for the film 'Battle of the Bulge'." Francis Phillips remembers him for telling us to say: "Gordon Bennett" in lieu of swearing.

Another teacher remembered by Michael O'Connor is Mr Donovan, who was "handy with his hands, slapping and punching some of the kids." It was Mr Donovan, who organised Michael's "one and only school trip to Lourdes in France at Easter 1967."

Terry recalls sport being taken seriously despite the lack of playing fields on the school site.

"We played football. We had to walk to Rough Hills, I think it was. We also played on the pitches at Dunstall Park. There was swimming at Heath Town Baths or Central, via a Don Everall coach: 20 mins to get there and 10 mins in the water, but they taught us to swim! Cross country in the winter involved a route along Steelhouse Lane, down Cable Street, across the road, past the Dog Track, around the East Park and back to Joey's - I was hopeless at it. We played cricket as well, but I can't remember any competitive matches against other schools. Joey's had a reputation, previous to my time there, for an excellent boxing team - we had to do that and I hated it. The competitive boxing against other schools had ceased by the time I attended - thankfully.

We had snowball fights with All Saints in my time. Any excuse to get one over on the 'Proddies' across the road! Joey's didn't do me any harm, came out with some GCEs and went on to have a reasonable career in the printing trade."

Plans to create a new comprehensive school for Roman Catholic children had been drawn up in 1969. In September 1971, the two schools of St Joseph's and St Patrick's School for Girls combined to form the basis of St Edmund's Roman Catholic (Comprehensive) School. The new school was based at the verdant Compton Park site on the west side of the town, a far cry from the terraced streets of Steelhouse Lane. Mr Pope was one of many teachers who moved onto St Edmunds when Joey's closed.

7

LIFE AT HOME

JOHN NEAVE

"I was born in No. 97, Gordon Street on 27 April 1937. My father had various jobs in his life but there was a depression in the Thirties. He was working at the AJS motorcycle factory in Blakenhall but the whole motor car industry went bust: Sunbeam went, and the AJS went. Then of course he had to find another job, temporary, and he was working on the racecourse, doing maintenance, painting, because there was a lot of unemployment in Wolverhampton at that time. That was before my time.

By the time I can remember, he was working in the Austin Motor Company in Birmingham, and he'd go there on the bus or the train, every day. And sometimes in the winter, we'd get terrible fogs. Sometimes he'd come back by road. He'd get off the bus and have a walk and get back on the bus, because it was going that slow! And sometimes by the time he got back to Wolverhampton, it was almost time to go back again! It was awful, he didn't get much sleep. He had to be back in Birmingham at half past seven in the morning.

I think my mother told me she worked at Baker's, making shoes. And when she was 21, they laid her off and she went to work for Edge's in Bilston. They were shoemakers as well, but it was a much rougher kind of work. When she was at Baker's she was making ladies' shoes, but when she went to Edge's they were making army boots, and it was very hard on the hands. Bakers was a high-class shoe shop, making good stuff they were.

All Saints: The History, People, Places

I started school at All Saints in 1942 during the War. They had air-raid shelters at the back of the school. We had a few practices, but fortunately we never had to use them. There were great holes in the playground because there was no money to spend on it. It was terrible, the school playground, but the school was fine. I remember the teachers. There were two sisters there, and they were always known as 'big' Miss Brown and 'little' Miss Brown. And there was Miss Jemmett, the Headmistress. I'm not sure but I think she was in charge of the infants department. And there was Miss Morgan, Miss Street, Mrs Smith... Miss Roberts. Mrs Smith's husband was a teacher at Graiseley as well. I was talking to Helen Rudd and she said there used to be a May Day at All Saints, with a maypole. I think I went around the maypole one year.

After I left All Saints, I went to Graiseley. Some of the teachers there got played up. They were hard, some of the kids. But I got on alright there.

When I left Graiseley, I went to Wolverhampton Art School and I loved my time there. I was already printing before I left school on a little tiny machine my father bought me for £9 and I was doing little jobs. Even before I left Graiseley, I was doing one day a week at the Art School. This was all printing, and one of the men who was teaching there, gave me this [shows Clive a wooden carving of a girl on a pony made by Norman Thelwell]. That man was a cartoonist, Norman Thelwell. He was teaching then, teaching Fine Art at Wolverhampton Art School until 1956.

He was the cartoonist for the News Chronicle from 1960 until it closed. He passed away about four or five years ago. He was a very nice fellow, I got on very well with him. He used to bring the linocuts that his pupils had done down to the basement, and I used to print them for him, you see, on the old machine we had there. He wasn't very big you know, a very little man, smaller than me, he was! He was a lovely chap though…

John Neave at work in Gordon Street in 2020.

When I was there, the Eagle comic came out. He was the one that did the cartoon strip in the Eagle comic called 'Chicko'. They were advertising for cartoonists to supply work for the new comic and he must have won the competition, and once he got that job, he was also doing cartoons for Punch and he was also doing them for one of the Sunday papers, I forget which one. And later on, I suppose he could make more money out of doing his cartoons than he could from teaching art, so he finished at Wolverhampton, stopped teaching there. But while he was there, he was a very interesting man, and I had a good time there.

Once I left school, I went more or less full time to Art School, and I'd come home about half past four and start printing in my shed down the garden, doing my own little jobs there, making myself a fiver a week, whatever it was. An apprenticeship only paid £3.50 a week, like three pound ten, that's how it used to be. So, I was earning myself a few bob and building a business up, which I did. And gradually it got better and better… But it's more of a hobby now, something I enjoy doing.

During the War, we had an evacuee. His name was David Coussins. We became big friends; we were always knocking about together. He was billeted at Mrs Rudd's, you see, and her husband, and Helen, in Gordon Street. He went to All Saint's school... and, anyway, the War was on, like, and we were big mates. Where I am now, there was a car park. This big car park belonged to the Royal Hospital and the doctors used to park their cars there. But during the War, like, anything was parked there. I wasn't with David that night, but there was this big low-loader, with the fuselage of an aircraft on, and the kids were climbing all over it. Anyway, David actually got into the cockpit of the plane. And the bloke came back and didn't even shout before he started the engine up and he drove off with David still in it. He didn't stop till Shrewsbury! The Rudds wondered, 'Where's David?' Twelve o'clock came, one o'clock. They were worried to death, 'where's the lad?' you know. Anyway, eventually, the police brought him back from Shrewsbury, and they weren't very pleased at all! I would say they were taking the plane back to be repaired somewhere, but where its destination was, I don't know. I think the driver had just paused here for a break. David would have been about 8 or 9…

At the time, there was this big yard at the back of where Helen lived and there were four or five horses stabled there, when I was a lad. And they'd come at half-past five, six o'clock. You'd see these shire horses walking up Gordon Street, and they'd be stabled in these stables. They had come off the canal, they were canal horses, towing the boats, you know. This was during the War. They would come off at Bilston Road, and they came up Eagle Street, Steelhouse Lane, and Gordon Street. They used to keep them overnight in the stables. We used to follow the horses round with a bucket and shovel, for manure for the garden!

In 1947, there was a terrible winter, and nobody had got any coal. Of course, everybody had coal fires, very few had gas fires. They relied on coal. The roads were blocked and the railways as well with the bad conditions. So, we went over Rough Hills, us kids, digging coal. It was very rough there. In my lifetime nobody ever got coal from there because it was terrible stuff. It used to fly out of the fire, bang! Very poor quality, but when you've got no coal at all it was better than nothing. And these old type houses like here, they'd all got outside loos. There was the coalhouse, then the toilet.

At No. 100, Gordon Street in those days there was this Italian man working from there, and his name was Tony Risi, and at one time he used to make ice-cream. Later, he stopped making ice-cream, but he had some big cold rooms there, and he used to make ice for the fish places, to keep the fish fresh. He had a wagon and he used to go round all the fish places to deliver the ice. There weren't many people who had refrigeration years ago. He sold the yard and he bought the yard that Helen was living in. That was at 103, Gordon Street.

The man he sold the yard at 100, Gordon Street to was a man called George Codd, a fish merchant… with a name like that, you couldn't believe it! C-O-double-D. And this George Codd, he had the only fish stall on the outside market in Wolverhampton, in front of St Peter's. He used to operate there, but he also had a wagon, and he used to deliver fish to a lot of the restaurants and works canteens in this area. He came originally from Milford Haven and his family had trawlers. He used to supply a lot of fish in Wolverhampton. Interesting times. He had his hair swept back and he always had a big American car. It looked a bit funny in Gordon Street. He had a shop as well in Broad Street.

My memories of the fellows going to work in the morning. They'd be walking to work along Steelhouse Lane in heavy boots with great big pop bottles full of cold tea. Because they were working in hot strip mills, they'd need the tea for their thirst, you know, to cool themselves down a bit. In Dixon Street and Major Street there were tar distilleries working there then. And they had steam waggons, 'Sentinels', made at Stafford or Shrewsbury, I forget which. In Steelhouse Lane they'd drop these hot cinders on the snow, you know. They went 'chug, chug, chug' chain-driven, quite a sight they were. There were a few of those…

Goodyears was a big employer, yes, that and Courtaulds. My aunty worked at Courtaulds, from when it opened to when it closed. I think it opened about 1922, I'm not sure exactly, been gone a fair while, ain't it, a big employer in the town, like Goodyears. It was in Whitmore Reans, down by the racecourse somewhere, where the new estate is today. Big factory…"

CLIVE HOLES

Clive remembers the 1950s:

"My abiding childhood memory of All Saints in the 1950s is of a tightly knit community in which neighbours were also relatives, workmates, and friends. Take my own family, the Graftons.

My mother and her four siblings (three sisters, one brother) were born in All Saints between 1901 and 1919. They all went to All Saints School, got married in All Saints Church and lived in the neighbouring streets, at least for the early part of their married lives. Three of the five never left the neighbourhood. Seven of the next generation were also born and went to school there. All these family members lived within half-a-mile of each other in All Saints Rd, Gordon Street, Sutherland Place, Vicarage Road and Steelhouse Lane. Only towards the end of the 1950s did some begin to drift away.

Three of the men worked for part or all their working lives for the Goodyear Tyre and Rubber Company in Bushbury. Others worked in small engineering firms in nearby Blakenhall. Before they married, all the sisters helped in the family business, a Steelhouse Lane newsagents, owned by the Grafton family for about fifty years. None went out to work after they got married, devoting themselves to raising their children. They met often, dropping into each other's homes for a cup of tea and a chat, usually in the course of their weekly shopping - which they also did entirely in All Saints.

It was not unusual for holidays to be taken with other family members in places such as Blackpool, the Isle of Man and Butlin's Holiday Camps. Several of the men were football fans, regularly attending Wolves or Walsall matches. Christmas was invariably a time of family get-togethers in each other's houses on a rotating basis: eating, drinking, piano-playing and singing. No cars were needed - all lived near enough to walk."

TERRACED HOUSING

"Up until the time my family left it in 1958, the many hundreds of terraced houses in the All Saints neighbourhood were pretty much an exact replica of the house I lived in at 80, All Saints Road and, size-wise at least, were unchanged from the time they had been built about sixty years before.

Terraced houses on the north side of Maxwell Road. Derek's father, Roland, lived at No. 31 with his parents and siblings during the 1930s and early 1940s.

It is thus possible for me to contextualise very accurately the raw data which emerges from the censuses of over a century ago, based on my lived experience of the mid-1950s. My comments can be taken to apply to the other neighbouring streets in All Saints such as Dartmouth Street, Gordon Street, Granville Street, Adelaide Street, Gower Street, and Maxwell Road. I had relatives and classmates who lived for many years in streets such as these. This was about a decade before the mass modernisation of the All Saints housing stock took place, when novelties such as proper bathrooms and inside toilets were first installed.

In 1901-1911, and still when I lived there in the 1950s, these houses all had an identical layout which I believe was the norm for all the terraced houses on the north side of All Saints Road.

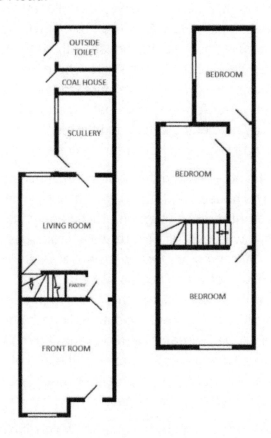

They each had five rooms and a scullery. Upstairs there were two medium-sized bedrooms and one smaller one at the back which could also serve as a storeroom/ box room. Downstairs there was a living/ dining room, and another room which looked out onto the street. This was always referred to in my day as 'the front room' and was only used at Christmas and on other special occasions. A small scullery overlooking the backyard was equipped with an electric cooker and a free-standing electric boiler and mangle for doing the washing. There was no bathroom in the modern sense and the only room in the house with running (cold only) water was the scullery, which was where we washed ourselves in the morning and where my Dad shaved. Small quantities of hot water for personal washing and tea-making were provided by an electric kettle, and for bathing we had a tin bath which was filled with hot water heated in the boiler.

We bathed in the scullery with the door to the adjoining living room closed. The house was heated by coal fires in the living room and the 'front room', though in practice only the living/ dining room fire was ever lit. There were fireplaces in the three upstairs bedrooms but they were never used, even in the coldest winter: hot water bottles were the norm, as was the chamber pot for any night-time calls of nature. The pantry, where all food was kept, was an unlit dark cupboard under the stairs. The unheated lavatory and the 'coal hole' were situated in adjacent small annexes at the end of a short (c. 20 foot) concrete yard. To reach either meant going out of the back door, whatever the weather.

This back yard led to a communal path which linked the backs of around ten houses to one another and ended with an 'entry' which led out to the street. This shared path was the main means by which the occupants of the houses communicated with each other: you simply walked along it, entered the neighbour's back yard, and knocked on the back door. People who lived in the street hardly ever knocked on their neighbours' front doors - that was for the milkman, the postman and visitors who were not neighbours. In All Saints Road, the terraced houses I am talking about all had a tiny back garden on the far side of the common path that ran along the backs if the houses. These gardens backed onto similar small gardens belonging to the residents of Maxwell Road, which was built in the 1890s in tandem with All Saints Road.

Back row left to right: Kenny Jones, who lived next door at No. 81, Jennifer Holes (my elder sister, aged 11), Pat Baggot (Jennifer's best friend from across the road), Yours Truly, aged 10; Front row. left to right: Lawrence Disley (my best friend's younger brother) from about six doors up, my younger sister Pam (aged 2); Surinder.

Clive thinks that Surinder's family was the first Indian family to move into All Saints Road.

All Saints: The History, People, Places

There were many extended families like ours in All Saints, and their members were known to each other: the Hickmans, Bickleys, Belchers, Stallards, Bagotts, Southalls, Owens, Blackwells, to name a few. Community bonds were strong and existed on several levels. A good illustration of this is what happened when my parents finally decided we would have to leave All Saints Road. My younger sister Pam was born in August 1956. This meant there were five of us in a small, terraced house which had only two decent sized bedrooms and a box room which was used as a store cum workshop. There was no bathroom (we washed at the kitchen sink and bathed in a tin bath in front of the fire) and only an outside toilet.

My parents looked at houses being built on two new private housing estates: one at Ettingshall Park, about two and a half miles away on the road to Sedgley, and the other at Coven, around six miles north of Wolverhampton, just off the A449 road to Stafford. My father, who is not from the area (he is Welsh), preferred Coven, where he thought the houses were better quality and it was only a couple of miles or so north of where he worked, at Goodyear's, which would make for a much easier daily commute.

My mother would have none of it. She talked as if Coven was halfway to the moon. Yes, the houses were nice, but she didn't know the area at all. It was 'too far away', and I would have to change schools just before the 11+... Above all (the real reason), she would feel cut off from her sisters, nephews, friends and former neighbours in All Saints! She put her foot down: Ettingshall Park it had to be, and we moved there in October 1958.

Life continued much as before, with my mother (and Pam, now a toddler in a push chair) catching the No. 58 bus on a Tuesday and Friday along the Dudley Road as far as the stop near the Coliseum cinema and walking through the back streets to All Saints to see her sisters and do a bit of shopping.

For me the newsagent's (always known as 'the shop') which one of my aunts ran in Steelhouse Lane also became one of the places I went to for home-cooked dinners during my last two years at All Saints School. Monday to Wednesday I went to Aunty Lal's in Sutherland Place, and on Thursday and Friday (my favourite!) to Aunty Hilda at 'the shop' in Steelhouse Lane, where there were usually apple fritters on a Thursday and always fish and chips on a Friday, all cooked by her expert hand, despite her being more or less blind from the effects of meningitis that struck in her mid-30s.

Job done, and everyone was happy!"

LEISURE

PHYSICAL RECREATION

"The All Saints neighbourhood was once well supplied with green spaces. At one end, where Vicarage Road became Pond Lane at the point where Caledonia Road went off at right angles, there was a large area of rough, uneven grass and cinders known as 'The Rec'. It had iron railings on two sides, but there were gaps where you could squeeze through and a large gate in Pond Lane which was usually left open.

This was where the kids from All Saints played football in the 'jumpers for goalposts' tradition. On one side of the Rec there was a corrugated iron fence with notices warning 'Trespassers will be prosecuted' - not that that ever stopped us! Over the fence there was a stagnant, weed-filled pond surrounded by mature trees, mainly willow but with some crab apples. It looked like a scene from 'Alice in Wonderland'. We often went 'scrumping' there, but the apples were usually too bitter to eat. The main attraction of the pond was the notices warning us not to go near!

Beyond the fourth, eastern boundary of the Rec was the Bayliss Jones & Bayliss (BJB) sports ground, and beyond that the Dixon Street playing fields, a large area marked out with football pitches where All Saints School played their matches described in other parts of this book.

Sad to say, many green spaces have been lost. The Rec and the BJB sports ground were sold off long ago and have been completely built over by housing developers. The Dixon Street playing fields are still there but are now partly a children's playground and partly a park area incorporating a fitness trail. The football pitch where we played our school matches is now planted with young trees. A photo was shown on page 88."

Clive Holes, Derek Mills

SATURDAY MORNING CINEMA

"'We come along on a Saturday morning, greeting everybody with a smile!' That was the first line of the rousing song which began the children's matinee show every Saturday at the Savoy cinema in Wolverhampton town centre, a half-mile walk from All Saints Road, recalls Clive. It was the anthem of the ABC Minors, the children's club (complete with lapel badge) which you had to join to gain admission.

In the pre-television age, every large cinema had such a club: in Wolverhampton: the Gaumont, the Savoy and the Odeon. The queues to get in were always long, the audiences noisy and excitable. The show would start with a community sing-song, with the words flashed up on the screen and live musical accompaniment from an organ. The whole thing conducted by a master of ceremonies up on stage.

It was an odd collection of songs, and always the same. I remember 'My old man said follow the van, and don't dilly-dally on the way!', a song from the Victorian music hall. Then there was 'Please Mr Porter, what shall I do?' another piece of Cockney Victoriana with a line which pleased the trainspotters: 'I wanted to go to Birmingham and they've taken me on to Crewe'. Oddest of the lot for a crowd of Wolverhampton under-12s was 'I belong to Glasgow' which contains the lines 'I belong to Glasgow, dear old Glasgow town; but there's something the matter with Glasgow cos it's going round and round; I'm only a common old working chap as anyone here can see, but when I get a couple of drinks on a Saturday, Glasgow belongs to me!'

But who cared? This was the prelude to the main event: two hours of old cartoons (Popeye, Micky Mouse, Donald Duck) followed by the main feature film, usually a past its sell-by date cliff-hanger from the 1930s such as 'Flash Gordon' or an adventure film featuring a character called 'Zorro' who always wore a black mask to match his black Mexican hat - which was even older!"

TELEVISION AND RADIO

"My Dad, Doug Holes, was early into gadgets. Was it something to do with him being in the RAF during the war? I don't know. So, at a time when it was still unusual, he passed the driving test in his early '20s and bought his first (second-hand) car in 1950. Our family was also one of the first in All Saints Road to get a television, also at the beginning of the '50s. I was born in 1948, so can't remember a time when we didn't have these things.

Our first TV was tiny: a nine-inch screen, and black and white only. It sat in the corner and wasn't on that much. The BBC, then the only channel, broadcast mainly in the early evening. There seemed to be a lot of 'test-cards' and breakdowns: a screen saying 'Normal service will be resumed as soon as possible' backed by soothing classical music seemed to constitute a large part of the output. However, it was still a marvel of technology (a word that didn't exist in those days) and it attracted the attention of the neighbours… and their children.

In the early 1950s, pre-school children's television consisted of a thrice-weekly 15-minute afternoon slot called 'Watch with Mother', a clone of BBC radio's 'Listen with Mother'. It featured 'Andy Pandy', 'Bill and Ben the Flower Pot Men' and, a little later on, 'Rag, Tag and Bobtail', and 'The Wooden Tops', all of them puppet-shows. I was fascinated by these characters, especially 'Bill and Ben' and the strange language these two used ('ickle pickle', 'flobadob'), as were some of the other kids from All Saints Road who came round our house to watch with me. This must have been when we were all pre-school, as the programme was scheduled for broadcasting during the day. But what goes round comes round. Now a grandad, I hear very much the same kind of words in the mouths of the Teletubbies whenever I watch kids' TV with my grandchildren.

Later on, when I was aged 8 or 9, 'Sportsview' with Peter Dimmock was my 'must-watch'… except I was never allowed to watch it! It was on too late, and the signature tune that started it was always the signal for bedtime. What I was allowed to see before ascending 'the wooden hills to Bedfordshire' were the mouth-watering opening credits, featuring clips of Stanley Matthews playing in what I think was the famous 'Matthews Final' of 1953. Sir Stan, as he was later to become, masterminded an improbable 4-3 win over Bolton in the Cup Final after his team, Blackpool, were 1-3 down with only 20 minutes to go. I can hear the signature tune now: de-rum, de-rum de-diddly-dum, de-rum, de-rum de-diddly-dum, de der-der-der-der dit-der!

Even after the coming of TV, radio (or 'the wireless' as it was known then) was still the dominant backdrop to life in All Saints Road. My mother was a devotee of the BBC Light Programme, the forerunner of Radio 2, and in the school holidays when we kids were at home, the day always began to the strains of 'Housewives' Choice'. At lunchtime it was 'Workers' Playtime', and tea was signalled by the strains of the harp which introduced 'Mrs Dale's Diary' a radio soap-opera which Mom never missed.

But for me, one radio programme stood out… Quatermass. This was one of the very early sci-fi programmes broadcast in the mid-1950s. It came on at about 8.00 pm, and I was absolutely terrified of it. I literally hid under the table throughout each half hour episode, but I wouldn't have missed it for the world. It was full of weird and frightening sound effects, as the earth was besieged by invisible alien life forms that took over human bodies without the humans that inhabited them realising it. Professor Quatermass (hence the name of the programme) was charged with defending the earth against the invaders. It was later transferred to TV, but was much more effective on radio, as the imagination was left to run riot. I still shiver whenever I hear the terrifying signature tune – 'Mars, the Bringer of War' from Holst's 'Planet Suite'."

TRAINSPOTTING

"A few hundred yards from the Dixon Street playing fields ran the two main railway lines to Wolverhampton: the ex-London Midland & Scottish (LMS) and ex-Great Western (GWR) Railways. The ex-GWR line is now part of the Metro tramline to Birmingham.

In the 1950s, the motive power on these routes was still overwhelmingly steam, and many youngsters passed their time during the summer holidays sitting next to the lines, note-book and pencil in hand, jotting down the numbers of passing locomotives and hoping for the odd 'cop' - an engine that the lucky spotter had not seen before - which would later be carefully underlined using a ruler and a red pen in the books published by the guru of trainspotters, Ian Allen.

I was lucky as my Welsh grandparents lived not far from the seaside resort of Porthcawl, and their house was only about two hundred yards from the main railway line connecting Swansea to London. Every summer, during Wolverhampton's 'Industrial Fortnight' when most of the big factories shut down, we visited them for our holidays. I would spend much of the time trainspotting, and 'copped' many locomotives that never came anywhere near Wolverhampton.

On warm summer nights, lying in bed with the windows open, I would listen to the tremendous exhaust beat of the heavy coal trains on the long ascent from Port Talbot, often with a second engine, the 'banker' pushing from the back. If I sat up, I could see through the window the bright orange glow of the firebox illuminating the fireman as he shovelled away. The engine itself was invisible, just the footplate was picked out in the pitch black.

Like stamp-collecting, this rather nerdy hobby did have its educational side. Take the ex-LMS's 'Jubilee' class of locomotives. A large number were named after overseas territories once ruled by Britain, like 'Leeward Islands', 'Straits Settlements' or 'Bihar and Orissa'... or battleships of the British fleet like 'Implacable' and 'Indomitable'. The ex-GWR's largest loco classes carried the names of grand English country houses such as 'Eynsham Hall', 'Frilford Grange' and 'Cookham Manor'. Kings, earls, duchesses, admirals, regiments, even Derby-winning racehorses all featured as engine names - it was as if the pre-BR railway companies had been constantly tipping their hats to the Crown, the Empire and the aristocracy. Trainspotting certainly improved my knowledge of colonial geography and the British class system.

After nationalisation in 1948, some names were changed to bring them into line with contemporary reality, as when 45610 'Gold Coast' was renamed 'Ghana' following that country's independence in 1958 - only to be consigned to the scrapheap six years later as 'dieselisation' took hold. Harold Macmillan's 'wind of change' was certainly blowing through the old Empire, and in the UK it was taking with it the steam locomotives named after its former colonies. These days things are much more banal: instead of riding behind 'Isambard Kingdom Brunel' when you catch 'The Red Dragon' service from Swansea to London, you're much more likely to be hauled by 'Reading Main Signal Box'."

HOLIDAYS

TRIPS BY CAR

"I remember what Dad's first car looked like though I am not sure of the make or year. It was old and black and the registration number was HON 758. It didn't have a self-starter - you had to turn the engine over with a starter handle which you inserted into a hole below the front of the radiator.

Dad kept the car in a lock-up garage at the top of All Saints Road, and we had a pair of wooden chocks which had to be carefully positioned to ease the car over the gutter as Dad gently reversed it onto the road. He hadn't been driving that long and it amused us kids sitting in the back to see him frantically turning the wheel as he attempted to complete a three-point turn without hitting the curb. 'Dad's being a mad driver again!', we shouted gleefully.

The Holes family on a Sunday picnic in Shropshire, c.1960; left to right: Clive, Pam, Jennifer, Mom (in the driving seat though she couldn't drive).

This ancient machine was soon replaced by a more modern car: a bulbous, cream coloured Austin A40 (AJX 470). Then there was a powerful green Ford Consul (JEA 532) with a bench seat in front that went like the clappers.

Clive in training for the next All Saints match.

Then finally, in 1960, came the first new car Dad ever bought a flashy two-tone maroon and grey Vauxhall Victor (312 JW) with the gear-change on the steering column.

These cars were a godsend, as on lazy summer Sunday afternoons they took us out into the countryside to lie on the grass, kick a football about, and have a picnic. Favourite destinations were around Stourport, Bridgnorth and Enville Common. The car also replaced the train as our means of transport for the twice-yearly trips at Easter and in the summer holidays to see our Welsh relatives. They also enabled us to go on trips for the day or the weekend, sometimes to North Wales resorts like Rhyl or Llandudno, but also, the highlight - to Blackpool in September.

The Blackpool Illuminations were a fixture in the calendar for many West Midlands families in the 1950s. Advertisements for full- or half-board in Blackpool's boarding houses would start to appear in the Express & Star in the summer, and it paid to get your booking in early. Most of the boarding houses were in streets a few minutes' walk from the promenade, just behind Blackpool Tower and its famous Ballroom.

The photo below was taken on one such trip in September 1959. We drove up to Blackpool on the Friday afternoon (I had to get permission to leave school early) and came home on the Sunday evening. Somehow the weather was always balmy on those mid-September evenings in Lancashire, as we strolled up and down the prom admiring the light displays and hopping on and off the trams that went to some mysterious destination called 'Bispham'.

Blackpool beach, September 1959; Aunty Lal, Clive, Mom, Pam, Jen.

In 1959, the Illuminations coincided with a football match on the Saturday afternoon between Blackpool and Wolves. Three days earlier, Dad had taken me to Molineux to watch Wolves thrash Fulham 9-0, so we were full of confidence as we entered Bloomfield Road. But - typical Wolves - it was not to be, and we were well beaten 3-1. We consoled ourselves with the thought that you can't win 'em all.

Saturday night in Blackpool was then (as now) 'Come Dancing' time. We kids sat on the side-lines with a bottle of pop and a bag of crisps as we watched Mom and Dad foxtrot and quickstep round the crowded Tower Ballroom, rediscovering their youth and occasionally bumping into other couples like themselves from Wolverhampton, Birmingham, Rochdale, Sheffield, you name it. Blackpool in the 1950s was a Mecca for the people of the Midlands and North."

EVENTS TO REMEMBER

THE 1953 CORONATION

"The biggest national celebration of the 1950s was the coronation of Queen Elizabeth II on 2 June 1953. Unfortunately, in Wolverhampton, it poured down most of the day, but that didn't stop the street parties in All Saints and elsewhere.

For the children, special events were organised. My sister Jen and I went to one of these at the Coach and Horses public house on Bilston Road. To this day, I don't know why our parents thought this was a good idea. My Dad's local was the Ring O'Bells on Dudley Road.

The children's party at the Coach and Horses pub, Bilston Road on Coronation Day, 1953. Extreme right: Clive (aged 4), Jen (age 6).

I don't remember much about the party beyond the fact that we knew hardly any of the other kids there. Perhaps that's why we look a bit miserable in the photograph, despite our party hats. I seem to remember taking a dislike to the boy standing dead centre in the front, who wore a jacket identical to the one I wore. The cheek of it! It was all a bit too much for a 4-year-old!"

CHRISTMAS

"For us children, Christmas was the highlight of the year. For our parents, especially Mom, it was a major logistical operation. Christmas Day really began late on Christmas Eve, when pillowcases were filled with presents (and always an apple and an orange!) and placed at the foot of our beds as we slept. By 5.00 a.m. on Christmas morning, we were awake and peering round in the dark to see 'if he's been yet' - though I'm not sure I really ever believed in him: how could someone the size of Father Christmas get down our chimney? And where did he park the reindeers?

Christmas morning was frantic, with Mom getting the turkey ready (we never had anything else at Christmas), chopping and preparing vegetables, making stuffing, steaming the Christmas pudding and generally being the domestic goddess that so many women had been trained to be by their own mothers back in those days. Meanwhile we played with our new toys.

One Christmas morning, I was surprised to find that one of my presents was a pair of boxing gloves. I can't think why, as I was never pugilistically inclined. A dictionary would have been a better choice. Anyway, I challenged my sister Jen to a boxing match, which, to my surprise, Jen - and more importantly Dad, as the 'responsible adult' - readily agreed to. I put one of the gloves on, and Jen the other, and we squared up to each other. Bang! Smack! One punch each. She winded me, and I made her nose bleed. With tears in our eyes, we both threw in the towel and called it a draw. My mother went mad, as she had to clear up the mess on top of the hundred and one other jobs she was already doing. Dad, meanwhile, smoked a Christmas cigar.

Every year, as soon as Christmas dinner was over, Christmas tea was the next thing on the agenda. This was part of a long-standing family tradition, whereby we entertained Mom's sisters and their families on Christmas night and either Aunty Lal or (more often) Aunty Lil did the same on Boxing Day evening. My earliest memories of these evenings, after the ham and tongue sandwiches, the pickles, and the Christmas trifle and cake had been eaten, are of Mom playing the piano and Dad singing a few 'solos' (he was an excellent tenor) and then a lot of family sing-alongs as the men sipped their beer or whisky and the ladies their port and lemon.

It seems the Graftons had always been good at performing, going back to the 1920s and '30s. Jeremy Walters, a cousin of mine (his grandmother and mine were sisters), comments as follows in his book, 'My Father's Wolverhampton, 1905-1931', page 62: 'Christmas was usually spent at the Graftons' home and their Christmas parties were scenes of mirth. The Man on the Flying Trapeze was one of their star turns [....] … Hilda, Lal, Kitty, Lil and Len provided much fun for their parents and visitors'. The five named were of course my mother (Kitty) and her four siblings, my uncle and aunts. Mom and Aunty Lal can be seen in earlier photos.

On Christmas Day afternoon 1958, a couple of months after we had left All Saints Road for Ettingshall Park, disaster struck. When Mom started to put the final touches to the trifle which would be served to our relatives in the evening, she found she hadn't bought enough cream. What to do? The shops were all shut. She had a bright idea - borrow some from Aunty Lil who lived in Vicarage Road a couple of miles away.

Dad was 'between cars', so driving wasn't an option, and there were no buses on Christmas Day. We didn't even have a phone (but then nor did Aunty Lil), so there was nothing for it except for Jen and me to *walk to my Aunty's and get some*! Why Dad couldn't do this I don't know, especially as on Christmas afternoon the BBC was showing the programme we as kids loved above all others: Walt Disney. But there was no choice, so off we trudged through the deserted streets carrying an empty basket, just as our most fave programme of all was starting. We got a lift back with our Uncle Ron, but the memory of that infamous Christmas chore still rankles!

But Christmas wouldn't have been complete without a trip to the Grand to see the pantomime. We usually went to the children-only matinee one Saturday afternoon before Christmas, when huge parties of overexcited children would shriek non-stop for a couple of hours. Everyone came laden with bags of sweets, but I have an abiding memory of being allowed to take a Mars bar only on condition that it was cut up into small slices to make it last longer.

The show itself was often scarcely audible for all the talking and shouting from the audience, often in indignant (or gleeful) response to wisecracks from the actors about 'the idiots who live in Bushbury' or 'posh Widow Twankie from Wombourne'. Then suddenly it was time to go home and meet our parents waiting in the theatre foyer."

A VISIT TO THE ROYAL HOSPITAL

On 28 December 1928, HM King George V decreed that the Wolverhampton and Staffordshire General Hospital should henceforth be known as The Royal Hospital, Wolverhampton. Clive has good cause to remember the importance of 'the Royal' to the residents of All Saints and beyond.

Unlike today, a lot of children's games were outdoors and seasonal and used materials to hand, or none at all: for the boys, conkers in the autumn, snowball fights and slides in winter, marbles and 'donkey-fights' in summer. None of these activities were controlled by teachers, they just happened. Sometimes there were accidents.

"When I was about six and still at All Saints Infant School", says Clive, "I remember some very cold weather when melting snow in the playground had frozen hard overnight and created the perfect conditions for a 'slide' - a patch of sheet ice about twenty feet long, rubbed smooth by many pupils taking a run at it and sliding with their feet side-on at 90 degrees. It looked great fun. I had a couple of goes but I couldn't get the hang of it and didn't go very fast. On my third or fourth attempt, I decided to really go for it. I flung myself down the slide, going faster and faster until… suddenly I was in the snow at the end of the slide, face down and not knowing how I had got there. I think I must have then blacked out.

The next thing I remember is that somebody, I didn't know who, had picked me up. I was draped over this person's shoulder with a lot of sticky red goo running down my face, and there was a handkerchief soaked in it… and my head hurt. I don't remember much about how I got to the next place, except that a car was involved, and the place was not the school, but somewhere else… I was on a table with lights above and people wearing hats and gowns looking down on me. They were doing something to my head.

I must have fallen sleep at that point, as I woke up at home on my mother's lap, with the noise of jangling keys - my Dad was coming through the front door. He should be at work, I thought, what's he doing here? On my head I could feel something like a hat. It was a thick bandage held by a large safety pin.

'You've had an accident', said Mom. Apparently, I had gone off the end of the slide and headfirst into the iron railings around the school playground. No ambulance or drama. Another child's father who happened to be in the playground and had a car just scooped me up there and then and took me round the corner to the Casualty department of the Royal Hospital to have my head stitched. Then this knight in shining armour brought me home. To this day I don't know who it was. Six stitches! I bragged about it for weeks.

That was my one and only encounter with 'the Royal', a building that dominated All Saints with its huge size and sheer scale. It still does - but its role in the neighbourhood has changed forever. There is more about the Royal Hospital in a later chapter."

THE NIT NURSE... AND NITS

"The late 1950s was a period of prosperity for Wolverhampton and the country. This is reflected in much of the account given of life in All Saints so far. Harold Macmillan, the Prime Minister for the second half on that decade, famously declared 'You've never had it so good!' and by and large that was true. It was a period of full employment, house-building and improved educational opportunity. What's more, Wolves had a fabulous football team!

All Saints shared in the general economic upturn which followed the ending of rationing in 1954. All Saints School, now a distant memory, can seem like a lost idyll with its photographs of beautifully turned out choirs and prize-winning country dancing teams. But, away from the 'golden generation' of the 1950s depicted, lay hidden stories of deprivation, squalor and cruelty for some.

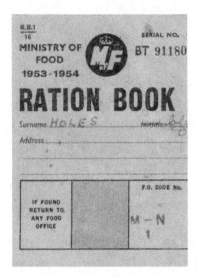

Clive's Ration Book from 1953/54.

Where we lived, in All Saints Road, the houses were all privately owned and either owner-occupied or rented from landlords. There were a few relatively well-off families, quite a number of middling ones, such as mine, and some which, for one reason or another, were disadvantaged. Patches of poverty and sub-standard, even squalid, housing certainly existed.

I was particularly friendly with the elder son of one such family which lived five or six doors away from us and got to know their circumstances well. Looking back now, I realise just how dysfunctional this family were. The house was absolutely filthy. I didn't go in there very often, but it looked as if it hadn't been cleaned for years and it smelt awful. I will call them the Johnsons, not their real name. I will call my friend Bill, and he was very talented: being particularly good at football. We shared many interests: football, cricket, stamp-collecting, trainspotting, and there was a period when we were inseparable best friends. One of the by-products of that, to my mother's horror, was that I got an infestation of head-lice from him which I passed on to the rest of the family.

School rituals come in all shapes and sizes, and a C of E controlled school such as All Saints in the 1950s certainly had its fair share. There were the daily ones like assembly and the morning milk break; weekly ones like collecting dinner money; occasional ones, like compulsory church attendance on certain Saints' days; and yearly ones like the Harvest Festival and maypole dancing. A less celebrated one, occurring unpredictably, was the visit of the nit nurse.

Nit nurses came into schools in Victorian times when standards of personal hygiene were low. They were only phased out by officialdom in the 1980s and '90s when it was felt that the responsibility for ensuring children weren't lousy should fall on parents, not the local education and health authorities. Besides, having their hair publicly examined supposedly subjected children to an embarrassing and potentially humiliating ordeal. But back in the 1950s, in the hey-day of the newly formed National Health Service, there was no such official prissiness.

Roughly once a year, the nit nurse would descend and each class would be called in and lined up, one after another, to have their hair inspected. The nurse was invariably a lady, and often a rather jolly one. She would delve deep into each victim's tresses, front, back, and sides, and especially behind the ears, searching for head lice and nits, or eggs, clinging to hair. Each examination took about thirty seconds. The nit nurse rarely had many customers who needed supplementary services beyond a cursory head examination and a clean bill of health… until one day I and a small number of other kids in my class were pulled out of the line after having our hair examined and asked to wait. Each of us was given a sealed envelope containing a letter addressed to our parents. We went back to class none the wiser. But the world was about to turn upside down.

I went home at lunchtime as normal and handed the letter to my Mom. She opened it, read it, and turned pale. 'What does it say Mom?' I asked, tucking into my Irish stew. She could hardly get the words out: 'It says you've got nits!' 'What does that mean?', I asked. At that precise moment a knock came to the front door. Without answering me, my mother rushed off to see who it was, and the next thing I knew the headmaster of All Saints, Mr 'Lanky' Lancaster, was standing in front of me with my mother, who by now was in tears. 'It's alright, Mrs Holes, it doesn't matter, it happens all the time,' said 'Lanky', or words to that effect. But my mother was inconsolable. 'Nits?! It says here he's got "a few nits"! Where from? How? I keep my children clean!' Now I was getting upset too. It seemed like this was all my fault. 'It's alright,' repeated 'Lanky'. 'Just pop round to the chemists on Vicarage Road and ask for a bottle of the special oil that kills hair lice. It won't take more than a few days of treatment.'

It was thoughtful of Mr Lancaster to have called in, as he had guessed how upset my mother would be by this social disgrace. Mom was no snob, but she fed and clothed us properly, taught us table manners, made us polish our shoes, and 'had standards' - my speech was regularly disinfected by her of all the 'dow's, 'cor's' and 'gew's' typical of Wolverhampton English, for instance, even though she was from very humble origins herself. Being told one of her kids had nits was for her... well, a disaster of Titanic proportions.

Needless to say, a family inquest was launched into how this could possibly have happened. And far from having, as the nurse's letter said: 'a few nits', my hair was found to be absolutely crawling with fully grown lice, which would shower onto a towel and scurry away every time my mother pulled the 'nit-comb' through my hair during her twice-daily inspections. As if that wasn't bad enough, my elder sister and *my mother herself* were lousy too!

It turned out that the epicentre of the outbreak was 'Bill Johnson' who lived in exactly the kind of domestic squalor which breeds head lice. Of course, I was totally blind to this. One of our hobbies of the moment was stamp-collecting, which involved us sitting for hours at a time at our kitchen table, heads locked together, peering at the latest new issues from Bulgaria or San Marino. His hair was so badly infested he had to have all of it shaved off, as in Victorian times, and came to school for a couple of weeks wearing a colourful turban. The poor lad was the butt of a lot of nine-year-olds' humour: 'Here he comes, the sheikh of All Saints Road!' was one jibe I remember. Kids! They are experts at ritual humiliation...

Bill Johnson' is just one example that I was aware of, but there were others. One poor lad I remember was always desperately embarrassed to take his shirt off during PE lessons. When he did, his ribs stuck out to such an extent you could have played a tune on them. He looked like a concentration-camp victim. This was a case of chronic malnutrition, pure and simple."

8

TRANSPORT

TRAMS, TROLLEY BUSES AND MOTORSPORT

In the early 20th century, Wolverhampton was at the forefront of innovation in several aspects of traffic management.

It was famously the first place in the UK to install automated electric traffic lights in Princes Square on 5 November 1927, followed by the first pedestrian safety barriers in the same location in July 1934, courtesy of Wolverhampton Steelway's Bilston Road works. It was also one of the first, after Kensington, London, in the same year to install Belisha Beacons to mark pedestrian crossings.

Wolverhampton was also, in 1902, one of only four UK towns to adopt an electrically powered system of trams. The first man to drive one was Alfred Skidmore.

"Growing up in All Saints in the mid-1950s", Clive recalls, "my curiosity was pricked one day when walking past the Cleveland Road Bus Depot with my mother. I noticed that inside the depot there were metal tracks that looked like railway lines which abruptly ended at the doors. 'What ran on these tracks?', I asked Mom, secretly hoping that the answer would be 'steam trains' which were one of my childhood passions.

She explained what they were, harking back to the trams that she could just about remember from her own childhood (she was born in 1915). This was somewhat misleadingly known as the 'Lorain' system, because 'Lorain' was the name of the company that manufactured the steel for the tram tracks; the system was officially known as the Brown Surface Contact System. However, this was a very short-lived innovation.

All Saints: The History, People, Places

From March 1921, Wolverhampton Corporation began the switch to an overhead line system of electrically powered trolley buses. This had completely replaced the trams by 1928 and was to last almost fifty years. At one time, Wolverhampton had the largest trolley bus network in the world - 46 miles of overhead lines with 59 trolley buses - operating out of the Cleveland Road depot. The buses themselves were originally manufactured by a company in Maidstone, Kent, and then by Guy Motors of Park Lane, Wolverhampton from 1926 until 1950, after which no more were built.

The trolley bus was a ubiquitous feature of everyday life in the Wolverhampton of the 1950s and early '60s. When my family moved from All Saints Road to Ettingshall Park in 1958, I used the trolley bus every day to get to and from school, getting on and off the No. 58 Dudley via Sedgley service at the stops on either side of Dudley Road near the Coliseum cinema. On the other side of All Saints, there was also a main trolley bus route down Cleveland Road and Bilston Road, and another serving Thompson Avenue.

The trolley buses were highly distinctive. Unlike the garish scarlet of the Midland Red fleet based in Bearwood, Birmingham, they had a smart two-tone green and yellow livery, with 'Wolverhampton Corporation Transport' written on the side. They were remarkably quiet, being powered by electricity, and as the driver took them up through the gears, they sounded a bit like a high-powered milk-float. They were surprisingly speedy, though excess speed was sometimes their downfall, as the rods which connected them to the overhead lines supplying the power had an occasional tendency to come adrift.

I remember witnessing one spectacular incident of this sort in about 1962, when playing football with friends in the fields opposite the junction with Dovedale Road in Sedgley. A No. 58 came barrelling along the Wolverhampton Road and suddenly the rods somehow became separated from the overhead lines and then got entangled in them, completely bringing down a 100-yard section. For several days afterwards, while the lines were being repaired, there was a replacement petrol-driven service… which, of course, was the shape of things to come…

The trolley buses I remember were all double-deckers. The rules were that standing was allowed on the lower deck only, and smoking was permitted on the upper deck only. This latter liberty often led to a dense smog on the upper deck, particularly at the end of the working day when the factories were disgorging their workmen. It was time to relax and light up a fag, but often, when I was on my way home after school and had stayed an hour for a kick-about, there would be forty-plus passengers all puffing away at the same time, and seemingly all going all the way to Dudley.

'12 please' they repeated one after the other to the conductor, twelve old pence being the adult fare from Wolverhampton to Dudley; it was '10 please' to the Green Dragon in Upper Gornal, and '8 please' to Sedgley Bull Ring. I think it was 5 old pence to my stop, but I was still a child so only 2 ½ old pence. I have always been a fan of the upper deck, and never a smoker, but I was definitely a passive one and probably on the equivalent of about 20-a-day for the two years I commuted to All Saints School on the No. 58 trolley bus.

These were the days of two-man bus operation - there was the driver, and there was the conductor. The driver drove the bus and was completely isolated from the passengers (and the conductor). The conductor issued colour-coded tickets from a machine attached to a leather strap which he (or sometimes she) wore across their chest.

The conductor was also in charge of safety and was the only person who could communicate with the driver, but only by pressing the bell - and woe betide any passenger who dared to press it! The system was one-ding for 'stop at the next stop' and two-dings for 'off we go' after passengers had got on or off ('alighted' was the official term).

To get the bus to stop the passenger had to make his way to the large platform area at the back of the bus in advance of arrival at his stop… but not press the bell. It was up to the conductor to spot the fact that there were passengers on the platform waiting to get off, and he would press the bell on their behalf.

On the other hand, it was up to the driver, not the conductor, to spot that there were passengers waiting at an approaching stop. But if the bus was already completely full, the signal from the conductor was three-dings, and that overrode everything: the driver would then not stop at any upcoming stop for a pick up and simply sail past, to the disgruntlement of the would-be passengers waiting in the rain – unless, of course, the conductor had alerted him to a passenger wanting to get off with the usual one-ding signal. The conductor would then decide how many new passengers could replace the 'alighting' passengers if the bus was almost full.

Complicated, or what? Seriously, this was the system as it operated on the Wolverhampton to Dudley route in the late 1950s! When buses were full, as they invariably were between 5 and 6 pm, chaos reigned as the conductor struggled through the crowds of standing passengers to get their fares and at the same time make sure he gave the appropriate 'ding' when one was necessary.

The one other job the conductor had was when the bus came off the overhead wires. Stored under the bus, in a long tube, was a bamboo cane around 20 feet in length with a hook on the end. The conductor would extract this cane and endeavour to re-attach the errant rods to the overhead wires using the hook. This was a skill I watched being deployed on the Dudley Road many a time. It was great street theatre and occasioned many a ribald comment from passers-by (which of course I didn't, as an innocent 10-year-old, fully understand), especially if the conductor was female - 'Ask the driver to 'elp ya gerrit back up' and such like.

Now, of course, the trolley buses which replaced the trams have also long gone, as has the Cleveland Road Bus depot which housed them. This building which used to be such a dominating presence in All Saints, like the Royal Hospital opposite, closed in 1993.

But no-one can halt the march of 'progress'. The first route to lose its trolley buses was the No. 32 to Oxbarn Avenue in 1961. Only six years later came the last act of the tragedy, when, on 5 March 1967, the No. 58, which had been the first service to be made operational in 1927, made its final journey from Wolverhampton to Dudley via Sedgley. No more trolley buses. The replacements were first petrol-, then diesel-powered. But as the economic and health costs of pollution have finally dawned on the transport planners, we have witnessed a reinvention of sorts. Hybrids are now the in-thing, and so, once again, is… the electric tram! Or, to give it its official name, the West Midlands Metro. We are back to where we were a century ago…so never say never. My Mom must be chuckling quietly in her grave!

CYRIL KIEFT AND MOTORSPORT

Wolverhampton's famous motorsport heritage is normally associated with the suburbs of Graiseley (Sunbeam's land speed record car and AJS motorcycles) and Blakenhall (Villiers engines used by many motorcycle manufacturers). Nearby was the home of Clyno cars. In the mid-1920s, Clyno, based in Pelham Street, was the third largest car manufacturer in the UK after Austin and Morris. Less well documented is the sports and racing car enterprise which was based in All Saints in the 1950s in a modest factory, the Reliance Works in Derry Street.

The man behind the business was Cyril Kieft, a native of Swansea, Wales. In 1939 he purchased W.H. Birkinshaw & Company Limited, drop forgers and edge tool makers at Reliance Works in Derry Street. Cyril was an immensely successful businessman and the new company became the country's largest manufacturer of picks for coalmines.

One of Cyril's hobbies was motorsport. After an abortive attempt to become a racing driver, he channelled his energies into building racing cars of his own design. His early 350cc and 500cc cars were built in Bridgend and the 500cc version caught the attention of Stirling Moss' manager, Ken Gregory. This led to Moss driving the car and a highly successful partnership ensued. In 1953 Kieft cars won the F3 Championship for the second year running. During this period, Moss, Gregory and Kieft became directors of a new company, Kieft and Company Ltd. The successes gave Kieft the opportunity to display his cars at the Earls Court Motor Show, both in 1952 and 1953. In September 1952, the Bridgend factory closed due to production difficulties.

Cyril announced that he intended to build a two litre sports racing car, and all production moved to the Reliance Works in Derry Street to take advantage of the highly skilled Wolverhampton workforce.

Stirling Moss walks along with his new works F3 Kieft 500 single seat race car. Photograph courtesy of June Tildesley (nee Kieft).

In an interview in the Iota magazine, Kieft described the town as "an extremely good area for labour of the right type. I now have men working for me who have been in the motor and motorcycle industry for many years". Gordon Bedson, the Chief Experimental Engineer at Vickers, was employed to design a Formula 2 car.

By early 1953, several models were in production at Derry Street, including a 500cc car for Formula 3, a 2 Litre car for Formula 2 and a 4.5 Litre model for Formula 1. The new cars were a great success and gained first and second places in the Lisbon Grand Prix.

The production line at Derry Street. Photograph courtesy of Frank Guest Motor Repairs.

Cyril's next endeavour was to produce a car using the world's first one-piece fibreglass body. To achieve this, a single moulding was made with cut outs for the doors and engine, etc. The new car, the Kieft 1100cc sports car, had a maximum speed of at least 110mph and a fuel consumption of 50mpg. Two of the cars appeared at the Earl's Court Motor Show in 1954.

An attempt to build a F1 car incorporating a Coventry Climax Godiva V8 engine ran into difficulties and it marked the end of Cyril Kieft's involvement in car production.

The car business was sold to a Birmingham based company and the Reliance Works factory switched to the manufacture of tungsten carbon cutting heads for coal cutters. Kieft acquired two drop forging machines for the purpose. After installation, the neighbouring businesses and residents complained about the noise, and he was forced to close the works. Production was moved to Witton, Birmingham in 1956.

Cyril Kieft outside the Reliance Works factory in Derry Street in the 1950s. Photograph courtesy of June Tildesley (nee Kieft).

Kieft race and sports car production in Derry Street may have lasted for less than four years, but for a short period of time Cyril Kieft brought the glamour and glitz of motor racing to All Saints.

A chance meeting in the '60s with the Wolverhampton racing driver Richard Attwood led to friendships with Formula 1 legends, Jack Brabham and Denny Hume. It revived his passion for the sport, watching grand prix races on television wherever he was on his travels.

Cyril continued to live in the Wolverhampton area but after the loss of his wife, Meg, he moved to Spain in 2002 where he resided until his death in 2004 at the age of 92.

The Reliance Works building in April 2021, now occupied by Frank Guest Motor Repairs.

9

THE PUBS, CLUBS AND SHOPS

PUBS

Several pubs and clubs existed in and around All Saints.

THE DARTMOUTH ARMS

The road and house development on the Duke of Cleveland's land incorporated a public house, the Dartmouth Arms. Built on the corner of Vicarage Road and Dartmouth Avenue, the pub is listed in Hitchmough's Black Country Pubs website as Dartmouth Arms Hotel, opening in 1891. The original owners were Ansells Ltd.

The Dartmouth Arms in 2020.

The pub's first licensee was Frederick J. Hibell, aged 28, described in the 1891 Census as a publican and brewer's traveller, born in Birmingham. As well as his wife, Fanny, and son Samuel, there were three other occupants: Maria

Pearson, a domestic servant; Harry Burrows, a hairdresser and Harry Day, a groom.

From the onset, the pub was used as a venue for inquests into deaths in and beyond the town, e.g.

- Oliver Whitehouse, a child from Cheslyn Hay, in November 1892;
- Mr H. L. Justin, a jockey injured in a race at Dunstall Park in May 1893;
- Thomas Gough, following an accident at Cannock Chase Colliery in January 1894;
- Richard Jeavons in a mining accident at Ashmore Park Colliery on 22 November 1894.

Gill Collins (nee Selvey) lived in The Dartmouth Arms as the daughter of the publican in the 1950s and ran it herself with husband Phil Collins from the 1970s to the '80s. Here are some of their memories in their own words:

Gill: "I was born in Cobden Street, but we moved to The Dartmouth Arms in 1953. Mom and Dad had kept a pub in Stafford and they offered them a pub here.

One of my earliest memories of the place is my birthday party. There was a big upstairs room. All my Mom's family came from round here, Gower Street, Adelaide Street. I had my cousins who lived in Gower Street, and my Aunt Dol and Uncle Ted, they worked in the pub as well... so it was a family-run pub. It belonged to Banks's Brewery of course, but it was family-run. Being a child in the pub was great. You'd got all the people there; you were never lonely. Being young, the old 'uns said: 'Come here, here's a couple of bob', you know, that sort of thing, 'Come and talk to us and sit by us'. I was always in the pub; a lot of my life was spent there."

Phil: "In the '60s we organised pub trips to see 'The Sound of Music' – six times that was, 'Dr Zhivago', there was two trips to that."

Gill: "They used to take their sandwiches on the coach and bottles of beer. It was more like a family than a pub. They all knew each other, they all joined in things together. You got people like Bert Foxall, and Ken Foxall, both from All Saints Church. And they used to organise things, they used to have pantomimes upstairs with the men. They had social evenings and all that."

Phil: "There were breakfast trips on a Sunday. You'd all meet at the pub at seven o'clock in the morning. Get a few pints down your neck first, then you'd go on a coach down Carding Mill Valley, Symond's Yat or Long Mynd, kick a ball about for two or three hours, have breakfast in the café, down to the pub, then get back in the afternoon.

Dartmouth Street was our living quarters when we were at the pub. It was at the back of the pub which now they've pulled down, as well as the first couple of houses of terraced housing where the car park is now. The living quarters now are upstairs in what used to be the Club Room. We used to have the Wolverhampton Table Tennis Club upstairs... I remember they used to send a message down on the dumb waiter for so many pints of this, so many pints of that, so many Guinness's, all on the dumb waiter. They used to have meetings up there and all sorts, weddings and things, but it's all gone now.

When they modernised it, they knocked that down, they wanted a car park... more and more people moved into the area, being on a bus route. Plus, the fact that the house next door; they knocked all their front room out, and the rear living quarters and kitchen out to extend the bar. We were getting a lot more Asians and West Indians coming in, saying they wanted a bigger bar, so they swapped 'em round—what now is the Bar was the Lounge and now is the Lounge was the Bar. That hasn't changed at all, apart from the fireplace..."

Gill: "And the Ladies' Snug's gone. Only ladies were allowed in there. That was for the old ladies from around here, the 'characters'. They wanted to be served by a woman. God help a man who went in there! They used to be on the half pints of Guinness, well, the bottles of Guinness -"

Phil: "- and Mackeson and stout -"

Gill: "- hang on, Hanson's stout and Banks's if you don't mind!"

Phil: "If you stand on the corner of Dartmouth Street and Vicarage Road you'll see where the door's been bricked up, that was the entrance to the Ladies' Snug. It was just a little area with a frosted glass hatch and a window. If we opened the hatch, it was: 'Go away you. Where's yer aunty? she'll serve us.'

They'd come in with their pinnies on a Sunday dinnertime, hair in rollers, that big-hair style... some'd bring jugs up, tek the old man a couple of pints back in a jug to have with his Sunday dinner... there'd be about five or six of 'em in the Ladies' Snug while their dinner was cooking at home, p'raps the old man would be out with his pigeons flying round. They'd have a couple of stouts, toddle off down the road with a jug of beer in their hand.

They used to come in at night as well, hadn't they? Slippers on, old wrap-around pinnies, headscarf round their head... if the hatch was open, they'd say, 'Shut the hatch!' so you couldn't hear what they was on about. It was only gossiping.

But once we'd left 'the Dartmouth', we didn't like to go back in again."

Hazel Skeldon and Emma Pursehouse lived in Gordon Street and Hazel, born in 1970, had strong ties with the Dartmouth Arms. "My Mom used to clean there, my sister, Sue, worked behind the bar, then I cleaned there later on."

Her parents, however, were drawn to the Cleveland Road Working Men's Club, nearby.

CLEVELAND ROAD WORKING MEN'S CLUB

Cleveland Road Working Men's Club was probably the centre of the social life for many from All Saints. It was no different for Hazel's parents. As Emma said: "they went there every night, d'ay they." There was always a bingo session. On Sundays, you had someone singing the old songs like 'Old Shep' which always set Hazel's Mom off. After the bingo, Hazel would usually sit on the step outside with the other young ones.

Hazel loved 'the Cleveland Road'. "It was brilliant. Everybody who went to the Cleveland Road came from All Saints. It had a massive sense of community spirit as well." Her Mom was heavily involved in getting coach trips up from the club. "From the Cleveland Road we used to go to Rhyl, Blackpool and one time we went to Barry Island on a double decker bus. There'd be two pick up points: the Cleveland and the Dartmouth. There'd be old people, teenagers getting hammered, all sorts. All round the area were rammed into the coach. One time we went to Blackpool and the coach broke down on the way home - the door wouldn't close. We were there for about six hours… oh my God it was such a laugh."

Christmas parties were another highlight. Everyone in the area knew that Hazel's Mom looked after some of the elderly folk, like Mrs Cotterill from Gordon Street, so when she started going to the club, they asked if she would like to organise the party for the old people. "She did something for kids as well. She used to rope someone into being Father Christmas. It was one of the old men from the club… can't remember his name."

Hazel Skeldon in Rhyl during a day out from the Cleveland Road Working Men's Club. (Photo: courtesy of Emma Pursehouse).

THE NEWMARKET

Hazel's parents were also regulars at the Newmarket in Cleveland Road. Her Mom used to say about the infamous barmaid, "Oh, she's got her tillies out again." According to Hazel, "Her top was low, really low… and when she was well into her shift, it was like down here!"

THE SUMMERHOUSE

The presence of a Summerhouse pub in Steelhouse Lane can be traced back to around 1849. The 1851 Census shows the pub was owned by Mr. John Lewis, a stone miner, originally from Lancashire and originally it operated as a beerhouse. These were premises which could only sell beer, often brewed on the property by the householder. It was the 1830 Beerhouse Act which introduced beerhouses to encourage beer drinking instead of spirits, particularly gin.

Emma would often visit the Summerhouse pub. The landlord was Norman who is still there. His two children, known as 'Mop' and 'Flop' went to All Saints School with Hazel. Hazel's parents never used the Summerhouse, preferring to go to the Newmarket or the Moulders Arms.

THE MOULDERS ARMS

The Moulders Arms in Kent Road was better known by locals as the 'Monkey House'. Back in the 1930s, the landlord kept a monkey in a cage inside a shed outside the pub. Over the years the tale entered local folklore.

The pub was a big favourite of Hazel, her parents and grandparents. "Really nice to sit outside…" When Hazel's Dad was ill in hospital, he would sometimes say: "Go and fetch your Nan and Grandad from the Monkey House and watch that monkey in the tree."

Some residents from All Saints adopted pubs on the outskirts of the neighbourhood.

THE RING O'BELLS

"This fine old boozer was not," says Clive, "strictly speaking an All Saints pub, as it was situated outside the parish boundaries on the Dudley Road, about 50 yards from the old Coliseum cinema in the direction of the town centre.

I include it here because it was my Dad's local for thirty years (c. 1948-78), for the first ten of which we were living in All Saints Road. He continued drinking there for twenty years after we moved to Ettingshall Park, only transferring his allegiance to The Old Ash Tree in Fighting Cocks when the Ring O'Bells finally succumbed to the wrecking balls which demolished much of this area in the late 1970s.

Back in the 1950s, kids of my age were not allowed in the bars of pubs - indeed I think it was illegal to bring children under the age of 14 into them. The Ring O'Bells was unusual in that, although the exterior façade was modest, it was quite a large pub with a big downstairs 'function room' which was regularly used as a playroom for drinkers' wives and their under-age children. It also had upstairs rooms for hire, and a large and well-kept terraced garden with two (!) full size bowling greens at the lowest level of the garden.

Clive Holes, Derek Mills

It was on summer evenings in the mid-1950s that I first made my acquaintance with the pub as one of the camp followers of the Ring O'Bells crown-green bowls team, in which my Dad was for many years a leading light. The team played in a Wolverhampton pub league, with matches arranged home and away a couple of evenings a week, and usually starting around 7.00 pm. The games would go on till nightfall, around 9.00 pm, and involved a dozen 'ends' (matches) between the members of the two teams.

Doug Holes (author's father) playing darts with 'Tosh' in the Ring O' Bells, 1961.

Unlike the weekend leagues played on a Saturday afternoon when the winner of each end was the first to score 21 points, in the weekday evening league the winner of each 'end' was the first to score 15. This kept the ends a bit shorter. Obviously, the players were supping pints throughout their evening of bowling, which they left at tables on the side of the green when they got up to play. This was the opportunity for kids like me to get their first surreptitious sips of that golden liquid which always looked so attractive (but tasted so bitter) backlit by the warm evening sun!

We also got to know the bowling greens of many Wolverhampton pubs: The Old Ash Tree in Fighting Cocks, The Stile in Whitmore Reans, even the Molineux Hotel, which in those days had one of the best teams (and best kept greens) in Wolverhampton, just like the professional football team next door.

Sometimes these summer evening idylls were disrupted, however. On one occasion I remember that one of the Ring O'Bells's upstairs rooms had been hired out to what sounded like a novice 'trad-jazz' band. Traditional ('trad') jazz, popularised by musicians like Acker Bilk ('Stranger on the Shore') and Kenny Ball ('Midnight in Moscow') was a very big deal in the 1950s and early '60s, and many sought to emulate their success. It was a warm, still evening after a very hot day and all the pub windows had been flung wide open. The sweaty, white-capped, besandaled bowlers were not amused as an extremely loud but very off-key rendition of 'Alexander's Rag Time band' began booming out from the distant upstairs room just as the match was starting. One badly but still excruciatingly loudly performed tune followed another, and the cacophony just went on and on and on. Finally, the bowlers' patience snapped, 'Put a bloody sock in it, why doe ya, ya wooden-'eads?!!' bawled one irate 60 year old between sips of his Butler's Bitter, 'Our dog's howling is more in tune than your bloody racket!' shouted another.

Many years later, at the age of 18, I finally went into the Ring O'Bells as a proper customer. It was Christmas 1966 and I was home at the end of my first term at university. I remember a coal fire roaring away in the bar, as my Dad introduced me to the landlady. 'I hear you've passed all your sustificates', she said: 'your Dad's really proud of you!' 'Yes',

I said, nodding in embarrassed agreement... And, sad to say, I think that was the first, and the very last time that I ever had a legal drink in the Ring O'Bells..."

Pubs like the Ring O'Bells and The Why Not in Steelhouse Lane are relatively recent casualties of widespread pub closures. Some older residents might also remember the Hen and Chickens in Eagle Street. Long gone is the Sutherland Arms in Sutherland Place which closed in 1931, as are the Queens Arms in Portland Place (1914) and the Barley Mow in Jenner Street (1914). In most cases, closure was soon followed by demolition.

This was not the case with The Steelhouse (Tavern) at the bottom of Caledonia Road.

The convenience store at the corner of Steelhouse Lane and Caledonia Road, the site of The Steelhouse Tavern.

It began life around 1858 as a beerhouse run by John Buckler, a bricklayer and furnace builder. Like many beerhouses it was eventually bought up in 1893 by one of the local breweries, William Butler and Co. Ltd.

A photograph found on the internet reveals it was known at one point in its history as the Nellie Revell Shop, licensed to sell beer and tobacco. Research has not revealed the date of the photograph or the origin of the name.

Significant alterations to the building were carried out in 1935. According to Hitchmough's Black Country Pubs website, it continued to operate as a pub until 1964 before closing. While Derek does not recall the building trading as a pub, he remembers it in the late '60s as a small but popular off-licence and general stores run by Mr Tye who had been head groundsman at Molineux.

Further alterations have taken place in the intervening decades and it now functions as a much larger convenience store, as shown in the 2021 photo above.

SHOPS

Clive Holes remembers the newsagent's shop that his mother's family owned and ran for about 50 years.

"The shop, at No. 241, Steelhouse Lane, sold newspapers, magazines, children's comics, sweets and cigarettes. No ice-creams or bottles of pop - such refrigerated items weren't available in your typical neighbourhood 'paper-shop' of the mid-20th century.

My maternal grandparents, Leonard Grafton (1874-1940) and Kate Rose Grafton (1877-1953) bought the shop in 1917. Leonard was a Brummie, from Aston, but Kate was born and bred in Wolverhampton.

Clive's grandmother Kate Rose Grafton (nee Perry).

They met when Leonard was lodging with the Perrys at 325, Bilston Road while working as a cycle tube picker (Kate's sister is also listed as working on cycles then).

Kate's father, Francis, was born in Wednesfield in c.1840. The Grafton's five children were Alice (known as 'Lal') (1902), Hilda (1903), Len junior (1907), my mother Kathryn ('Kitty') (1915), and Lillian ('Lil') (1919). Len junior spent much of his working life at Goodyear's. His four sisters helped in the shop in the years before marrying, and, in the War, worked in local munitions factories.

It was very much an All Saints family. Leonard and Kate got married in All Saints Church, Wolverhampton in 1901, all the children wed in All Saints Church and continued to live in streets nearby at least for the early part of their married lives: All Saints Road, Gordon Street, Sutherland Place, and Vicarage Road. Some never left the area and died there.

My mother Kitty, a very bright girl who passed the school leaving examination, was not allowed to take up her place at the Technical High School, as she was needed to help her parents run the shop. This disappointment remained with her for the rest of her life.

In 1940, Leonard Grafton, at the age of 66, fell seriously ill with scarlet fever, and died of pneumonia just a few weeks later. Such premature deaths were common in the era before antibiotics. One of his sons-in-law, George Sutton, who married Hilda in 1929, took over running the shop and eventually bought it from his mother-in-law, who went to live with her youngest daughter, Lil, in Vicarage Road.

To the Grafton children who grew up in it and to the next generation, like me, 'the shop' was much more than a small business. On Saturday mornings there was a 'gathering of the clans' at which Aunty Hilda would ply everyone with tea, often with a sly drop of whisky slipped in, and home-made cake. At these get-togethers, all the local gossip would be chewed over, along with the doings of everyone's kids. These kids, my two sisters and me among them, loved going to see their Aunty Hilda, as not only would they meet their cousins, but they would have the run of the comics in the shop for a couple of hours without having to spend their pocket money on them - just don't tear them! - the Eagle, the Wizard, the Hotspur, the Beano, the Dandy and Bunty for the girls.

It is hard to imagine now the level of service provided by the average paper shop then. Almost everyone took a national morning paper, out of a choice of five or six, and most took the local evening one, the Express and Star, six days a week. Then, during the football season, there was The Sporting Star ('the Pink') on a Saturday evening and a wide range of Sunday papers. Everyone expected their choice of all of these to be delivered through their front doors at breakfast time and in the evening, come rain or shine. I well remember, as a child in the 1950s, the queues of paperboys and girls waiting to fill their delivery bags in the shop. My mother and her sisters had pitched in in their childhood too.

Our 'paper shop' was just one of around half-a-dozen small businesses at the Cleveland Road end of Steelhouse Lane. I remember a fishmonger's, a greengrocer's, a quaintly named pub, the Why Not, a baker's that sold freshly baked bread and cakes, and even a draper's, Wiltshire's, on the corner of Sutherland Place. The nearest butcher (Price's), where my Mom bought her meat, was just across the Cleveland Rd/ Bilston Road roundabout, next to a large pub, the Horse & Jockey, and on the other side of it was a hairdresser's (J. Davies) where my Dad used to take me for the regulation short back and sides. Thus, it was perfectly possible in the pre-supermarket era to do a 'big shop' in Steelhouse Lane without ever venturing 'into town', and when we lived in All Saints Road my mother did this every Tuesday and Friday (fresh fish day), popping into Aunty Hilda's for a cuppa, a sit-down and a chin-wag when she had finished. Shopping 'in town' was for non-food things such as clothes, toys and more expensive items like electrical goods.

There were also small shops in surrounding streets. We lived at No. 80, All Saints Road, and next to us, at 79, there was a shop run by a Mrs Milroy, a good friend of my Mom. It was basically just a terraced house like all the others on our side of the street, but the front window had been converted to accommodate a shop display of jars of sweets and cakes. At lunchtime when me and my elder sister came back from school to have our dinner, 'afters' would often involve a trip next door. We were each allowed to choose a cake from the tray which had been delivered that morning to Mrs Milroy's. I think they cost 3d (three old pence) each.

Further up All Saints Road on the corner of Vicarage Road was a bigger and posher establishment called Bowdler's which had a wider choice of sweets and bubble-gum, with which you got full colour picture-cards of football teams, usually fifty in a set, which ensured you carried on spending 1d (one old penny) for months to try and assemble a complete set! Somehow you never did. Other shops of the time were Emm's, a chemist's shop on Vicarage Road, and a popular fish and chip shop, owned for many years by Dave and Margaret, on the corner of Vicarage Road and Dartmouth Street.

The Suttons ran the shop successfully until the mid-1960s, when they sold to an Indian family and retired to live in a house around the corner in Gordon Street.

Thus, after almost 50 years, what was always simply referred to in the family as 'the shop' acquired a new owner, Mr Sidhu. The photograph above (courtesy of Ned Williams) was probably taken in the late '70s. It had also acquired a new, distinct appearance with a display of porn magazines adorning the window. It lost custom from Asian ladies but became a regular port of call for the local prostitutes buying cigarettes and condoms.

The late '70s saw the appearance of a video shop, Sangeet Videos, on the corner of Raby Street and Vicarage Road. The shop was owned by Surinder Singh Bahara. Surinder went on to open his own cinema in Bilston in the '80s, showing a range of Bollywood titles. Not satisfied with showing Bollywood films, he went on to produce the first Punjabi movie filmed in England. The award-winning film, Yaari Jatt Di, shot in various parts of Wolverhampton, was released in 1987.

Sixty years on, small local shops of the type I've described have all but disappeared from All Saints. 'The paper shop' in Steelhouse Lane which my family once owned was demolished in the 1970s, along with all the neighbouring shops and businesses. These would include Adey's shop, opposite Mr Tye's off-licence, remembered affectionately by all workers and schoolchildren on their way to and from Bayliss, Jones and Bayliss and All Saints School. Remembered particularly by a group of lads in the '50s who stole and ate a bar of chocolate called Ex Lax only to discover it was a laxative!

However, a phoenix has risen from the flames. A new-build shop (perhaps these days you'd call it a 'convenience store') now stands in splendid isolation about 50 yards from where our shop once stood. It is, I believe, owned by the same family that bought ours back in the 1960s: the Sidhu's. It looks rather lonely but, whenever I walk past on one of my periodic trips down Memory Lane, it seems to be doing a roaring trade. Steelhouse Lane still lives, after all!"

10

ALL SAINTS AT WAR

THE GREAT WAR (WORLD WAR ONE)

When Britain declared war on 4 August 1914, celebrations were held throughout the country. The mood was optimistic with many people believing it would be a quick and simple affair that would be over by Christmas.

Inevitably, there were soon concerns about food shortages. Reports of 'buying of provisions and stores in excess of present requirements' circulated in parts of the country. On 6 August 1914, the Express & Star published a letter from the Mayor of Wolverhampton, Frederick Howard Skidmore. This was an appeal for all residents to be calm and considerate'. He referred to the 'hardships and privations' that the soldiers and sailors would be suffering overseas and urged Wulfrunians 'to exercise the strictest economy in domestic life'. The message was taken on board in Wolverhampton and indeed the rest of the country and rationing was not introduced until 1917.

Large numbers of men responded to the wave of patriotism sweeping the country and rushed to enlist. Groups of friends, workmates and relatives from towns created the 'pals' battalions, a uniquely British phenomenon. The government wanted 100,000 volunteers and began a large recruitment campaign, featuring Lord Kitchener, which bombarded the public with posters. This was so successful that within a month 750,000 people had volunteered.

Many of these will have been the members of the Territorial Force, the volunteer wing of the British Army, created in 1908. The logbook of All Saints School, dated 24 August

1914, reported that two teachers, Mr R. Piper and Mr Pugh, had been called up with the Territorials.

Recruitment figures in Wolverhampton were impressive. They hit a record high on the morning of 31 August 1914, when it was reported that 62 men had enlisted. By the time the local paper was published, scores of men were still entering the Town Hall.

On the same day, there was also an article about the formation of the 2nd Battalion of the South Staffordshire Regiment. As part of Kitchener's call to arms, Hon. Colonel T. E. Hickman formed a new battalion of local volunteers to go into service with the South Staffordshire Regiment. Recruits had to be male, between 19 and 30 years of age, and were asked to bring another possible volunteer with them. Men were being despatched daily from Wolverhampton to the barracks in Lichfield and the newspaper estimated that over 1,800 men from Wolverhampton and district had already volunteered for the new battalions.

On 5 October, a civic farewell was given at St Peter's Church for the 6th Battalion of the South Staffordshire Regiment as it left for war.

Recruitment continued at a pace. In early October, the Express and Star reported on efforts to recruit men who had come to watch a Wolves Reserves match at Molineux. It proved increasingly difficult to avoid enlisting. Some did. For a variety of reasons, a significant number of men were unwilling to enlist and many of these became the recipients of the 'white feather'. The Order of the White Feather was founded in August 1914 and women would hand white feathers to young men who they deemed to be cowards for avoiding military service.

By the end of the year the Wolverhampton and District Recruiting Committee had been formed, and recruiting techniques were developed. The committee, consisting of teachers, clergymen, political agents, and members of various societies, visited every man between the age of 18 and 40 to explain the necessity of going to war, and to encourage enlistment. Lady committee members visited men's wives, while the men were at work, to stress that their husbands should join up. A man and a woman would then call on the family in the evening to try and persuade the man to enlist. Talks were given at factories during the lunch hour, and everything was done to assist the recruitment drive. Skilled recruits received 9s.11d. per week, unskilled recruits received 8s.9d. per week, with a separation allowance for married men of 12s.6d., plus 2s.6d. for each child.

The logbooks from All Saints School show that the war impacted on the school in a variety of ways. In April 1915, another member of staff, Mr Charles Wixon, left to join the army. Teachers were periodically recruited to assist in wartime administration. In October 1915, the school was closed so staff could assist in the compilation of the National Register. Later in the year, there was a surge of volunteers and the school was closed again on the afternoon of 10 December so that male teachers could help to complete the attestations. In 1918, the school was closed for two days to allow teachers to write out the Ration Cards.

A resident of All Saints, Benjamin James Owen, enlisted on 11 Dec 1915. At the time he was married, living with his wife Sarah Ann Williams at 2 Court, 2 Eagle Street at the back of the Summerhouse pub on Steelhouse Lane. He worked as a dry grinder near to his home,

Benjamin became a member of the Territorial Army reserve on 12 Dec 1915 and was mobilised in the 4th Battalion of the

Lincolnshire Regiment on 12 April 1916. A year later, on 25 April 1917, he was captured but in attempting to escape, Benjamin was wounded. This was witnessed by a neighbour who apparently was also in the same regiment. Showing incredible bravery and determination, Ben crawled about the battlefield for four days, drinking water from the bottles of the dead. He was eventually spotted by French officers and picked-up. (Photo below courtesy of Robbie Bennett).

Benjamin James Owen, Sarah Ann
and their first child, Benjamin Joseph.

Benjamin had suffered injuries to his shoulder and one lung. He was treated in Northumberland War Hospital, Bosworth, in Newcastle-on-Tyne, being admitted on 19 May 1917. He was discharged from the army on 11 February 1918, returning to his wife in Eagle Street.

Over thirty years later, his first child, Benjamin Joseph shown in the photograph above, was to fight with distinction in World War 2. An account of his remarkable military life is included in the section on that war.

There is a wretched postscript to Benjamin's life. His wife Sarah Ann died in 1929 a few weeks after giving birth to their sixth child, Dorothy, who was brought up by her aunt and uncle. Benjamin, himself, died in 1935 at the young age of 41 from pneumonia, a lung disease probably exacerbated by the wartime wound.

Benjamin's debt to the hospital in Newcastle was shared by many thousands of servicemen. Trench warfare resulted not only in fatalities but a wide range of physical injuries and psychological traumas which required specialised treatment and convalescence in hospitals at home and abroad.

In Wolverhampton, The Royal Hospital in Cleveland Road played a crucial role throughout the war years. At the time of The Great War, it would still have been known as Wolverhampton and Staffordshire General Hospital.

Just a few weeks after the assassination of Archduke Franz Ferdinand, the War Office informed the hospital managers that it would be designated as a military hospital with wounded service personnel given precedence. Space was set aside in the newly built King Edward VII Wing with thirty five beds made available in the Edward and Alexandra Wards. Following the outbreak of war, the whole of the residential medical staff had reported for military duty leaving the hospital seriously depleted. For the first time, the hospital was forced to accept the employment of female doctors, a decision regarded so 'revolutionary' that it made the national news.

The first group of wounded soldiers were transferred to the hospital on Tuesday 27 October 1914. The journey from the battlefield to auxiliary hospitals like 'the General' was slow and laborious. From the frontline, casualties passed through a series of medical units in which they were assessed, given painkillers and had dressings applied, checked and refastened. The treatment was provided by teams of medical officers and Royal Army Medical Corps (RAMC) orderlies. The physical movement from unit to unit was carried out initially by stretcher bearers and then by motorised or horse-drawn vehicles. Not until the wounded reached the Casualty Clearing Station, up to ten miles away from the frontline, were their injuries formally classified and any necessary basic surgery carried out. Those requiring specialised care were taken by ambulance trains to hospitals in France. The final leg involved a transfer by train or road, accompanied by medical staff, to one of the channel ports like Le Havre. Once back in England, the casualties reached their hospital destination via the rail network. Casualties earmarked for 'the General' arrived at the town's Low Level Station before a final journey by way of motorised or horse-drawn means.

Most of the soldiers admitted on the 27 October had been fighting four days earlier in the Battle of Armentieres.

As the number of wounded soldiers being treated at the hospital increased, temporary buildings were erected in the hospital grounds. Most of the surgery carried out involved removing infected tissue. Antibiotics had not been discovered and medical staff resorted to traditional treatments like poultices, antiseptic fluid and even leeches to combat infections. Wounds consequently took longer to heal and some men might spend weeks in hospital, nursed by volunteers from the St John's Ambulance and Salvation Army. The doctors, nurses and porters were only part of the team who kept 'the General' ticking over. The staff in the pharmacy, laundry, kitchens and stores provided essential support.

Schools organised collections. On Friday 21 May 1915, the pupils of All Saints School donated fifteen shillings for 'supplying comforts' to the soldiers and sailors engaged in the war. The money was forwarded to the Overseas Club. The Red Cross and Salvation Army were also actively involved in fundraising. Various events were organised. On 27 December 1915, a charity football match was held at the Molineux Grounds in aid of the General Hospital, the Express & Star Tobacco Fund, the Express & Star and Mr J. B. Dumbell's Soldiers and Prisoners Comforts Fund, and the Mayor's War Charities Fund. The match was held between A. Bishop's XI (captained by Wolves' wing half Albert Bishop) and A. Groves' XI (captained by Wolves' centre half Albert Groves). The match attracted a good-sized crowd of 15,000 and £469 1s 2d was raised for the respective charities. Some of the money was used to supply patients with free cigarettes and beer. Other items like chocolate and fruit were handed out and tickets to the town's two theatres were available.

Wages of one shilling a day were given by pay and welfare officers.

The brutality of The Great War, epitomised by trench warfare in northern Europe, has been well documented. The battles at the Somme and Passchendaele are two which sadly come too easily to mind. However, this was a war fought in many parts of the world, such as the Balkans where Russia was supporting Serbia in its fight against countries of the Austro-Hungarian Empire.

Company Quarter Master Sergeant Thomas Roberts, from No.15, Maxwell Road became involved in this conflict. He enlisted in the Royal Army Service Corps at Wolverhampton on 21 May 1915. Initially, he was sent to Salonica in Greece to serve with 605 Company Motor Transport, landing there in 1916. On 5 March 1916 Thomas was posted to the British Mission with the Royal Serbian Army and was later awarded the Serbia Gold medal for his outstanding service. Thomas survived the war and was aged 26 years on discharge.

Conscription was introduced in January 1916 through the Military Service Act. This imposed conscription on all single men aged between 18 and 41, but exempted the medically unfit, clergymen, teachers and certain classes of industrial worker. A second Act passed in May 1916 extended conscription to married men.

In the summer of 1917, Mr Pugh returned to teach at All Saints School. Along with Mr Piper, he had joined the army at the start of the war. Following a severe wound in the leg while serving in France, he was classified as Army Reserve P, a designation for disabled soldiers whose services are 'deemed to be temporarily of more value to the country in civil life rather than in the Army'.

The Great War, later to be known as World War One (WW1), ended at 11am on 11 November 1918. Scenes of rejoicing were witnessed in the streets. A Service of Thanksgiving was held in the afternoon in Wolverhampton's Market Place, attended by the Deputy Mayor and conducted by the Mayor's Chaplain. There are no records of the day being celebrated at All Saints Church.

The celebrations may well have been restrained as the country was now fighting another enemy, Spanish Flu, a pandemic that was to kill 228,000 in Britain, with a quarter of the population affected. Over 50 million people worldwide died. Like many schools across the world, All Saints School was severely affected, closing on 8 November 1918, and not reopening until 8 January 1919, eight weeks later.

Two weeks later, on 24 November, Lloyd George the Liberal Prime Minister spoke eloquently at The Grand Theatre, Wolverhampton of a bright future for the men and women of the country.

"Our work is not over yet - the work of the nation, the work of the people, the work of those who sacrificed. Let us work together first. This the appeal that I am making today. What is our task? To make Britain a fit country for heroes to live in."

The significance of this famous speech was to resonate for the next two decades as one outcome was an ambitious programme of council house building described earlier in Chapter 4.

WW1 DINNER FOR PRISONERS OF WAR

During the Great War of 1914-1918 some 7,335 officers and 174,491 other ranks of the British Army were captured by the enemy, a great number of those during the last seven months of the war. Following the end of The Great War in November 1918, soldiers and prisoners of war were repatriated.

The Comfort Fund, set up jointly by the Express and Star and Mr James B Dumbell, the Managing Director of the Turner Motor Manufacturing Company Limited, to send parcels to the troops and sailors was mentioned earlier in the chapter. Their generosity extended beyond the end of the war. In March 1919, the proprietors of the Express and Star organised a dinner and entertainments (the "Peace Dinner") at the Baths Assembly Rooms for all the local servicemen who had been listed as prisoners of war. Over 900 men were invited, including a number from the All Saints neighbourhood:

HALDRON, WH, Sgt., 109, Steelhouse Lane,
BLONDON, A, Cpl., 324, All Saints Road,
HATFIELD, G, Lce-cpl., 195, Steelhouse Lane,
BAKER, A, Pte., 1st South Staff, 3, House, 2 Court, Jenner Street,
BAILEY, E, Pte., Northumberland Fusiliers, 95, Granville Street,
BEAVON, G, Pte., 5 Court 3 house, Steelhouse Lane,
BLOWER, CE, Pte., 20, Portland Place,
DAVIES, S, Pte., 7, Melbourne Street,
DYKE, TC, Pte., Northumberland Fusiliers, 7, Melbourne Street,
EVANS, H, Pte., 95, All Saints Road,
EVANS, TH, Pte., 250, All Saints Road,
GREEN, J, Pte., 83, Dartmouth Street,
HENSTOCK, H, Pte., 22, Vicarage Road,
HODGKISS, R, Pte, 14th Northumberland Fusiliers, 6, Vicarage Road,
LOWE, P, 45, Maxwell Road,
MOORE, F, Pte., 74, Granville Street,
NICHOLLS, J, Pte, 58, Maxwell Road,
OVERTON, CG, Pte., 8 Maxwell Road,

PARKES, WA, Pte., 56, Sutherland Place,
PEASLAND, H, Pte., 112, Granville Street,
PLATT, J, Pte., 10, Granville Street,
PRESTON, FJ, Pte., 80, Vicarage Road,
WILKINS, FB, Pte., 69, Sutherland Place.

THE GREAT WAR TREES

On 10 November 1919, Wolverhampton's mayor, Councillor Thomas Austin Henn of Dunstall Ward (and Henn's Jewellers) proposed to plant a thousand trees across the town to "stimulate local patriotism…"

In the following February the Staffordshire Advertiser reported he would ask for money to plant the trees to improve the outlook of those "who dwell in a drab and monotonous environment". It would cost £1,200, nearly £61,500 in today's prices. The money would be raised by the pupils, parents and staff of Wolverhampton's schools, not as one might have expected by the Borough Council.

All Saints Road was chosen as one of those 'drab' environments. The planting of the trees at All Saints on 22 March 1920 was the first in that scheme. At the ceremony, the mayor was accompanied by his children Frank and Molly, and Mr T. Wesley Henn, his grandfather. The event was reported in the All Saints Girls School logbook, shown above. The headmaster of the Boys School, Mr Boon, described a large assembly of parents and pupils who watched the trees being planted on the south side of All Saints Road and near the school.

Many of those trees are still to be found in All Saints Road, a legacy of that ceremony, along with others planted later in nearby Vicarage Road, Mason Street, Silver Birch Avenue and Thompson Avenue. An event, commemorating the centenary of the mayor's 'Green' tribute to those who fell in The Great War, was due to take place on Sunday, 22 March 2020. It would have been a celebration of the day when pupils, elected by fellow pupils at All Saints, St Joseph's and Dudley Road Schools, planted 30 trees in All Saints Road.

Memorial trees in All Saints Road.

Sunday's celebration at The Workspace, All Saints Action Network (ASAN), All Saints Road, would have been attended by the Mayor of Wolverhampton, Councillor Darke, accompanied by John Henn, the great grandson of Mayor

Thomas Henn. However, due to concern over the Covid-19 pandemic, the event was postponed.

From the Left: Shobha Asar-Paul, Chief Officer of All Saints Action Network (ASAN); Councillor Claire Darke, Wolverhampton Mayor; Phil Collins of All Saints Gardening Club; Zee Russell, Ettingshall Councillor.

Nevertheless, five fruit trees donated by the school were planted on the All Saints School site so that the centenary was marked, albeit earlier than originally planned. The photograph above (courtesy of Claire Darke) shows one of the saplings being planted next to All Saints Church, where a plaque commemorates 91 men who died in WW1.

During the years following the 1914-1918 war, memorials were put up with public funding or by private and public subscription. In many cases a Roll of Honour was inscribed with the names of the fallen, both civilians and military personnel, in a wide range of settings such as churches, public buildings, factories, railway stations and schools.

One such memorial, shown below, is found at All Saints Church. 91 men from the All Saints area are listed on a brass plaque. Brief details about three of those men are given below. It is impossible to do justice to their bravery, their fortitude, their sacrifice.

By 1911 George Arthur Wainwright was living with his grandparents, William and Charlotte Street, at No. 28, Granville Street, working as a bottler at an ale and stout brewery. In October 1911 he enlisted in the 3rd Dragoon Guards (Prince of Wales' Own). At the outbreak of The Great War, he had already served in the Army for three years, first in Egypt, before going to France. He first fought in France on 31 October 1914 but was killed in action on 6 November 1914. He is commemorated on the Ypres (Menin Gate) Memorial in Belgium.

John Bywater was another professional soldier who lost his life early in the war. He was born in Wolverhampton in 1883 and married Annie Britton Godfrey in 1906 in Aston. In 1911, they were living at No. 2 Court, Eagle Street, Wolverhampton, together with two children, John and Rose.

John was a labourer for a nut and bolt manufacturer and later worked for Bayliss, Jones and Bayliss before joining the army.

The Great War memorial at All Saints Church.

John served in the South African War. When the First World War broke out, he was called up to the 2nd Battalion of the

South Staffordshire Regiment, disembarking on 12 August 1914. On 30 January 1915, he was reported missing, but it was later confirmed that he had been killed in action on 27 October 1914. He is commemorated at the Oosttaverne Wood Cemetery in Belgium, as well as on the Monmoor and Victoria Works Memorial.

Joseph Horace Belcher was born in 1897 at No. 247, All Saints Road. On the day of the 1911 Census, he was an errand boy at an ironmonger's shop, but later became a library assistant at the Wolverhampton Free Library.

He enlisted on 7 October 1914, aged only 17, and served in the North Midland Field Ambulance Section of the Royal Army Medical Corps as a private. He received the Victory Medal and the British Medal. Joseph Belcher was killed in 1917 on the Western Front in France and is buried at Tyne Cot in West Vlanderen, Belgium. A plaque, produced by Wolverhampton Free Library after the tragic death of Joseph and another of their library assistants, is to be found at the library building in Snow Hill.

The Great War became known as 'the war to end all wars', a phrase said to have been coined by the American President, Woodrow Wilson in January 1918.

Following the end of The Great War, a peace agreement, the Treaty of Versailles, was signed in June 1919. The stringent conditions imposed on Germany included the loss of territory and military resources, as well as severe economic reparations. The consequent humiliation is deemed by many to be responsible for creating the political vacuum eventually filled by Hitler's National Socialist German Workers Party, the Nazi Party.

Clive Holes, Derek Mills

Despite the establishment in the same year of the League of Nations, with its ambitious aim to maintain world peace, another war on a global scale broke out in 1939.

WORLD WAR TWO (WW2)

On the morning of 3 September 1939, the British people received the inevitable radio message from the Prime Minister, Neville Chamberlain, that Britain was at war. The ultimatum to Germany to withdraw its armed forces from Poland had gone unheeded.

Preparations for war had been progressing at varying rates over several years. One major concern was the impact of bombing. Over 1,400 civilians had been killed and 3,400 injured during German bombing in WW1 and as early as 1935 the government had been making Air Raid Precaution (ARP) preparations. Local authorities were responsible for raising and running the ARP services as well as training volunteers for duties such as stretcher parties, first aid posts and rescue parties. Volunteer numbers were still low when the government set a target in 1937 of one ARP warden per 500 civilians, requiring tens of thousands to come forward. It was not until the 'Munich Crisis' of 1938, that people volunteered in significant numbers. The 1939 Register completed on 29 September 1939 showed which residents had been designated as ARP wardens. A gentleman at 28, Maxwell Road is listed on the register as an ARP warden.

Not all preparations had been completed at All Saints Infant School by 3 September 1939. The school did not have any air raid shelter protection. The logbook for All Saints showed that the school did not reopen after the summer holiday break until 30 October. 74 pupils who lived within five minutes' walk of the school were invited to attend school on a half time basis. 31 attended in the morning and 34 in the afternoon. Parents were informed by the school that if an air raid warning was given, staff would supervise the return to their homes.

By December, a shelter had been built at the back of the school and all pupils were invited to attend school on a half time basis. The normal school routines continued but were complemented by weekly air raid shelter drills and regular checks on the pupils' gas masks. By April 1940, the last two air raid shelters being erected were sufficiently well advanced in construction that all pupils were invited to attend all day. Normality returned in time for the May Day pageant. The May Queen, Kathleen Jewkes, was crowned and there were the usual displays of dancing by juniors and infants.

Several residents were now serving in the armed forces. One such person was John 'Jack' Biddle from No. 70, All Saints Road who joined the Royal Navy in May 1939. John was to be involved a year later in a major naval tragedy.

John was serving as an Able Seaman on HMS Esk, an E-Class destroyer, one of five ships laying mines along the coast of Norway. On 31 August 1940, they ran into a new German minefield off the Dutch island of Texel and two of the ships including HMS Esk sank. There was a considerable loss of life with as many as 135 crew members from HMS Esk reported killed, including the ship's commander. Having jumped into the sea, John was picked up by a British ship with another survivor. A newspaper report writes of John visiting relatives of friends from HMS Esk a week later to pass on his condolences.

Clive remembers the Biddle family well, as they lived only ten doors away from his home in the 1950s in All Saints Road. John had left the family home by then but his brother, Reggie, still lived there with his parents.

By November 1940, All Saints began to experience regular air raid warnings. A lot of the damage to buildings was self-inflicted. The listing for No.122, Steelhouse Lane describes the damage caused by A.A. (anti-aircraft) shell splinters.

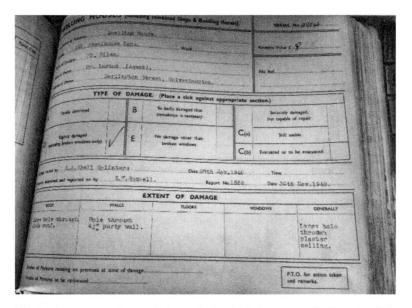

Wolverhampton's register of air raid damage listing for 28 November 1940. (Courtesy of Wolverhampton Archives).

On 4 December, pupils and staff at All Saints School retreated to the air raid shelters on three occasions during the day. Two weeks later, an all-night 'warning' meant that some pupils were too tired to attend school.

Far more serious damage was inflicted elsewhere as the war progressed. Sievwright's garage and Tatlows in Cleveland Road were both set on fire on 31 July 1942. The same bombing raid was probably responsible for the severe damage to a house in Caledonia Road shown below. (Photo: Express and Star).

The long-awaited invasion of northern France took place on the beaches of Normandy on 6 June 1944, D-Day. Across the country, hospitals like 'the Royal' received casualties from the campaign.

Newspaper reports and newsreel footage in cinemas of the D-Day landings captured the attention of the nation. A photograph, taken at the time, show large crowds assembled in the grounds of the Royal Hospital to watch and greet the arrival of these injured servicemen.

We have already described the wartime experiences of John Neave and his family who lived in Gordon Street. Otherwise, there are no other memories that have been shared by residents who lived through that time. Fortunately, we can draw on the astonishing military memories of an audacious local man, Benjamin Joseph Owen, thanks to his brilliant book, 'With Popski's Private Army', first published in 1993, and an interview he gave to the Imperial War Museum, a year earlier.

BEN OWEN – A LOCAL HERO

Ben's father, also named Benjamin, had fought in The Great War and his military life has been described earlier. We now look at Ben's career in the army.

Ben was born in 1917 in Eagle Street, off Steelhouse Lane and the family later moved to Rough Hills. At the outbreak of the war, he was already an experienced professional soldier having joined the Royal Artillery as a 15-year-old. Dissatisfied by 'orthodox' soldiering, he completed commando training and served with the 8th Army in the victorious desert campaign in North Africa.

Following the end of the campaign, Ben's unit was transferred to Taranto on the southern coast of Italy, to prepare for the allied invasion. Ben was already aware of the exploits of Popski's Private Army (PPA) in North Africa and when he saw a notice inviting applicants to join what he later described as "a strange unit", there was no hesitation. In many respects Ben's assessment was correct. The unit was run quite informally: there was no saluting and no drill, officers and men messed together, every man was expected to know what to do and get on with it. There was only one punishment for failure of any kind: immediate Return To Unit (RTU). At the interview, Ben was introduced to its charismatic leader: Major (later Lieutenant-General) Vladimir Peniakoff, known informally as Popski. When asked by Popski why he wanted to join his army, Ben's surprising reply was: "For a bit of fun."

Only 11 out of 60 applicants were accepted in October 1942 for PPA, formally known as Special Forces Unit, No.1 Demolition Squad. Ben and the rest of the successful applicants travelled the following day to Bisceglie near Bari, the headquarters of PPA.

A month earlier, PPA and its jeeps had landed from the sea at Taranto, Italy, along with the 1st Airborne Division. Within a few days, it had carried out reconnaissance operations nearby, gathering critical information about the strength and positions of the German forces. Consisting initially of only two 12 man patrols: 'P' commanded by Popski and 'B' commanded by Bob Yunnie from Aberdeen, the quality of their intelligence reports persuaded the allied chiefs to expand the unit from 12 up to over 80 men, hence the recruitment of Ben Owen and his colleagues.

From October for three months, Ben joined the patrols on intensive training in the mountains, moving rapidly in 'sawn off' jeeps, with no windscreen or hood, mounted with two Browning machine guns. A third patrol 'S' led by a 'Springbok' named John Campbell was created, as well as the 'Blitz' patrol, which used a supply vehicle and acted in a support capacity.

Following training they moved in January to Minturno, north of Naples on the Mediterranean coast. Their orders were to carry out missions behind the German lines to demoralise their troops.

The first one was a disaster. Ben was one of six members of 'B' patrol ordered to destroy two bridges in a nearby valley. At 7.30 pm in darkness, they moved down the valley with the 'skipper', Bob Yunnie, at the front and the explosive expert at the back. After about 200 yards, Ben recalls a bright flash and the realisation that someone had set off a shrapnel mine. The cylindrical mine propelled vertically to head height and exploded, releasing metal fragments and steel balls. One of Ben's colleagues was hit by shrapnel in the neck and killed instantly, shrapnel hit Paddy McAllister in the spine, paralysing his legs. Ben was blinded in one eye and caught shrapnel in many parts of his body including his arm which hung loose across his chest. Only Bob Yunnie and one other were uninjured.

Ben was ordered back, with two others, to the line where soldiers of the Scots Guard were providing support. Ben refused because of Paddy's condition and, with help from Bob Yunnie, he started to drag him back. The retreat was painfully slow with hidden slit trenches and shell holes hampering progress. Periodic bursts of fire from the Germans, during which Ben was shot in the leg, added to the ordeal. It was almost four and a half hours later before they reached an ADS (Advanced Dressing Station) where Ben and Paddy received much needed medical care.

The blindness in his one eye was temporary but Ben was to stay in hospital for four weeks before discharging himself. Popski was under the impression that Ben had left the hospital and deserted the army when Ben made an unannounced but welcome return to the unit.

Ben was to stay with PPA for the rest of the war. Their meticulous training prepared them for amphibious, mountain and parachute operations. Ben completed the skiing despite a leg that "neither bent nor straightened properly" after being shot in that first mission.

PPA became involved in numerous clandestine and front line roles in Italy: locating targets for the Allied Air Force, chasing Germans out of rear-areas, capturing German troops and equipment and saving bridges from being blown up by retreating German troops. By gaining the trust of farmers and partisan fighters, they acquired valuable intelligence about the German forces and this was wired back to headquarters.

The jeep was the mainstay of the unit's operations. PPA may have been run informally but before you ate and slept at night, there was one rule for your jeep that had to be followed. Ben explained it in an interview at the Imperial War Museum in December 1992. "When you returned to headquarters, you restocked your jeep and everything, ready to go away immediately - and sometimes you did go away immediately - and then you had your sleep or your dinner. Just like the cavalry where you looked after your horse before you looked after yourself."

'With Popski's Private Army', republished in 2006, covers the two years Ben spent in PPA. It gives an absorbing insight into the life and mindset of a professional soldier: a brave and resourceful man, exposed almost daily to a series of brutal and dangerous experiences.

Following the end of the war in Europe, they made a dramatic entry into Venice via amphibious craft. The book includes a wonderful picture which captures that event with one of their heavily armoured jeeps, surrounded by admiring and excited locals, parked in St Mark's Square - the only wheeled vehicles to have been there.

They were disbanded in October 1945 following a short spell in Austria. Several annual reunions took place including one organised by Ben at the Black Horse, Thompson Avenue.

A FAMILY AT WAR

Ben was not the only member of this remarkable Owen family who made an important contribution to the war effort.

Jim was in the special police force; younger brothers Ken and Eddy were both in the Territorials before joining the army. Eddy was mentioned in dispatches for his bravery. His sister, Marion, was in the ATS (Auxiliary Territorial Service) as a spotter on the guns. Ben's cousin Jack (John) Owen, also from All Saints, was a pilot in the air force, flying Whitleys. On his 33rd mission, while searching for a suitable drop zone for supplies for the French Resistance, his plane crashed into a hillside in Normandy. Jack is buried in Vire. Dorothy was too young to serve in the war but enlisted in the

ATS in 1948, the year before National Service was introduced.

Ben died in 2008, aged 91, bringing to an end an extraordinary, perhaps unique, story of an All Saints family serving with great distinction across two world wars.

VE (Victory in Europe) DAY

There are no records of church services at All Saints to mark the end of the war in Europe on 8 May 1945. That is not to say VE Day passed unnoticed. Celebrations in Gordon Street were picked up by the local newspaper. A photograph of a very impressive 'Hitler Guy' in the road gave a flavour of the festive mood in the neighbourhood. Flags of all sizes were flying along the whole length of the street with no one apparently put off by the inclement weather.

Moms and kids would now be waiting eagerly for husbands and Dads to return home from campaigns in Europe. In the Far East, fighting would continue for another three months until the dropping of the atom bombs on Hiroshima and Nagasaki brought a horrendous end to several brutal campaigns.

On VE Day, Derek's father, Roland, was serving in Burma; an infantry soldier in the Worcestershire Regiment, part of the 19th Indian Division ('the Dagger Division') of the 14th Army. Having played a major role in the liberation of Mandalay in early March, the Division was making rapid progress to liberate the port of Rangoon, the capital of Burma, before the onset of the monsoon season.

Letters were sent home to my mother and to relatives. He was at pains to play down any dangers he faced: "The Gurkhas are looking after us", "It's safer than a Saturday night in Wolverhampton" were typical reassurances.

Like many servicemen, Roland spoke little about his experiences. In later years, reminiscences would very occasionally be revealed: talks by officers to boost morale on the troopship to India; his first sight of Japanese soldiers, much taller by far than the officers had suggested; a platoon patrol across an unidentified minefield. He remained proud of his involvement with the 'Dagger Division' but, above all, he would constantly stress his deepest respect and admiration for the expertise and bravery of the Gurkha soldiers.

The Burma campaign had been overlooked by the news media which focussed on the war in Europe. This lack of recognition during and after WW2 led to the 14th Army becoming known as 'The Forgotten Army'. When Victory over Japan, VJ Day, was announced on 15 August 1945 the national celebrations were muted compared to VE Day.

Roland was not to leave South East Asia for home until January 1946. He was demobbed in February and returned to his peacetime job at John Thompson in Ettingshall. Following his service in WW2, he was transferred to the Army General Reserve. He was called up for Reservist Training in July 1952 and completed a 15 day programme in Preston. To the relief of Roland and his family, there was to be no involvement in any of the conflicts that occurred after WW2 and he was discharged from Reserve Liability in 1959.

Relatives commented after his death in 1978, that his wartime experiences had left a permanent mark on the man. Inevitably, this impacted on my mother. For the rest of her life, she had no time for Japan or its goods. We carelessly bought her a Sony TV on one occasion and had to persuade her it was made in South Korea before she would agree to use it.

POST WW2 CONFLICTS

The decades following the end of WW2 were witness to several post-colonial conflicts in which British troops were involved, notably the 'Malayan Emergency' (1948-60), the Mau-Mau Uprising in Kenya (1952-60), the Cyprus Conflict (1955-9), and the messy end of the Aden Protectorate in South Arabia (1960s).

MALAYA

Here is a first-hand account by John O'Gorman, an All Saints resident, of life as a British soldier in Malaya during the Emergency. John's chilling account first appeared in the All Saints Parish News of September 1979.

"The worst pain is caused by magazines of ammunition hanging from your belt and rubbing your hips till they are quite sore. Not one of the eight members of our patrol minded the leeches, the smells from the black murky swamp waters, or the thorns that tore your jungle green army issue uniform to shreds. Nor did we mind living in twilight down amongst those 300 foot trees with vines and creepers trailing about. Sometimes it would relieve the pain a bit to take the weight of the magazine pouches in your hands. Yes, that felt very nice. We couldn't always do that though, because while we held a loaded and cocked rifle in the one hand, the other one held either a prismatic compass or a machete to hack at those thorns, creepers, and vines, which always seemed to me to be made of elastic.

I well remember the 21st of March 1954. I was serving with the 1st Battalion of the Royal Hampshire Regiment. We had been taken into the jungle in helicopters, then there was a long march until we arrived near the edge of our search area, which was a swamp covering many miles of jungle. This was the type of place for Communist Terrorists (CTs) to hide in and feel quite secure. They knew that any Security Forces would make quite a noise thrashing their way through this swamp and jungle, giving them plenty of time to pack up their camp and melt away into the trees.

It was on the second morning in the jungle that we found ourselves moving through this swamp, searching for any island of land on which the CTs could be camping. At last firm ground – what joy! Things would be alright now. T.H. was at the front acting as leading scout. T.H. was a National Servicemen, about 19, full of humour, loaded with common sense, a good man at maintaining a straight line through the jungle when given a compass bearing by his Patrol Leader... CRACK! I knew at once that it was a rifle shot, and whoever let that one off would get 28 days 'inside'. There was always somebody letting a round off by accident... CRACK! 'Bandits!' I heard someone shout. I went down on one knee and froze. My mind thought 'If I run away, I shall be court-martialled. If I stay here, I shall be shot. What I shall do is turn to my right, go forward, and that will take me past their left flank. Then I'll turn around, come back, and shoot them in the back'. At the time it just didn't occur to me that being behind the CTs' backs would put me in front of my own patrol. Being excited by fear and the fear of being afraid didn't help me to think logically. Meanwhile, a strange frustrating fog seemed to settle around my eyes. Having made up my mind to shoot them in the back, I set off climbing a slight rise through the trees. I had gone no more than twenty paces when I suddenly saw lying down some twelve paces in front of me: two uniformed terrorists, both wearing the five-pointed red star in their caps. Both were firing rifles at me. The fog which still seemed to be around my eyes did not prevent me from seeing their fingers squeezing the triggers on their rifles, and smoke coming from the breach. It was at this moment that I heard the THUMP of our Bren gun, coming up the slope behind me spraying the trees with automatic fire. I only hoped the Bren gunner would see me there in the trees. While our Bren gunner was spraying the trees and I was firing like mad at the two CTs, I had an urgent thought go through my head. I didn't mind being shot in the stomach, but I didn't want to be hit in the teeth. So having clamped my jaws firmly together, I carried on walking and firing at my two CTs. Although I was alone at this moment, I was not so much lonely as frustrated with myself. This shooting at each other didn't seem to be getting anywhere. The CTs could not get all the practice they needed for hitting targets like me in the jungle, and while in barracks neither could they get their rifles zeroed by qualified armourers. The main thing was they had very little ammunition to practise with, while we had a government spending £1million a day on us.

All of a sudden, I found my Platoon Commander by my side, 2nd Lt. L.W. He carried an American carbine which fired single shots or automatic. This particular weapon only had a killing range of 300 yards, but as you could only see about 10 yards in the jungle, it was good enough. Nice chap, 2nd Lt. L.W. National Serviceman about 23 years of age. Always made Sgt. J.T. and me feel important, and he was the chap who had answers when Sgt. J.T. and I couldn't find one in our Military Training pamphlet. As soon as my commander appeared firing by my side, I saw one of the terrorists drop his rifle, turn, and start to crawl away. I thought he was going to escape. I ran up to him, but he then collapsed onto his side. His face resting on his right arm, his brown eyes glazed over after he had seen me looking down on him.

It took a year for us to learn that my patrol of eight men had been ambushed by fifteen Communist Terrorists. My Platoon

Commander had his compass, which he was carrying on his belt, smashed by a bullet, otherwise we were all safe. Two of their men died."

ADEN

Eric Gittins_has earlier recalled his time at St. Joseph's. He left in 1963, went onto Wulfrun College before joining the RAF in '65.

Following basic training at Swinderby in Lincoln, he went to Locking in Weston-super-Mare for Electronics training. Eric was then posted to Aden, arriving in April '66. He was based at RAF Salt Pans, the receiving station for all the armed forces in Aden.

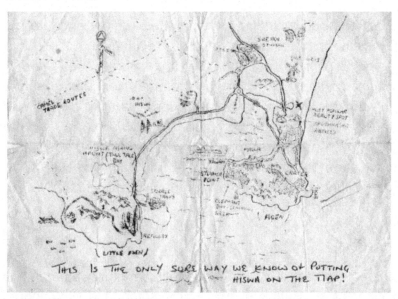

RAF Salt Pans, Aden, shown to the east by an X. (Map courtesy of Eric Gittins).

"I knew it was a hot spot and could have issues but was concerned about being away from parents to some extent.

The role I had at RAF Salt Pans was radio communications, on the receiving side. Ensuring that the transmissions from other parts of the world were kept in constant communication, getting the transmission side to change frequencies according to the ionosphere variation. Sunspots caused havoc at times.

The workplace was about 1km up the dust track and was heavily fortified with bomb-blast walls, high security fence and the army on patrol after lunch. Some of the billets were brick, others were corrugated iron, but all had air-conditioning, and needed it! One day we checked the temperature outside in the shade and it was 120°F or 49°C and very dry, no doubt a lot hotter in the sun.

Salt Pans had a cinema, used in the evening, and later for the evening shift, but it was reel by reel change, not like auto changing. Ended up getting my projection licence there. If you wanted to go to Malla for shopping, you always had to go with at least two others, as security, but if you were with an officer, then that officer was not allowed to go into the shops with a firearm. Whoever was with them had to stay outside and look after it. All staff at Salt Pans and Hiswa (the transmitting station) had to have a full gun licence. By early '67, the shopping was getting limited as the forces were only allowed to go to the main road shopping due to the problems with the locals.

There was 'Mad Mitch', Colonel Mitchell, the Commanding Officer of 1st Battalion, Argyll and Sutherland Highlanders who took his troops into the Arab area of Crater to calm the unrest. The locals were not sure of them as they were in kilts!

One member of Salt Pans who had been reposted to one of the other RAF camps was caught outside of curfew and was challenged by an Army patrol. He responded in Arabic, as he was of Indian/Arabic descent. He was challenged again, and I believe ignored the request and was shot. He was taken to the local hospital and when his identity was realised, he was taken to the RAF hospital at Steamer Point. His name appears on the memorial in North Staffordshire.

RAF Salt Pans, around 1967. I'm 4th from right middle row, looking to my right. (Photo courtesy of Eric Gittins).

Some 50+ years later I am still in contact with Sgt Vic West, front row to my immediate right. I was also godfather to one of his sons. Sgt Dave Black, sixth from left, I caught up with at RAF Cosford, in 1970.

The Arab-Israeli War of '67 caused a lot of issues and soldiers' deaths; four were murdered locally. On one occasion, the Army camp at Salt Pans, the living quarters and the 'tech' site were set up to be mortared. One hit the mess tent of the army, but fortunately no one was there."

Despite these hazards, there were opportunities for servicemen to enjoy rest and recreation time. Eric was a member of the Salt Pans cricket team. "I started off as being

6th or 7th wicket down. By about the 5th match I played in, I was first wicket down.

In 1967, I was posted back to RAF Cosford where I stayed until I was demobbed at the end of '70. During which time I moved from repairing electronic equipment to repairing the equipment that we used to fix them."

Eric moved to Melbourne in '76 with Jan and daughter Sue, attracted by a well-paid job in TV repairs. Fast forward twenty years and in '95-'96 Eric was awarded a Bachelor of Education degree to teach in schools, going on to become Head of Technology (Materials) at two schools, before finally retiring.

11

ALL SAINTS IN TRANSITION

1960 - 1999

It may well be that 1960 marked a watershed for All Saints School and its neighbourhood. Indeed, an Inspector's Report for November 1962 noted that the "area in which the school is set appears to have changed considerably since the last inspection nine years ago... many houses had been demolished, many families had been rehoused with some vacated houses occupied by immigrant families: 19 immigrant pupils now attended the school". At a Governors meeting a year earlier, Mr Lancaster had stressed the teaching difficulties experienced with the intake of Indian pupils who were unable to speak English.

Over the next decades, the challenges posed by those changes in housing, population and employment intensified, overwhelming what was described in the 1950s as a 'respectable working-class community'.

IMMIGRATION

In the '50s and '60s there was considerable immigration from the Commonwealth countries in Asia, Africa and the Caribbean. The immigrants came to work in the factories and new public services, at a time when the country desperately needed workers from its former colonies to regenerate its post-war economy.

However, they received a mixed welcome. Housing, for example, became one of several issues they experienced. Many immigrants were blocked from buying a house because of racism. Renting a council house from a local authority was not an option because they lacked residential qualifications. Consequently, many were forced to find rented accommodation in older, often decaying housing stock in inner city neighbourhoods like All Saints.

As one of the major industrial centres in the country in the '50s and '60s, Wolverhampton attracted many immigrants. Their arrival did not pass without controversy. In a speech to a Conservative Association meeting in 1968, Enoch Powell, MP for Wolverhampton South-West, made the following explosive statements:

"It almost passes belief that at this moment 20 or 30 additional immigrant children are arriving from overseas in Wolverhampton alone every week... We must be mad, literally mad... It is like watching a nation busily engaged in heaping up its own funeral pyre."

Despite this contentious forecast, All Saints evolved by the 1970s into a multi-ethnic community: Asians, working class White people who had lived there a long time and Afro-Caribbeans. Growing up in the '80s, one ex-resident was only aware of three cultures: White, Black and Indian. Many of the Indians were Sikhs from the Punjab. He cannot recall any Pakistani people in the neighbourhood, nor any Chinese. The influx of East Europeans, largely from Poland, was to take place much later. The memories which follow provide us with a valuable insight into their experiences during this period.

HERMAN WILLIAMS

Herman came to the UK from Hanover, Jamaica in 1961 at the age of 17. He lived initially in the home of his cousin in Lea Road, in the Pennfields area of Wolverhampton.

Herman Williams at the ASAN (All Saints Action Network) building in September 2022.

Herman was attracted by an assurance from the UK government of plentiful jobs and good wages, but aware that these outcomes had not materialised for all the immigrants who had left islands like Jamaica. Letters and phone calls to relatives and friends back home had sometimes painted quite a different picture of life in England, flagging up problems with accommodation, jobs and racism.

Despite these warnings and a lack of financial support to pay for the fare to England, Herman joined individuals with a diverse range of skills and experiences who came over from Jamaica. These included pig-farmers from what once had been a thriving community on the island. Like Herman, they came in search of a better life and better-paid work.

Back home, Herman was a carpenter by trade. He signed on at the labour exchange and was found a suitable job. His colleagues were fascinated by the technique he used to saw wood but otherwise he was ignored. He soon discovered that carpentry was not well rewarded. He needed money and looked for work in heavy industry which dominated the West Midlands area in the early 1960s and which was relatively well-rewarded. He took on a succession of jobs in foundries, where he learnt to be a steel moulder. Then, one day, his boss told him that the furnace man was off sick - would he like to try his hand at looking after the furnaces? Herman accepted.

Now in his late 70s, Herman looks back at that fateful day with these words: "so me start do de furnace job: tip it out, not running the metal, just clean it out, you know". It all sounded very simple. But things went terribly wrong. A few days later, while he was inspecting some damage to the interior wall of one of the furnaces, a work colleague accidentally pressed the wrong button on the control panel with disastrous results. "… all de ton of coke come down from inside de furnace. Messed up de furnace and fell on me - I'm sick! I was in hospital about three months." This was long before the days of Health and Safety and automatic compensation for industrial injuries. Herman just got his normal pay for those three months, and nothing in the way of compensation. He never went back!

In those early years in England, Herman would wonder why he was only getting a little bit more money in a factory job here than he was getting from being a carpenter in Jamaica. "When we was working in Jamaica, we used to do carpentry. I mean, about that job… when we come here, they wonder why I'm going get a little more than them, when we work in factory, than when we're doing carpentry…"

After two years living in locations around the city, Herman moved to Vicarage Road to be near his place of work. He remembers settling into life in the All Saints neighbourhood. He refers to "… Trinidads living on the other side… and struggling English people, you know… Well, we met plenty [neighbours]. I was getting on alright".

Herman would socialise in pubs like the Summerhouse in Steelhouse Lane. He recalls West Indians playing dominoes in one corner, Asian playing cards in another with the dartboard area occupied by White British. Years later, when he took his son Jackie there, they were both made welcome and they built up a comfortable friendship with the pub's regulars. The only drawback was the small and overcrowded bar with a lack of seating that put off many West Indians who didn't like standing with their drinks.

In sharp contrast to the relaxed atmosphere that Herman experienced around All Saints, he faced racism in the town centre. He recalls two such occasions involving young men that Herman refers to as "teddy boy".

"But if you go in town, teddy boy are there… We… went in town and the teddy boy, them with brick… run, we have to run… home. Another time, we take bus again and one of them took the bus, another teddy boy… and the bus [conductor] stop and saying, 'I'm not going further', and we have to come off and run, go home..." Herman and his friends didn't even recognise where they had been dropped off by the bus crew!

Herman recalls another similar event, "Well, [we would] have a drink and ready to go home, you know Broad Street down there...the time we live at Heath Town... and ready to take the bus... some of them come, some that not even going that way... all the girlfriend say, 'No, no, no, no!', but them want a fight... them girlfriend try to stop it, but them still... we have to run."

Herman gave no date for these two incidents, but similar events nationwide in the '50s and '60s, in some cases far more horrific, had led to the introduction of The Race Relations Act in 1965. The law banned racial discrimination in public places and made the promotion of hatred on the grounds of colour, race, or ethnic or national origins an offence.

Since his arrival in the town, he has been a member of the congregation at the Seventh-Day Adventist Church, nearby in Oxford Street. Services take place on a Saturday, their Sabbath, attended predominantly by members of the Black community.

Herman has had little to do with All Saints Church, either as a place of worship or as a community hub. He remembers visiting the building with a friend and being made welcome. He was drawn instead to the community centre set up in the old St Joseph's School building after the school's closure. It had become another popular meeting place for All Saints' residents. "... at night times, weekends, all of us round there... everybody come together". When it was finally demolished in the 1990s, Herman travelled to a community centre in Whitmore Reans, but visits came to a halt when he gave up drinking for health reasons.

He reflects on his plans back in 1961. "… well, to be truthful, every Jamaican come here for five years… they come, spend five years, and come home… make that fifty, sixty."

Herman did not go back. He settled in England, worked and raised a family and has made the city his home for the last 60 years.

SHOBHA ASER-PAUL

Shobha, Chief Officer at ASAN, the All Saints Action Network organisation based in All Saints Road on the site of the old school. She arrived in England with her parents in 1968.

Both parents were qualified teachers in India but were not allowed to take up a teaching post in England immediately. After a year working in a biscuit factory in Southall, London, her Dad was accepted onto a teachers refresher course in Wolverhampton.

"For me, my younger sister and our parents, a rented room in a terraced house on Vicarage Road would be the family home for the next 10 months. Our landlords were an Indian family; they had a son who was a bully and terrorised my sister and me. One time he spilt boiling hot water on my arm just before a school summer event. His mum slathered my scalding skin with a cream - I can still feel the pain of the burn, made worse by being outside on a scorching hot day.

At 86 years old and over 50 years later, my mum still finds it difficult to talk about that time. Arriving from a comfortable life in New Delhi, my Dad was compelled to follow a dream of living in the land of Shakespeare, Bertrand Russell and new beginnings. For my mum it was the polar opposite; she never wanted to leave her family.

My sister went to St Mary's School and I to All Saints School. I don't have much recollection of my school but I remember my sister crying desperately at hers and hating school dinners.

We made friends with other Indian families in the area - many of them recently arrived and most of whom we are still in touch with to this day. One of our best memories is of Mr and Mrs Roberts and their kindness. They lived on Maxwell Road. We don't recall how we met but they used to invite us over to their home. An immaculate parlour room that had a glass cabinet with china crockery and a winged armchair; we had our first Victoria Sandwich cake made by Mrs Roberts. They helped us feel welcomed and connected us, Mrs Roberts was like a granny figure; my mum would wear one of her best saris and style her shoulder- length hair curling it out at the ends when we went over.

There was a corner shop on Vicarage Road selling sweets, groceries and everything else run by Mr and Mrs Jetley. Mr Jetley wore a brown/ caramel colour cotton overall jacket in the shop - just like Arkwright in Open All Hours.

We were aware of Enoch Powell's views on immigration. After we left Vicarage Road, I found myself walking towards Mr Powell in a street in the Merridale area of the town. As we passed, he smiled. I was astounded, considering the negative impact that his opinions had on families like mine."

SURJIT BANGOR

Surjit is a member of staff at ASAN.

"I'm from Punjab, from a little village called Raipur between Jalandhar City and Hoshiarpur. I was nine years old when we came here in 1969. And our sister was already here. Our sister was the one who called Dad over. He came a couple of years before us. And then me and my two brothers; we came with Mom.

We lived in Gordon Street, in the middle, with our sister. When we first arrived, it was completely different to what we were used to. Money was very difficult. Then we moved and rented a place in Granville Street.

We moved again when my parents bought a house at No. 85, Gordon Street. It had a kitchen but there was nothing in the kitchen, just a ceramic sink, no hot water. There was a coal house, and the toilet was at the end of the house. It didn't have a bath so we used to go to the Wolverhampton Baths to have a bath once a week. The house became the subject of a compulsory purchase order by the Council to create the hospital car park. And once they had done the car park and marked it off, the hospital was shut. And we ended up with no home so the Council provided us with the house at No. 71, Vicarage Road. I was the middle one, I had an older and younger brother. In the winter, I had to clear the snow, make a path to go to the toilet, and get some coal and light a fire.

When it came up for sale, my parents bought it. And what my Dad said was: 'What we'll do, we'll buy this house, … if the Council sell. That's OK, because the family's going to grow' - because we are three brothers... and he very kindly bought that house for me. That was £7,500, and I've been there since, very happy. Then we bought No. 69 after, next door. So, we've got two houses together for the extended family."

SCHOOL

"For primary school, with my age at that time, I was 9, I was sent to Eastfield Language Centre. It's on the Willenhall Road. And that's where anybody coming here who didn't speak English would go... I didn't know even one word. And everybody from all over the world, they go there, you spend a year or two there, then they find you a school.

By the time I went to school I was secondary school age, I went to St Joseph's. That's why probably my English is not that good, because I've been moved from school to school. From St Joseph's, which was a boys' school, then to St Patrick's on Coalway Road, that was originally a girls' school. They had amalgamated together, so half of the school, our boys, went over there. Some of the girls came over here, depending on their age. And then after a year or two, both schools closed, and we moved to St Edmund's. It was a mixed school near to where the Wulfrun College is and St Peter's School. They are right next to each other."

SETTLING IN

Surjit remembers the impact of Enoch Powell on race relations. "There was lots and lots of it, racism. And people were scared to go out. But locally, like in 'the Dartmouth', we had lots of Asian community life in here, in the olden days, but now people have moved out. But in the pubs, like, you would meet people, and they were really good.

I remember my brother's wedding. It happened in Gordon Street, and twenty, thirty people were in the house. Dad knew the gaffer at the Dartmouth Arms... everybody used to be very friendly... and I remember exactly. He said to me: 'Surj, there's about twenty, thirty of you in the house. How you going to manage with the food and the drink?'... then he said: 'Well I'm closing the pub now, why don't you bring all the food over here? The tables are still set up, why don't you come and eat here?' That was very nice of him. Everybody was very, very friendly, in that respect."

My son, he was born in 1988, and he was the first kid in the family, so they wanted to have a little party. I remember there were woodwork and metal work sheds here on what are now the outside courts, and they became a community centre. And that's where we had a little party for him. That's just across the road here.

We didn't expect that many people. We only invited one or two people from the house, but all the families turned up, and we ended up using both community rooms. They are not there now. I got a video, there's a big party going on. That's in the old days how we associated with people. And I tell you, people look at it now, my kids, and they say: 'Dad, even then, plenty of booze!'"

INDIAN OR ENGLISH

"We try to go back to Raipur every second or third year. We've got a house over there. Everybody when they first came over here, my parents, their intention was not to stay here long... some people might say they were well off there and they only come here for just... I think if you were really well off, you don't need to go to another country. You go there for holidays; you don't go to stay... but we came to better ourselves.

Our parents came here and I've been listening to everybody, and they used to say: 'Spend ten, fifteen years, then go back.' But it never happened. I had the same feeling. My beautiful house was over there, and we said: 'What we will do is, once the kids start going to secondary school, then we'll retire and we'll go and live over there.' But then living over there compared to over here now. For myself, I am more British than Indian. I mean here, I could go anywhere I want. India - it's where I was born, but now it's different altogether from what I remember. We could not go and live there independently. We would have to rely on somebody all the time, and my kids.

Surjit at work at All Saints Action Network (ASAN).

I got three kids: two boys and a daughter. We have taken them when they were young. But now they'd rather go to Europe, America, Canada. They love India for holidays, that's what they say... but to go and live there now, no. This is our country and... it's very, very difficult for us to go and live there. When I go there, I like to stay at least a month. There's a lot to see. India's a massive country.

English is their native language but they speak Punjabi with my Mom and Dad and us as well. We didn't know English at all, not a word. And Mom and Dad spoke Punjabi... in fact my son, when he was the only child in the house, he was left with Mom and Dad. We were working... and they are pure Punjabi, and that's how he picked up Punjabi.

We were worried, when he went to school, what was going to happen. But the teacher said: '... he will learn... he was born here; he will learn English. It won't be a problem for him... in fact, where he stays will be good for him. He'll know his mother language and English as well'. But they have all done well. Our youngest one, he is mostly English, he lives in Edinburgh now, and sometimes we try to speak Punjabi to him."

COMMUNITY RELATIONS

"When we came here, the parents, they wanted to go and meet people, so what do they do? 'Let's go to the temple.' Like every Sunday, you go there, go to the temple and meet people. And the temples were the first point. Everybody's going to be there, so-and-so's going to be there. Let's meet him. Then the weddings. It doesn't matter who you are, if you are Sikh, Muslim, Hindu, and you live in the street, you are invited. Temples of all denominations provide a welcome. Always food in the kitchen for whoever visits.

And you meet somebody in the pub, and you are invited. We never had a bad experience with our neighbours. So, it's all been good."

PHIL AND GILL COLLINS

Phil and Gill, who ran the Dartmouth Arms from the late '60s, remember the arrival of Asian families in All Saints.

Gill: "When we were at 'the Dartmouth', we had quite a few Asians, not so many West Indians. There was a crowd of, I won't say older men, but middle-aged West Indians who used to come in and then you got the Asians.

Used to get them in, some were on shifts weren't they, and you used to get them in at different times and it was quite amusing because you got talking to them. 'I can't go home until so-and-so time, until so-and-so's gone onto their shift', cos there was that many living in the same house."

Phil: "If they went to work at 10 o'clock and were on from 10 to 6, the chap would come home to a nice warm bed, wouldn't he? When a lot of these Asians started moving into the country, if the house wanted a lot of work doing to it, the Council would sell it to them cheaply. I mean you could get one on Vicarage Road for about £12,000, a terraced house."

Gill: "It was a lot less than that, Phil, when they came."

Phil: "Late '60s, '70s, early '80s... The houses on Vicarage Road, opposite 'the Dartmouth'. You've got a little bit of a garden in the front and a big garden at the back that goes through to the alleyway. We used to watch them coming in, the Asians.

There'd be four or five families in one house. And when they'd see another house come up for sale down the road. Well, there used to be an Asian guy come to 'the Dartmouth' once a month in a big white Rolls Royce with his bodyguard, go upstairs, and they'd [Asians] pay into a divi club, well we call it that, I don't know what they call it. It's like, he used to take 10% of their wages... he put it into the bank. He was a loan shark. And then if a house come up for sale, they'd go to him and apply for cash to buy the house with and he'd lend them the money.

About three or four times a year he'd come in his big white Rolls Royce. He'd go upstairs and they'd all troop up there one at a time and come down with a wage packet. He'd pay them so much of the interest back out after he'd deducted his profit, and then they'd stay in the pub all night long until it was spent. And at the end of the night, you'd be picking empty wage packets off the floor."

Gill: "We got the pub in 1969, so it was just before then when all this was happening, so I'd say '67, '68 when this went on."

Phil: "I know at one time on Vicarage Road, there was an Indian guy called Mr Midda. He had a lock-up garage and he used to make anoraks. I was working in furniture delivery in them days for Times Furnishing, or Cavendish Woodhouse. And at the warehouse, where I worked in Oldbury, we got this order come through for Mr Midda: seven bed-settees... seven bed-settees in that house?! Anyway, we thought somebody had made a mistake, but we banged them on the van and went in to deliver them. We went in one door and took all the bed-settees in and we come out four doors down the street! He'd cut holes in all the walls... archways through the walls, so the first house you went in was for all the women, the middle two houses for the kids to watch television and play in, and the end house for the men, and they had one big communal kitchen.

There might have been eight or nine families in there. The men slept downstairs, the women slept upstairs with the kids, and that's how it was. There were no three piece suites in the house, they'd got all these bed-settees in each room so they could sleep at night. Most of the furniture was just a coffee table with an incense burner on it, and cushions or bean bags to sit on the floor. They had a big communal kitchen where the women cooked the meals. The men were at one end, the women at the other end. Whether they watched television, I don't know, or whether they'd just sit there and the kids would be playing in the middle. They'd all be extended families: sons, daughters, uncles, aunties, grandads, grandmothers.

If a house down the road come up and a young couple was getting married, they'd go to this bloke. 'Can we have the money?', 'Yes' and go and buy it and they'd move out. Then somebody else would come from India and they'd move in.

The bottom end of Vicarage Road where they've built Mike Swain Way down to where Banga Travel is, they had all those houses there. They've pulled them all down now, so I don't know where they've moved to."

Gill: "And Mr Midda's two big eldest sons used to go round in a white van once a week and collect all the bundles up from the various houses - right half of the anorak, left half of the anorak, the right sleeve, the left sleeve - then they'd take them down his workshop ready to be made up and then down to the market. And that was expected of all the kids in those days. Once they'd come home and done their homework, then they'd go upstairs and they'd be on the sewing machines till it's time to go to bed. If you came up on the bus, it used to stop outside 'the Dartmouth'. At night, you could look through the windows and I used to watch them.

They still do it now... we see in the morning now, the Asian women trotting off down the road. Just down Cable Street, down the bottom there, there's quite a few Indian places making clothes."

There were times when tensions would come to the surface. Gill and Phil Collins recall an incident at the Dartmouth Arms after they had left.

Gill: "It was alright when the first man took over."

Phil: "But then rough people started going in there. One landlord came in there who was from down Pleck in Walsall, Tommy Norton, and the brewery put him in there to sort it out cos he was handy with his fists.

You could see, the one night, there was two families of Sikhs there, with their turbans on, big men, and they'd be staring at another family sitting at the other end of the room and you'd think there's somat going to happen in a minute now, it's boiling up. It was yap, yap, yap to each other. We couldn't understand the language but Tommy knew there was somat gooin on... and then they all kicked off the one night. Tommy dragged the one outside by the scruff of his neck, knocked him to the floor. Then he picked up a pool cue, took the man's turban off, cracked the cue across his head and offered a brusque piece of advice: 'Get that stitched!'

By then the police had turned up, the riot squad... all piled out. They had a right go at each other, and they arrested Tommy and put him in the back of the van. He said: 'What ya doing that for, I'm the landlord throwing 'em out!' They'd got him in the back of the van; they had to loose him off!"

HAZEL SKELDON AND EMMA PURSEHOUSE

Hazel and Emma from Gordon Street witnessed two contrasting aspects of race relations around the All Saints neighbourhood.

Hazel recalls one incident: "Everybody got along. There was a lot of Asians in the street and there was a riot one year. There was a knock on the door, my Dad opened the door and a few Indian families came in because they were scared... and my Dad just let them in."

Racism did exist and, in some instances, it was clear for everyone to see. The management at Cleveland Road

Working Men's Club operated a racist membership policy. On one occasion, Emma had made her way to 'the Cleveland' when she saw Paul Hines, Hazel's brother-in-law, standing outside. "The club would let his kids in, but not your brother-in-law who was black." Hazel's parents protested about their policy and took it to the club's Committee. Their complaint was dismissed and as a result they were barred from the club. They started going next door to the Newmarket pub instead.

In the meantime, they found out about a similar case in London where a racist policy had been successfully challenged. A representative came up from London, explained Paul's legal rights and helped him to get allowed into the club.

HOUSING

The School Inspector's report of 1962 had identified the demolition of many houses nearby. To halt further deterioration of the housing properties, the Council in 1971 designated the zone bounded by Gordon Street, Steelhouse Lane, All Saints Road and Vicarage Road as a General Improvement Area (GIA). This led to the Council investing nearly £350K on the environment and its council-owned housing.

While the investment led to tangible benefits for residents living in council-owned properties, only 43 out of the 245 properties in the private sector were improved. To address this imbalance, a proposal was put forward in 1974 to create a Housing Action Area (HAA).

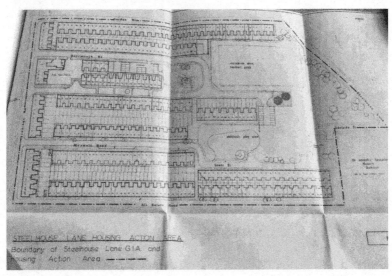

The plan above shows the proposed layout of the zone labelled the Steelhouse Lane Housing Action Area. It was hoped that the financial package associated with a HAA would encourage more property owners to invest in home improvements. (Courtesy of Wolverhampton Archives).

This recommendation was based on:

- the physical state of the housing accommodation in the area;
- social conditions in the area.

The council also surveyed the standard amenities of properties across the neighbourhood by ownership and tenure.

Hazel Skeldon lived with her parents and brother at No. 40, Gordon Street in the 1970s. The terraced houses in Gordon Street date back to around 1900 and by 1970 a large number still lacked amenities like hot and cold water and inside water closets.

Table 3 - Standard amenities by ownership and tenure (total properties)

Standard amenity	Ownership		
	Council	Private	
		Owner-Occupied	Tenanted
1. Fixed bath or shower	129	75	34
2. H & C water supply at bath/shower	128	62	34
3. Wash-hand basin	128	62	34
4. H & C water at wash-hand basin	128	62	35
5. Sink	130	143	102
6. H & C water at sink	129	71	35
7. Water closet (inside)	128	61	35
TOTAL PROPERTIES	130	143	102

The data in the chart above (courtesy of Wolverhampton Archives) revealed the marked contrast in the amenities available to the householders. Of particular concern was the disparity in the supply of hot and cold water for private tenants.

Little had changed since the 1950s when Clive Holes lived in the area. Hazel can vaguely remember the outside toilet being replaced by an indoor one.

"The only thing about Gordon Street, we never had no heating in any of the houses, they never put it in for years. The bathroom was... god, no heating, It was black [with mould], and every time you painted it over, and the council came to do it, it would just come back again. We used to have calor gas in each room to keep us warm, yeah, condensation on the windows, I used to hate that. ... and then the lofts. You could get all along the street in the lofts. It did cause a few problems... and laughter!"

In February 1980 the Council Housing Committee made the crucial decision to carry out a clearance scheme in All Saints. Large areas of Gordon Street, Steelhouse Lane and Sutherland Place would be demolished. The Chief Environmental Health Officer defended the decision explaining that the main concern was a block of houses (Nos. 41-61) in Sutherland Place where all the homes lacked stability and the only solution was demolition. There was strong opposition from the residents to the scheme. The Express and Star quoted Mr Harry Hickman, from No. 47, Sutherland Place: "We have done all we can to keep this community alive - but we can do nothing now." The impact of this clearance scheme on the neighbourhood cannot be overestimated. The decline of All Saints had gained momentum during the 1970s, but this scheme may well have been the 'straw which broke the back' of the residents' spirit.

For some children in the '80s, Gordon Street was a no-go area. One ex-resident recalls: "Gordon Street was trashed when I was growing up. It was very horrible because a lot of the houses were boarded, smashed up and then again you would have the brothels. My Mom warned me: 'Don't ever go round.'"

When Emma Pursehouse first visited Gordon Street, the landscape was quite different. "I know when I first started coming to your [Hazel's] house, there was more of a street!" The houses in Sutherland Place and Gordon Street had been the target of the clearance scheme mentioned earlier. Sutherland Place was demolished and the road closed as part of the ill-fated Tesco superstore plan. On the Sutherland Place side of Gordon Street, the houses to the east of No. 70 were demolished in the late '80s. The houses on the opposite side, below No. 42, were also knocked down in the '90s. New houses were built on the site. Hazel's family home at No. 40 was one of those demolished and they moved to No. 57, further up the road.

Phil Collins who has lived in the area since the 1960s reflects on the changes.

"Dartmouth Street, that's gone. Gordon Street, half of that's gone. They only pulled it down as far as John Neave's (No. 70). They couldn't come past there - he wouldn't let them! All those streets used to go down as far as Steelhouse Lane at one time, but they blocked them all off and turned the bottom half into a kids' play-area and a seven-a-side football pitch, but that too disappeared over time.

Wolverhampton Council did a lot of modernisations around the area. But most of those houses on the right-hand side of All Saints Road going up were run by Midland Park, not the Council. As far as I know, it's a private housing group. They did a lot of renovation. If you walk up the street, you can tell the ones that the Council own because they've had new rooves on, new chimneys on. The ones that are privately owned have got the old slates on."

SOCIAL ISSUES

By the early 1980s, the magnitude of the social issues in All Saints was being picked up at a national level. In 1984, members of the Archbishop of Canterbury Commission, examining the role of the church in the life of Urban Priority Areas, visited All Saints. They were shocked by the poverty and squalor.

UNEMPLOYMENT

Our knowledge and understanding of unemployment and other social issues in the neighbourhood is boosted by a publication, 'In Our Own Words'. It arose from a 1998 project, 'Something is Brewing in All Saints', organised by The All Saints Women's Resource Centre.

'In Our Own Words' comprised stories collected from local people. Their words give a snapshot of everyday life in All Saints at the close of the 20th century, a real eye-opener: relentlessly bleak but with small sparks of hope. Typical titles of these sketches are 'life on the dole', 'ageism', 'give me a chance', 'life as a single parent', 'my life of hardship and illness'. The picture they paint is a cocktail of educational underachievement, unemployment, deprivation, drug abuse and prostitution. Against this, there is, in some of their accounts, a fitful display of the community spirit for which All Saints was once well known. A selection of these have been incorporated into this article and others in this chapter.

In the '80s, the town went into an economic decline. Many of the town's major employers made staff redundant. It is estimated that in the 1978-1984 recession, 25,000 jobs were lost in the town and average earnings in the borough moved from near the top to near the bottom of the national figures. Heavy and light industry had created prosperity for the town but that sector suffered the most harm from the recession.

Stewart and Lloyd, the steelmakers in Bilston, closed in 1979, Star Aluminium in Blakenhall closed in 1981. Others like John Thompson at Ettingshall and Goodyear in Bushbury began downsizing in the '80s. The most prominent factory in the All Saints neighbourhood, Bayliss, Jones and Bayliss, closed the steel side of the business and the works were sold in the 1980s.

The economic and social impact on homes and shops in the All Saints neighbourhood was devastating. The damage was also visual. Once the factory buildings were demolished, particularly on the site of the Monmore Works, an unappealing vista of dereliction was revealed, extending from All Saints Church across to Cable Street.

Working class areas like All Saints were particularly affected. A White male of 36: "My father was on the dole when I was a kid. I can't remember him having a job at all. He was always drunk and hitting my mom, and he was in and out of jail. He was a very nasty man to me, my brothers and sisters."

Many Black people perceived there was covert discrimination over employment. A Black male, aged 36, gave his opinion on this controversial matter: "When I was on tip-top form and went for an interview, once people saw the colour of my face there was prejudice there."

Some refer to supplementing the social security benefit payments with work 'on the side' and the constant risk of being 'grassed', in one case by someone from their own street. A female interviewee recalls that "… you sometimes have to resort to making what money you can, no matter what it takes".

PROSTITUTION

It is debatable whether the start of prostitution and kerb crawling was one of the main factors in the transformation of the All Saints area or one of its outcomes. As far back as February 1970, the Birmingham Post reported that the Borough Engineer would be improving the street lighting between the Royal Hospital and All Saints Road following complaints about an alarming increase in the number of prostitutes.

The All Saints area of Wolverhampton was to be blighted by prostitution for decades, almost becoming a byword for it. The Sandwell Evening Mail of 29 December 1987 reported that more than 700 people living in the All Saints and Walsall Street areas of Wolverhampton had signed a petition calling for a 'major initiative' from the police, council and local MP to clean up the streets. One of the signatures on the petition may well have belonged to Doris Skeldon who lived at 40, Gordon Street. Doris was the mother of Hazel who describes her childhood memories of the prostitution problems in the neighbourhood in the '80's and '90's.

"When we lived in Gordon Street after our friends moved out… a known prostitute moved in there and it turned into a brothel. It was absolutely awful. By the '80s, there was a lot of brothels in Gordon Street. I was so scared to come out of the front door and walk down the street. Even my Dad, they used to stop my Dad as soon as he went out the door. My Mom used to kick up a fuss and she got up a petition to get them out. When that didn't work, she got up a petition to block off the bottom of the street – the cars were racing up and down all the time. She started it, went round with it to neighbours and passed it onto the MP. It helped when the street was blocked as it slowed down the flow of cars."

This only addressed part of the problem. Hazel remembers her sister Sue walking down the street with a pushchair and kid and getting propositioned. She recalls another incident: "I was waiting at a bus stop in Steelhouse Lane … I was so scared, I phoned my Mom because a car kept going, backwards and forwards, backwards and forwards. The car had stopped by me and my Mom came walking up, kicked the car and had a go at him."

It was just as likely to happen in broad daylight. Emma Pursehouse who lived with the Skeldon family was "on her way to work in her overalls when I was propositioned by some flipping bloke on a bike".

A report from the City Council housing officials accepted that people want to leave an area affected by prostitution and it adds to the spiral of decline. It went on to describe the All Saints area as "an example of the decline that has accelerated over recent years and can be seen as directly attributable to the growing problems of prostitution and kerb crawling".

One male interviewee was asked in prison by inmates if "there were as many prostitutes as they say there is in All Saints". Another male interviewee claimed that "All Saints is not to blame for me being jobless but it plays a big part at interviews because half the gaffers drive round the red light district and don't want to be seen by their employees, do they?"

The interviews with three young prostitutes flag up the familiar factors which can push vulnerable women towards prostitution: a lack of qualifications, failed relationships with parents or partners, unemployment, financial problems and drug use. A distressing account is given by a White female, aged 30.

"When I officially left school at fifteen, I had not taken any exams. I tried to find a job, but not listening at school and not being able to read properly had taken its toll. I got a job in a Cash and Carry but I couldn't read the boxes properly and got the sack". Eventually, virtually unemployable, she turned to prostitution: "That's how it began. She told me what to do and how much to charge.... The first punter I went with, I froze. When I got out of the car I vomited, but each time it got easier. Well, not easier, but I'd block it out of my mind. I'd get high before I went out on the beat."

The ongoing dangers associated with a life of prostitution were brought into focus in 1990 when the body of Gail Whitehouse was found lying in some shrubs and bushes in Steelhouse Lane by two 17-year-old youths. She had been strangled. Gail was a familiar figure in the red light district of Wolverhampton. A backlog of fines for soliciting, totalling about £4,000 had been quashed earlier in the year by a judge to give her a fresh start. She was last seen on the night of Monday 3 September around 10 pm, apparently trying to get into a lorry tractor. Her body was found on Thursday 6 September about 75 yards away from where she was last seen.

The problems associated with prostitution were to continue into the new millennium. In 2002, a survey revealed that Wolverhampton had the third busiest street vice trade in the country with the hotspots identified as All Saints and Horseley Fields.

DRUG AND ALCOHOL ABUSE

Unemployment was a contributory factor in other issues. Hazel Skeldon and Emma Pursehouse recall: "Nobody had work, could get work, so a lot of drinking took place. Groups of drinkers would hang around passages in Gordon Street and elsewhere."

Emma and Hazel do not remember drugs being a problem in the mid-'80s at first. At some point, it changed. Coke was still an unaffordable drug in the '80s but by the '90s, heroin and cocaine were widely available. Hazel is convinced that her family and friends were affected by drugs. "Without a doubt.... drugs so easy to get, you got dragged into it. It wasn't just our street; it was all along Vicarage Road as well."

Hazel's brother, David, who was Emma's boyfriend for about 8 years became an alcoholic and then a drug user. He died because of this. Hazel's sister, Sue, also died from alcohol related problems. Other family members have been affected by drug problems.

David Skeldon and Emma Pursehouse. (Photo: Emma Pursehouse).

A lot of the young men in the area were constantly in and out of prison too. Drugs really became a scourge of the area.

Clive Holes, Derek Mills

Emma can name about ten people they hung around with who did not make it to past the age of 50.

In 1989, Emma Pursehouse wrote a poem, 'An Ode to Dave's Dreams'. This is a selection of three of its verses.

Broken windows, battered doors,
Kids on corners, playing at whores,
Painted faces, pulling their tricks,
Glass bottles, cars on bricks.

Father's drunk, living in a pub,
Mother's whole life is polish and scrub,
Colours it up with bingo and booze,
Awake all night to the black man's blues.

Blame it all on twists of fate,
All of your chances coming too late,
Take the torment of the silent shout,
You knew the way; the way was out.

© Emma Pursehouse, 1989.

ALL SAINTS CHURCH AND COMMUNITY

The situation with All Saints Church has been a recurring concern, going back many decades. We have heard that the warning bells were ringing as far back as 1965 with Father Morris's damning comment about the parish.

That particular financial crisis was addressed but another appeared in the early '80s. A survey of the church building revealed that considerable expenditure would be needed to rewire and carry out major repairs to the roof. The cost would be completely unaffordable. Rather than accept the church's redundancy, the community groups considered another option, its adaptation into a community centre.

On 25 April 1984, Mike Swain, the community worker at the Steelhouse Lane Community Project (SLCP) had sent a letter to the Chief Executive and Town Clerk at Wolverhampton Council. The letter concluded:

"... that probably the cheapest solution for community development would be the adaptation of All Saints Parish Church to include both a worship area and community facilities."

This 'reorder' was eventually agreed between Lichfield Diocese and the Council with funding, estimated as £282K, included in the Inner Areas Programme for 1980–1990.

Our knowledge and understanding of the outcome of this complex matter is boosted by a booklet, 'The Fall and Rise of All Saints', published by Barnardo's in 1990. The charity became involved with the All Saints community in 1986. Their representative, Peter Smith, was given the brief to work with the church and community groups, to help them to identify their needs and achieve their expectations and to gain resources. Between September 1986 and April 1991,

Peter witnessed the 'fall and rise' of the outlook for the church and community.

In 1986, when he made his first visit to All Saints, it was designated the "most deprived part of the most deprived ward in Wolverhampton". As Peter turned into Gordon Street to visit the Steelhouse Lane Community Project (SLCP), he was confronted by small, densely packed, terraced houses, some with broken windows, some boarded up; open land, where houses had been demolished, full of rubbish and broken glass. He wrote that it was "like turning into a nineteenth century industrial neighbourhood".

He found several existing groups were already set up and supported by the Junior School Head, Mr Werry, and members of the community. The church community was represented by the Steelhouse and District Community Association (SDCA), set up in 1977. Steelhouse Lane Community Project (SLCP), based in Gordon Street, was set up in 1978 in response to crises in the area and funded by the Commission for Racial Equality. It drew much publicity in 1984 when Mike Swain, a project worker, took 18 unemployed youngsters on an expedition to India, covering 13 countries over nine months. In Vicarage Road, the All Saints Haque Centre (ASHC), an advice and drop-in centre, was set up in 1983, with financial support from the British Council of Churches, to give attention to the special needs of the Asian members of the community.

Unfortunately, it very soon became clear to Peter Smith that the proposed community centre had become a battleground for these groups, with each looking to dictate its future role and management. Despite a shared interest in the future of the neighbourhood, there was discernible distrust of each other. To compound these existing problems, the vicar, Father Alan Brannigan, confessed he was out of his depth in community work and did not enjoy living in this multi-racial area with its problems of prostitution.

What followed over the next five years was a roller coaster of hope and despair. Invitations from the church, SLCP, ASHC and SDCA to help in the preparations for the completion of the new community centre were followed by frustrations caused by building work delays and disagreements. At a public meeting in March 1987, Lichfield Diocese was accused of holding up the transfer of the church building into the hands of the Council. Work was now scheduled to start in the summer, three years since the proposal was put forward and agreed. This did not come to pass. However, following the departure of Father Brannigan at the end of the year, the diocese appointed a replacement, Canon John Edge. His impressive rhetoric at his interview was more than matched by his actions over the next few years, making a considerable contribution to the welfare of the community. He became affectionately known as 'Father John'.

Gill Collins, the present churchwarden remembers Father John: "… he'd even got the teenagers coming into the church. He was great. Everybody got on well with him. He was the type who would stand in the street and have a drink with you or have a dance with you or whatever was going on."

Another public meeting was held in February 1989. To the amazement of the residents, representatives from four council departments, COPEC Housing Association and the Police attended. Each presented their existing strategies for addressing many of the numerous housing and social issues. Not only were the residents unaware that these progressive initiatives were already in place but these various agencies were unaware of what each other were doing. However, it did raise everyone's spirits that, at last, the residents were being taken seriously. The local MP, Dennis Turner, was also in attendance and asked to be kept informed, offering his help where possible.

At the AGM of the Community Centre later that year, the church warden said: "I think the future looks good for the community." While progress with the community centre was now in full swing, problems continued with the 'chapel' at the chancel end of the church building. There were even rumours that the Council had run out of money and the work could not be finished. At the start of 1990, the 'chapel' resembled a builder's tip, separated by a huge partition wall from the splendidly furnished community centre.

Despite this, the official opening of the community centre took place at 7.30 pm on Friday 2 February 1990, following an earlier Candlemass service in the 'chapel', still without lighting or heating. About 100 attended a joyous ceremony. It began when three elderly couples representing the White, Asian and Afro-Caribbean residents were welcomed as special guests and received bouquets from local children. Councillor Ledsam from the Leisure Services Department unveiled a plaque. Entertainment was provided in the main hall by the school choir, the school Bhangra dancers and a local Asian musical group. The evening concluded with a multicultural buffet laid on by residents.

All Saints was now in possession of a new community centre, two full-time community workers based in the neighbourhood, funding from the Inner Areas programme, new housing plans, a police strategy to control prostitution and kerb crawling and new social projects like the All Saints Women's Resource Centre. Their 1998 project, 'Something is Brewing in All Saints', was highlighted earlier in the chapter. This vibrant group, based in Gordon Street, was established in the late 1980s and led initially by a resident, Gail James. It drew support from many quarters including Bilston College which at the time was very active in promoting women's education. A team of five: Linda Nevill, Barbara Sutherland, Marilyn Burrill, Alan Leavesley and Jane Seabourne worked productively with the All Saints women's community by organising courses in assertiveness, confidence building, as well as an education programme designed to develop skills in community activism.

One account by a female, aged 31, illustrated the opportunities that this admirable Resource Centre presented to residents.

"When I heard about the All Saints Resource Centre, I couldn't wait to see what they had to offer. They were really friendly and helpful, but most of all they were really understanding. I enrolled on a computer course and I was petrified because I had never touched a computer before. After that first day, all my fears were blown away and I really enjoyed the course… After a while I started to do some paid and voluntary work there, which really boosted my confidence and made me realise I can do more for myself."

When Bilston College closed in 1999 and merged with Wulfrun College, its involvement in women's education was not pursued. The inspirational Gail James left the neighbourhood. The Women's Resource Centre was viewed as a source of optimism for the future of All Saints, but its association with the community, after the publication of the 1998 book, is unknown. If its splendid work did indeed end abruptly, it was a significant loss for the neighbourhood; a blow to the optimism expressed in 1990.

SCHOOLS

GROVE SCHOOL: 1970-1999

At the turn of the 20th century, the area which stretched between Caledonia Road and Pond Lane was the site of a brick works. Following its closure and demolition, the land fell into neglect.

At the start of WW2 in 1939, a large neighbourhood air raid shelter was built on land adjoining Caledonia Road. At some point, another piece of the land was developed into a playing field, 'The Rec', incorporating a football pitch used by locals and the 'home ground' of All Saints School's football team until 1958. By the mid-1960s, 'The Rec' and surrounding area had become an embarrassing eyesore and due a significant transformation. In 1968 it came in the shape of two new schools: Grove Junior School and SS. Mary and John's Roman Catholic School.

Proposals for a new school in the neighbourhood dated back to the 1950s. An Education Development Plan of 1957 had recommended that All Saints School should be demolished and rebuilt on the site occupied by St Joseph's School. This scheme was abandoned. When Grove Junior School opened in Caledonia Road in 1968, it provided an attractive alternative for local parents. SS. Mary and John's R.C. School opened a year later. Built in only four months, a national record for a school, Grove Junior School opened as a two form entry school.

The logbook records: "… on 9 September the first intake, made up of two classes of infant children transferred from Dudley Road School, joined us. 157 children were admitted on the first day of whom approximately 85% are coloured [sic] immigrants".

Construction work in 1968 on the two new schools.
(Photo: Grove School).

The staff consisted of: Headmaster, Mr Ernest L. Rhoden; Deputy Head, Miss Yorke; Heads of Maths and English and six class teachers, all of whom were in their first year of teaching.

The school generated immediate national and international interest. In October, the school was visited by Miss Marie Rawlinson from California; Renee Short, MP for Wolverhampton NE; the secretary of the Council for Community Relations; a LEA Inspector and a BBC TV crew. In 1971, Ernest Rhoden wrote, '… that the school had been built in a national record of four months did not have as much news value as the fact that it would have an immigrant intake of 90%'.

To put this astonishing media interest into context, a survey undertaken in Wolverhampton in 1962 showed that there were approximately 1,000 immigrants in the town's schools.

Clive Holes, Derek Mills

In January 1967 there were 4,500 immigrant children in the schools. By January 1969, this figure had risen to 5,566, almost 12% of the total school population. In Grove School nearly 90% of the children were immigrants.

Preconceived concerns soon dissipated. In October, the governors spoke of the "wonderful work" being carried out by the teachers and announced they would not be pressing for a redistribution of some of the coloured [sic] pupils to even out the ratio of immigrants to white pupils. They expected the percentage of coloured [sic] pupils would decrease in time to 60%.

The official opening of the school, shown above, by The Right Hon. Edward Short, MP, Secretary of State for Education and Science took place on Tuesday, 10 December. The presence of Enoch Powell, the controversial local MP shown sitting at the back of the stage, with his back to the wall, added to the extensive media scrutiny. (Photo: Grove School).

In February 1969, a newly formed Parents Association said they were impressed with the education the pupils were receiving. It hoped more Asian parents would join the Association's committee and suggested the introduction of English language lessons for Asian parents.

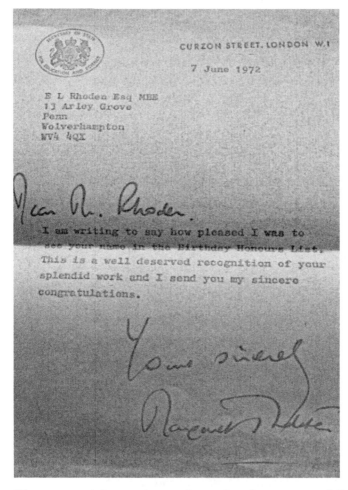

CURZON STREET. LONDON W.1

7 June 1972

E L Rhoden Esq MBE
13 Arley Grove
Penn
Wolverhampton
WV4 4QX

Dear Mr. Rhoden.

I am writing to say how pleased I was to see your name in the Birthday Honours List. This is a well deserved recognition of your splendid work and I send you my sincere congratulations.

Yours sincerely

Margaret Thatcher

The congratulatory letter from the Secretary of State for Education and Science, Margaret Thatcher.

A year after it opened, the school was praised in an article in the Race Relations Bulletin. It wrote that, despite prophesies of doom, the quality of education had not fallen, only one pupil could not read or write English and children had not been taken out of the school. ... two morals could be drawn from the last twelve months. "First, there is no reason why a school with a high proportion of coloured children should be a second-class school unless it is allowed to become so. Secondly, nothing succeeds in dispelling traditional fears in race relations save sane, cool, courageous leadership."

Ernest Rhoden's exemplary leadership was recognised in the Birthday Honours List in June 1972 when he was awarded the MBE. The letter is shown courtesy of Grove School.

Mr Ernest Rhoden, the school's first headmaster, with a group of ecstatic pupils. (Photo: Grove School).

In September 1974, the Infant School opened on an adjacent site to the east of the Junior School. It was initially known as the Dudley Road Annexe because of the main source of its intake. Reception and Nursery classes were incorporated into the school in 1976 and 1980 respectively. 1980 also marked the retirement of the Headmistress, Mrs S.G. Dimmack and the appointment of Mrs J.E. Garbett.

The leadership of Mr Rhoden and the Local Education Authority (LEA) was put to a stressful test following an incident at the start of the summer term in 1979.

On the 24 April, Mr Preminder Singh Bhamra escorted his son, Kulbinder, to school. The child was wearing a large yellow turban which was not part of the agreed school uniform. The father argued that his son had taken part in a religious ceremony and should now be allowed to wear it. Mr Rhoden contested that the turban was not one of the five essential points of the Khalsa and furthermore there had been no consultation regarding this addition to the school uniform, as laid down when his son was admitted to the school.

The matter escalated quickly and the Community Relations Officer, Mr Elder, told Mr Rhoden that unless he allowed Kulbinder to attend school wearing his turban, legal action would be taken against Mr Rhoden under the Race Relations Act. By the following day, the Express and Star carried a front page story of Kulbinder's 'banning' from school. On the 26 April, Mr Elder warned of demonstrations which materialised the following day with picketing by the Indian Workers Association (IWA) and the Socialist Workers Party.

The crisis continued into May with further demonstrations. On the other hand, there was overwhelming support for the actions of the school; a petition with 2000 names supporting the Headteacher and LEA was handed in to the Education Office.

At a meeting on 9 May a compromise was put forward whereby Kulbinder would be allowed to wear a small, removable turban in school colours. This was agreed by the Director of Education and Education Committee, and somewhat reluctantly by the parents and school managers. The consensus was that the whole issue had been planned and politically motivated by a member of the Indian Workers Association.

At the end of the month, the Head Teachers Association issued a writ for libel, on behalf of Mr Rhoden, against Naranjan Singh Noor, a member of the IWA, regarding two letters he had written and circulated in which he accused Mr Rhoden of racism.

Kulbinder returned to school in mid-June and left a month later for secondary school transfer.

On 8 February 1982, the libel case against Mr Noor was finally heard at Birmingham. Members of staff, parents, ex-staff, school governors and members of the Education Committee spoke in support of Mr Rhoden. The jury were unanimous in their verdict and awarded Mr Rhoden £5,000 damages and costs estimated at £42,000.

These protracted events, and the toxic atmosphere they created, failed to undermine the impressive progress that had been made by the Junior School since it opened. The school's diverse achievements in 1982 were summarised in the logbook: boys and girls teams won football and netball trophies; the school choir was successful at the Wolverhampton, Catshill and Tamworth festivals; individual pupils won prizes in art, essay and music competitions. Most leavers had swimming awards and good academic achievements. Mr Rhoden and his staff could be justifiably proud.

Unfortunately, in 1983 tragedy struck not once but twice. On Saturday 5 March, a wing of the Infant School was damaged by a fire, later treated as arson. Although many pupils returned to some classrooms by the following Wednesday, the nursery children did not return until after the Easter holidays. Then on 12 November 1983, the logbook recorded the sudden death of the Junior School Head, Mr E.L. Rhoden, MBE. Two years earlier he had suffered a heart attack while collecting supplies for the week's camp at Pwllheli. One can only speculate whether the stress from events over the last few years had been a contributory factor.

Up to 1991, the Junior and Infant Schools were managed as two separate schools. A Governor's meeting at the start of the year discussed the proposal to amalgamate the two schools and Mrs Garbett's application for early retirement. Both were rejected.

At the time of the discussions, there were 87 pupils at the Infant School. Of those 87, 13 were in the Reception class with the remainder in Years 1 and 2. No mention is made of children in the Nursery classes. At the Junior School, there were 128 pupils spread across Years 3 to 6. In July, 38 pupils transferred to secondary schools with the vast majority going to Colton Hills and Parkfields, two comprehensive schools relatively close to Caledonia Road. One pupil was accepted at the Girls High School, having passed their entrance exam. Mrs Garrett would have to wait until December 1994 to retire when the Governors also unanimously agreed to amalgamate the two schools into Grove Primary School.

In January 1995, Grove Primary School started a new term with Mrs Thorpe as Acting Headteacher, a post she officially took up in June. Her tenure was relatively short. Following an incident in November 1996 involving a complaint she made against a member of the LEA, Mrs Thorpe announced she would retire in March 1997. A week earlier, the Primary School had undergone its first Ofsted inspection. The report which came out in late December highlighted many positive features. Mrs Thorpe was praised "for providing clear leadership and direction". It also emphasised that "the children enjoy coming to school and appreciate the stability and opportunities to learn which are provided".

At the end of February 1997, Mrs Thorpe retired and Mrs Bonser was appointed in her place. A logbook record was no longer completed by the school and we have a lengthy gap in our knowledge about Grove Primary School's progress.

ST JOSEPH'S SECONDARY MODERN SCHOOL FOR BOYS AND ALL SAINTS SCHOOL

The fortunes of All Saints School and St Joseph's School became intertwined in the 1970s. After 57 years in the All Saints neighbourhood, St Joseph's School closed in 1971 and the pupils relocated to St Edmund's School at the leafy Compton Park site in the west of the town.

In 1976, the pupils from All Saints Infant School relocated and took up residence in the old St Joseph's classrooms. In the mid-1980s the Education Committee approved a scheme to update All Saints Junior School, providing a large activities hall for the pupils and a facility for community use. Despite the two schools operating on two separate sites, they amalgamated during the summer holidays of 1991 to form All Saints Primary School. In July 1993, the Junior School pupils moved into the Infant department building prior to the start of work approved earlier. The St Joseph's site was to remain the home of the Infant department until April 1994 when the new Junior department building opened for pupils. It marked the end of the St Joseph's building as a school and within a few years it was demolished.

Over the next few years, the All Saints School's logbook paints an optimistic picture of the school. When the Queen visited St Peter's Church in 1994 to celebrate its millennium, pupils from the school were chosen to line the approach. In 1996, the Director of Education opened the new school library. The school was submitting a National Lottery bid in 1997 for playing fields to be laid out on the old St Joseph's School site. An Ofsted Inspection in 1997 'praised' the school in overcoming the amalgamation of the Junior and Infant Schools, moving into a new building and a change of Headteacher.

However, longstanding issues with surplus places and budget deficits were soon to be addressed. This is covered in the 1999-2020 sub-section.

THE ROYAL HOSPITAL

The Royal Hospital has always been held in high esteem across the town and it deserves a few paragraphs outlining its expansion after The Great War.

The period between the wars was one of great change. Many new members of staff were appointed. This was due in part to the foresight of Edward Deanesly, a consultant surgeon. He convinced the hospital's governors that to attract the best medical staff they should be paid as full time hospital clinicians rather than having a private practice and a small honorarium for their work at the hospital. Old departments were refurbished and new departments were created including a diabetes clinic, venereal disease (VD) department, ear, nose and throat (ENT) department and orthopaedics. Moreover, new outpatient and casualty departments were built and a radiotherapy service was established after a supply of radium was purchased for £4,000, a massive investment, in 1929.

Construction of a new block of wards and operating theatres commenced in 1937. The wing with four storeys and its bay windows became a distinctive part of the hospital grounds.

During the Second World War it again received many wounded servicemen and women. It also welcomed an intake of junior doctors attracted by its reputation as one of the best provincial non-teaching hospitals in the country. When the blitz of London began in 1940 and the city's medical schools were moved out of danger, the Middlesex Hospital sent students to the Royal Hospital. Some of these, delighted with their professional experiences, returned after qualification as residents and later settled in the town as consultants and GPs.

In 1948, the hospital was handed over to the newly created National Health Service. Its facilities and finances were both in good shape, reflecting the quality of its medical care and administration for nigh on 100 years. During the '50s, in addition to its excellent male and female Nurse Training School, it established both Physiotherapy and Radiography Schools of similar note. The quality of care and training of staff was well-regarded throughout the UK and beyond with increasing numbers of overseas medical, nursing and physiotherapy students arriving.

The 1960's saw many of the wards renovated. Throughout the sixties and early seventies, a new theatre suite, an Intensive Treatment Unit (ITU) ward, plus a coronary care unit were established. However, talk had already begun to move the hospital's facilities to the New Cross Hospital site. Indeed, the ITU ward opened by Sir Keith Joseph in 1972 was the last significant development at the hospital and the following twenty years saw little in the way of development.

The Royal Hospital has always been an integral part of the All Saints community. It could be argued that its opening in 1849 marked the birth of the neighbourhood that eventually extended south beyond All Saints Church and School. As far back as 1874, the Bulls Head pub, a stone's throw away in Bilston Street, had been used as a venue for hospital inquests. Other local pubs were also used for this purpose. The Newmarket pub in Cleveland Road, opposite the hospital, was the venue for an inquest in 1861 into a boiler explosion at the Rough Hills colliery of Messrs Aston and Co. which resulted in the death of the head engineer. Mr E.T. Wright from Monmoor Iron Works was called as an expert witness.

Roy Stallard, a former nurse and nurse tutor who started work at the hospital in 1954, takes up the story.

"Up to its closure in 1981, the Bulls Head was used by hospital staff and doctors. With its intimate atmosphere and panelled walls, doctors relaxed while they waited for the hospital's call-out system to 'request' their prompt return. The Horse and Jockey pub, nearby, was used for staff parties. A wide selection of shops like Doody's in Steelhouse Lane were conveniently located. The 'ladies of the night' became part of the All Saints landscape in the '70s and could be seen plying their trade in Sutherland Place by night staff.

Even the Cattle Market in Bilston Street played a part in hospital life. Animals would occasionally escape and make their way into the hospital grounds. On one occasion, an elderly lady was woken late at night by their noise outside the ward. 'Am I in heaven?' she asked the nurse who came to her aid.

By 1970, the new ring road was creating access problems for the hospital. The buildings were old, it was difficult to expand the site and many clinical specialities were already being transferred to New Cross Hospital in Heath Town. Following an NHS Trust meeting in 1996, Roy Carver, chairperson of the Trust, used his casting vote and the decision was made to close the Royal Hospital. Demonstrations by the staff were low-key but news of the closure led to many vitriolic letters being sent to the Express and Star.

One by one, many of the specialities moved away to the 60 acre New Cross site and wards closed. Accident and Emergency (A&E), ENT and the Children's Department, all housed in relatively new facilities, were first to go in early 1997. All staff who wished to transfer were redeployed to New Cross. The Trust attracted staff by promising new state of the art departments for Heart and Lung, Eye and A&E. There would also be a Women's Hospital incorporating a new neo-natal department. The Nursing School at the Royal would now come under the auspices of Wolverhampton University."

This new nursing arrangement was a bitter blow for tutors like Roy. The Nurse Training School was a highly respected institution, attracting 60 students each year onto its three-year course. In his opinion, "The university nurse training has had a catastrophic effect on practical nurse training - all theory etc but can't pass a naso-gastric tube! The Royal would go along for years without a nursing exam failure."

The Royal Hospital closed on Tuesday 24 June 1997 after more than 148 years of care and dedication to the citizens of Wolverhampton. It may be of little consolation, but the new hospital group encompassing the hospitals at New Cross, West Park and Cannock is known as The Royal Wolverhampton NHS Trust.

Roy retired in 1998 and his energies and expertise are now being utilised as a hospital historian. With help from staff at Bantock House Museum, his aim is to set up a museum which celebrates the work of the NHS and Wolverhampton's hospitals. So far, over 300 items have been collected, many of which are donations from folk supporting the project. The museum, managed by a Heritage Committee, is currently in the process of being moved to a more permanent home in the library section of the education centre at New Cross.

1999 - 2022

ALL SAINTS CHURCH AND COMMUNITY CENTRE

Although detailed statistics are not yet available for the 1921 Census, it is safe to assume the composition of the population of the All Saints community has continued to change since the 1970s.

The data for the 2011 Census, released by the Office of National Statistics (ONS), showed that White British (35.9%) made up the highest ethnic group. The other main groups were Asian Indians (23%), Afro-Caribbeans (12%) and Polish (6.7%).

Moreover, a summary (Appendix 4) of the 2011 Census data for the areas north (e.g., Maxwell Road) and south of All Saints Road (e.g., Bowdler Road) shows a significant difference in the ethnicity of the population.

- Much lower % (21.5) of White British residents on north side compared to south side (51.0)
- Much higher % (19.0) of Afro-Caribbeans on north side compared to south side (5.9)
- Much higher % (10.0) of Polish residents on north side compared to south side (3.2)
- Similar % (23) of Asian residents on both sides.

Two residents with very close links to the church, Gill (churchwarden) and Phil Collins (caretaker) reflect on these changes and the impact they have made on the church congregation.

Phil: "What it all comes down to is most of the houses in All Saints now: Gower Street, Maxwell Road, Gordon Street -

there's a lot of East Europeans, Asians, West Indians living there and they go to their own churches and places of worship. They don't come to All Saints... so the congregation has dwindled down.

Gill and Phil Collins at All Saints Church in September 2020.

... when they opened the likes of Pendeford, Perton and Telford, they all wanted to get out of - as they classed them

- the 'slums' of terraced houses. They wanted a house with a garden for the kids to play in. So, when the Asians started moving in, and the Eastern Europeans - they're not used to having a garden - they give them all the terraced houses. Five or six families would live in one house, then move to another one, then buy another one, and buy another one... they were buying up factories as well and turning them into temples... there's one a hundred yards from here. The office that was part of it is now Alisha's Supermarket, which is a Polish supermarket. We've got a big influx of Polish people now in this area, but their church is down on the Stafford Road.

The main factory part is now a little Sikh temple. They're having a big construction built, the framework's going up. Obviously, they're collecting money, and they'll have their own temple there. It's a family, a disagreement with the head man of the main temple, and they've broken away from the main temple and got their own, so obviously they go there."

Phil: "... then the Hall got demolished. It's all gone now and nobody bothers. I mean they've had some good parties down there on Saturday nights, Sunday afternoon."

Gill: "You can count the congregation now on the fingers of two hands. Regular Sunday services have just started again after the coronavirus lock-down. We used to average about thirty-ish, twenty-five, thirty a week."

Phil: "But now it's about five... there'll be the vicar and two others and their two children, I think that's it. Phil Bennett... he's moved out of here to Perton, but he kept on coming to the church until lockdown. He's struggling on his legs now... and then there's Ken Mackintosh, he's a West Indian guy and he's also the Church Treasurer. Our congregation was made up of older people and they've either moved out of the area or passed on."

The tone of the conversation with Phil and Gill comes as no great surprise. One respects their local knowledge and their opinions on the factors which have contributed towards the dwindling numbers. The tendency among many members of inner city churches across the country to emphasise the movement of long established families out of the area and the incursion of immigrants is well documented.

Father Barnett, the vicar of All Saints, made the following blunt statement about his congregation in January 1977:

"Almost complete dependence on priest in decision-making and for leadership... Those who are very dedicated and keen (20 people) tend to make it quite difficult for newcomers to get involved and so feel wanted... Overall impression of church activities and worship is of a small group of people who are not very confident in what they are doing."

Gill had great respect for Canon Edge who was appointed vicar in the mid-1980s.

"While Canon Edge was here the Church was really doing well. And then, when he went to Chester, the next one who came in, he was more interested in himself, and what he was doing. He didn't care about the congregation. He wouldn't go out and even visit people... and that's when it started to go downhill. The younger ones didn't come, and it's just never really picked up."

One senses that church members continued to measure the success or failure of the church by the strengths or weaknesses of the incumbent vicar. The Archbishop of Canterbury Commission in 1985 advocated that those churches in Urban Priority Areas, like All Saints, needed to adopt a different approach to survive. The Commission believed that such churches must become 'local, outward looking and participating'. It put a greater onus on church members to achieve those three aims.

Following the opening of the new community centre in 1990, Peter Smith from Barnardo's, in cooperation with the church, carried out a survey of 41 active members. The main points that came out of the survey were:

- elderly membership – mainly aged over 60
- 87% attended at least once a week
- nearly 80% women
- only 4 Afro-Caribbeans
- only 2 of the 41 had joined in the last ten years
- very few interests outside church
- only 8 out of the 41 were involved in community activities.

When the members were asked in the survey what the church contributed to the community:

- 32% replied that it provided the vicar and his visiting;
- 24% could not think of anything;
- One person replied: "Not a lot but trying."

Many in the survey emphasised the importance of the church for providing friendship and social events. This led Peter Smith to question why members were not making more effort to extend this friendship to others in the community and organise social events of a multicultural nature.

When the project finished in 1990, he was alarmed that the church members still had little to do with non-members in the community. He wrote: "… with a largely ageing congregation in which only two members are recorded as having joined within the last ten years, the future does indeed look bleak".

All Saints: The History, People, Places

That prediction from Peter Smith may have finally come to pass. It would be too easy to say that a golden opportunity to act on recommendations and build up the congregation after 1990 came and went. In fairness, it is a national issue. The Independent newspaper reported on 23 Oct 2011 that membership, across the country, of the Church of England by those under the age of 26 has fallen by a fifth in three years. The Guardian newspaper recently revealed a 40% decline in church attendance over the past 30 years. The 2021 Census data shows that England and Wales are no longer majority Christian.

Despite his reservations expressed earlier, Peter Smith drew hope from his experience on a summer's evening in 1990. He wrote of the church choir rehearsing in the chapel, while in the adjacent community centre, one room was occupied by a discussion group, in another a Bhangra dance practice was in full flow, while the junior football team trained upstairs. He wondered at that moment whether "the dream of the church and community centre of a splendid communal building and a new sense of cooperation, leading to the renewal of a long neglected area, was at last being realised."

Back in 1984, the incredibly difficult decision to reorder the church was taken. Opinion is still divided. From the perspective of Rev. Sarah Schofield who spent twelve years at All Saints from 2006 to 2018 (one of, if not, the longest incumbencies in the church's history) she is still very grateful for the decision in 1984 to reorder and retain a place of worship in the chancel. Had they not done so, she believes depopulation in the area coupled with the later closure of the school would have made it unlikely that the amazingly warm and gifted group of people she knew as All Saints church would have still been gathering in the old building.

She arrived in All Saints just as several women were murdered in Ipswich, and sex work was something they had in common. Along with her congregation she was determined to set up something that provided a safe place for women, especially the sex workers based around the church. Initially they lacked confidence and waited patiently for the experts to come along to tell them what to do.

It was seven years before they linked up with a non-Christian charity which had some experience of supporting sex workers in other parts of the country. A start was made, drawing on the enthusiasm and skills of residents from a range of faith backgrounds. After three years, thanks to the Near Neighbours grant, more people became involved, some as professionals, some as residents or members of other congregations (Christian and non-Christian) and some in more than one capacity.

This venture became known as the Warm Welcome project. With a grant from the Church Urban Fund, the vestry was transformed into a small kitchen with a microwave and dishwasher. The church could now provide hot drinks and meals at a night-time drop-in session for sex workers. Volunteers and specialist staff were available to advise on drugs, sexual health and housing. In 2015, the church had the confidence, some would say the impudence, to re-schedule the Maundy Thursday service on a Wednesday so that sex workers could attend their regular Thursday sessions in the church.

The Warm Welcome project was one of six shortlisted in 2017 for 'The Marsh Awards for Innovative Church Projects': a competition to find the Christian congregations running the best community activities in a church building. As well as the Warm Welcome project, the award organisers also flagged up other groups at All Saints making use of the church buildings and facilities. These included a parent support group and Changing Lives charity.

Near the chancel, a change of dry clothing has been provided for the sex workers during wet weather.

While the spiritual life of All Saints Church moved in a positive direction during this period, the fabric of the building continued to cause serious concerns. As caretaker of the church and vicarage buildings, Phil Collins has followed its fortunes, some would say its misfortunes, over recent years. These were his thoughts in an interview held in September 2020.

"It [the Church] still belongs to the Diocese of Lichfield, but the Council pay this peppercorn rent per year for it. The Council are tenants but the Diocese still owns it. And the Diocese won't sell it until the Council have done the work on it that needs doing. It needs a new roof and things like that."

Ambitious plans had been put forward to address, once and for all, the long-term structural repairs to the church building.

Nevertheless, there remained a frustrating lack of conviction by the City Council to fulfil these plans and understandable caution by the Lichfield Diocese.

"They [Council] put the fire-alarm system in, and that's all they've done. That was about three or four years ago. They've done nothing else since. They don't want to spend the money. There was getting to be more and more damage each week with the youth club, so they stopped the youth club because they ran out of funding."

One incident clarifies the frustrations experienced by Phil.

"They [Council] came about 18 months ago and put scaffolding all round right up to the top of the roof. Somebody from Gough's the builders came on a Saturday morning and replaced about fifty tiles on the front of the roof, and they said: 'We'll be back next Saturday to have a look at the back and take all the shrubbery out of the guttering'. But on the Monday the Council scaffolders turned up to pull the scaffolding down again. I said: 'What you doing that for?' They just said: 'The job's finished now, we need the scaffolding for another job.' I said: 'But they haven't done the back, they've only done the front'. 'Too late, mate'. When the chaps from Goughs turned up on the next Saturday morning, they said: 'Where's all the scaffolding gone?' It was the Council – they had said the job's finished."

ALL SAINTS VICARAGE

Phil's grievances are not only aimed at the City Council.

"The old vicarage on Vicarage Road was built in the 1950s. It was lived in right until they built the new vicarage in Gower Street which is in what's now called Adelaide Walk. It became derelict. Keepmoat, the building firm, won the tender to build the new housing development at the bottom of Raby

Street… and what they said was: 'We'll take the vicarage off you, we'll build you a new one.' Keepmoat was going to turn it into two flats. Everything went wrong."

Phil witnessed a catalogue of problems for the old vicarage involving vandalism, fly-tipping and squatters.

" … somebody came in one day and opened the up and over garage doors, to see what was left inside. The next thing you know, they were dumping rubbish in it. We had a couple of girls, prostitutes, living there… The police turned them all out and they had to come and board it all up.

… When Keepmoat started on the new vicarage, they hadn't got the space to build it in. They had to move the fence on the park eight feet, so they could get the footings down. They couldn't expand out, so they had to build up, three floors up. So, you've got a kitchen-diner downstairs, a downstairs loo, and an office. Then you go up a flight of stairs to the en-suite master bedroom, and a living room. Then you go up another flight of stairs to the main bathroom and three more bedrooms.

With Amanda, the new vicar, being disabled, she uses a mobility scooter. She could manage to get up the stairs, but she didn't use the top. But it's there, if in the future we get a vicar who's got children."

Phil and Gill continue to devote their time and energies to the parish church of All Saints.

SCHOOLS

ALL SAINTS SCHOOL

The school was to go through its last Ofsted inspection in 2000. The inspectors described the school as "set in an area of significant unemployment …" 173 pupils attended of whom 108 were girls. 70% of the pupils came from minority ethnic community backgrounds and 33% spoke English as an additional second language.

The inspection reported that the school was "highly effective" with a headteacher who "successfully inspires the staff and pupils to work hard..." The provision for the nursery and reception children is "very good and is a strength of the school." It judged that "the school has made very good improvements since the last inspection in March 1997."

It is 60 years since Clive and I left All Saints School but on reading the 2000 Ofsted report, our attention was drawn to the report that "Standards in music are above national expectations in both key stages." Nothing changes!

Mrs Wheeler retired in 2001 after seven years as Headteacher. Mrs Val Currall, a consultant Headteacher employed by the Local Education Authority (LEA), took over while the provision of education in the All Saints area was being examined. In November 2001, Education Department chiefs set out a consultation document for developing Early Years and Primary Education in the All Saints area. Projected figures for 2002 showed that there would be significant surplus places in three of the schools in the area. The document was distributed to parents in early November. It included the rankings for each of the four schools in the area. The document stressed the difficult situation at All Saints: the small numbers and the high proportion of surplus places meant it was becoming increasingly difficult for the school to continue to operate effectively.

	Sites and Buildings	Quality of Education	Pupil numbers	Finances	Overall
All Saints	4th	3rd equal	4th	4th	4th
Grove	3rd	2nd	2nd	3rd	2nd equal
SS. Mary and John's	1st	1st	1st	1st	1st
Graiseley	2nd	3rd equal	3rd	2nd	2nd equal

The Governors of All Saints were saddened but not surprised by the proposals in the document. On 14 November, they passed a resolution which supported the idea of an amalgamation if All Saints closed. It recommended that the newly formed school would have Church School status.

In mid-January 2002, the LEA Lifelong Learning Cabinet discussed the issues and the outcomes of the informal consultation period. They proposed the closure of All Saints School and a merger of All Saints Primary School with Grove Primary School to create a two form entry community school on the Grove School site. This would take effect from 31 August 2002.

This decision was greeted with profound disappointment by the staff and governors at All Saints. Despite the attraction of modern facilities and a playing field at Caledonia Road, the proposal had been opposed by many parents and residents. The Ofsted inspection of All Saints School in 2000 had reported on the positive feedback from parents. The majority thought that teaching was good, children liked coming to school, they worked hard and were helped to become mature and responsible individuals. An 800-name protest petition was handed in to the City Council in December. Demonstrations which took place outside the school in January and February 2002 generated press coverage. In April, the governors submitted a letter voicing their concerns about the merger.

The LEA were not swayed and in June the LEA Cabinet meeting formally approved the recommendation to close All Saints Primary School and merge it with Grove Primary School.

On 12 July 2002, All Saints Primary School closed. Around 95% of the pupils transferred to Grove Primary School and all but two members of staff took up teaching positions at Grove in September. At the time of the merger, Grove Primary School was described as "an attractive, happy place where there is a caring and orderly atmosphere in which children and staff enjoy their work."

GROVE PRIMARY SCHOOL

In the absence of relevant information, the school's initial progress after the merger in 2002 is unknown. However, one can be confident that any progress had stalled badly by 2014. An Ofsted inspection expressed deep concerns about the effectiveness of the school and rated it as 'inadequate'. This had significant repercussions. It is Government policy that if a school funded by the local authority is judged as 'inadequate' by Ofsted then it must become an academy.

Academies receive funding directly from the government rather than the LEA and are run by an academy trust. It has more control and can dictate on policies such as admissions and the curriculum.

Another inspection quickly followed in June 2015 and found "a culture of bad teaching and unruly classes", according to an Express and Star article on 21 September 2015. The latest rating meant the school had been in special measures for two years. The ongoing problems at the school resulted in the original academy sponsor withdrawing from the academy conversion process during the early summer.

The inspection report noted that the school had now arranged support through St Martin's Multi Academy Trust (MAT). By March 2016, the school had become part of that Trust, joining another two schools from the Bilston area of Wolverhampton. Lynne Law took over in April 2016 as interim executive headteacher to become the third head at Grove Primary in five months.

ALL SAINTS ACTION NETWORK (ASAN)

The closure of Wolverhampton's Royal Hospital in 1995 was to have an unexpected, far reaching impact on the All Saints neighbourhood.

Deeply concerned about the effect of the closure on the future of the area, a group of residents and agencies came together to discuss the issue. A dominant figure in these deliberations was Mike Swain. Having worked in All Saints since the 1970's, he was deeply committed to improving the quality of life for everyone in the area. Mike had already played a central role in the decision to 'reorder' the All Saints Church building in 1984 and had gained positive publicity for the neighbourhood when he organised a trip to India for a group of youths from the area.

The outcome of their meetings was the creation in 1998 of a social enterprise and development trust, ASAN. Its mission was to work with partners to create a sustainable organisation, responsive to local needs through the development and management of enterprise, employment and social projects. Mike Swain was appointed as its founding Chief Executive.

The possibility of using the All Saints School site for an alternative community use had been mooted by the Council at the time of the closure proposals. Fortunately, the school did not suffer the same fate as St Joseph's School and its buildings became the base of this new community enterprise.

In 2007, work started on the refurbishment of the school buildings. The two buildings were reborn as The Workspace, a £1.6M development, completed in 2009, providing office rentals, an on-site day nursery and conference facilities.

Under the leadership of Mike Swain, the organisation went from strength to strength. Its key achievements included securing New Deal for Communities funding of over £1M from the government for the area, becoming the accountable body for the local Children's Centre and the development of The Workspace as a community owned asset. This entailed an active role in developing the plans for the regeneration of the Vicarage Road and Raby Street areas.

Tragically, Mike Swain died on Wednesday 14 September 2011. In the intervening period, a memorial garden, alongside the church, has been dedicated to Mike. Using the donations from people who knew this highly influential man and via voluntary efforts, the garden has been attractively landscaped with a greenhouse, seating and planting. The area is meticulously maintained by Phil Collins from the All Saints Gardening Club and kept open to the public during office hours.

Clive Holes, Derek Mills

Shobha Asar-Paul, Chief Officer of ASAN, with Jim Barrow (left) and Clive Holes (right) at the gate to the memorial gardens.

Surjit Bangor has been with ASAN since 2006 and recently described his time working for them.

"I worked like about eighteen years for a furniture store in Bilston. We used to make furniture and after that, a little break and then I used not to work. And obviously, for the 'Social', you need to prove what you been doing like, applying for jobs. So... that's how I ended up at ASAN.

I was unemployed and then all of a sudden, this job came up and I applied for it only... so as to get a letter, a refusal letter from ASAN saying: 'No, he's not useful for this'. But I ended up getting the job. I had applied for the job to get a refusal letter to claim unemployment benefit, but I actually got the job! Mark Woodall from Wolverhampton Council was my line manager. There was about twenty-five of us, and he short-listed me and I told him then, I said: 'Mark, I really don't want the job, only reason I done this is...' He said: 'Surj, you can't tell me that now, I could have had (...) but I wanted you.' Then one day he came and knocked my door and he said: 'Give it a couple of weeks. If you don't like it, then I'll do a letter to whoever you want'. And I done that and now I'm here!

It's brilliant. Ever since then I enjoy it. It's that good. And I was doing the community maintenance. We used to go down old people's houses, do anything we can do for them: gardening, recycling. We still do recycling. Recycling is... if you are the resident of ASAN, all you have to do is become a member, an ASAN member, free of charge, then you are entitled for recycling a three-piece suite, washing machine, anything like you want to get rid of. Book it with us, and we'll take it away for you and take it to the tip. Just people living within All Saints parish. We got over 600 members and they are entitled for the two libraries. Like you borrow the book from the library and we return it, and they do the same with the tools here.

Mike Swain started all this. We used to work for Mike Swain, He used to live in Gordon Street. I knew him before I come here. Mike Swain has done a lot for the area. The guy was extremely easy to talk to. You could go to him any time. He never used to say, 'Oh, I'm the Chief Exec' - always very approachable, like."

HOUSING AND THE ENVIRONMENT

Peter Smith's Barnardo's report in 1991 had painted a brighter future for housing and the environment. The local authority was seeking to ratify the area as a Housing Renewal Area and embark on a seven year improvement scheme. The COPEC Housing Association planned to build new housing on vacant plots.

Information about the outcome of these two ambitious plans is not available. However, despite everyone's good intentions, they were not sufficient to address the area's longstanding problems. By 1999, All Saints was still recognised as one of the country's most challenging neighbourhoods with soaring crime rates, prostitution and the poor health of residents.

NEW DEAL FOR COMMUNITIES

In 1998, the Labour Government set up the New Deal for Communities programme, costing £2bn, to regenerate some of the country's most deprived neighbourhoods. Wolverhampton Council submitted a scheme, the All Saints and Blakenhall Community Development (ABCD). The submission was successful and in 1999 it was awarded £53M over 10 years as part of this programme. This equated to funding of just over £4,600 per person and company during the decade.

Despite their ongoing involvement in the New Deal for Communities programme, the city was still ranked 28th out of 354 Local Authority Districts in 2007, with 1 being the most deprived. A report in 2008 by Broadway Malyan, commissioned by the City Council, identified All Saints and Blakenhall as one of the four most deprived neighbourhoods in the city. Their depressing report highlighted many long-standing issues.

282

"Most homes in the All Saints neighbourhood are privately owned two storey pre-1919 terraced homes with very small rear gardens or yards. There are very few modern homes with appropriate amenity space and generally very little choice in house type and tenure. This unsustainable mix of properties has resulted in a fragile housing market typified by low values, low demand, empty homes and a poor quality private rented sector.

The All Saints area has a significant problem with empty properties - with over 10% of the residential properties being empty in relation to 4.91% Citywide. Many of these have been empty for a long time… In general, BAME (black, Asian and minority ethnic) groups are housed in poorer quality housing, mainly the private rented sector, living on very low incomes or dependent on a range of state benefits. There are significant issues of anti-social behaviour, prostitution and drug dealing. These problems are exacerbated by the empty homes. They have led to the stigmatisation of the area and have inhibited its regeneration."

The outcome of the New Deal programme generated mixed opinions. A report by the Department for Communities and Local Government thought the £2bn scheme had not been successful. These findings are disputed by the ABCD executive director Tim Clegg.

He dismissed the report as "out of date" and said: "We have supported local businesses, cut crime, improved housing, transformed our parks and open spaces and built a new school and community buildings. The improvements that we are beginning to see will result in a better educated and healthier community who will in turn get better jobs and contribute to a stronger, longer economy."

When the programme wound down, most of the New Deal projects were handed over to Wolverhampton City Council and with the cooperation of the Homes and Community Agency (HCA) they formed the basis of their Local Investment Plan covering 2010-2014. Wolverhampton City Council's aim was to create a residential environment for All Saints that appealed to a wide range of people - both existing residents and residents who would be attracted to move to the area. Some key historic buildings would be re-used and derelict land and buildings would be redeveloped to preserve and enhance the townscape character.

Wolverhampton City Council identified four linked projects to achieve this vision:

1. The Royal Hospital and Bus Depot

The ring road had brought about the demise of the bus depot by isolating its building in Cleveland Road from the town centre. On 1 November 1993, all operations were transferred to other garages, the majority going to Park Lane, Fallings Park. It functioned temporarily as an indoor car park when it was leased by All Saints Action Network (ASAN) but was boarded up in 2017.

The project would include:

- the refurbishment of the former Royal Hospital main building (a listed building) for a health centre;
- new flats and housing - 300 dwellings;
- small scale shops and service accommodation;
- apartments and employment space on the site of the former bus depot;
- conversion of the former nurses' home into flats;
- hotel and conference facilities.

2. Vicarage Road and Raby Street regeneration area

A lengthy consultation with the local community, including All Saints Action Network (ASAN), identified several priorities.

- Family orientated housing
- High quality environment
- Improved traffic management
- High quality urban design
- Community involvement to ensure long term sustainability
- Improved public spaces and amenity areas
- Sustainable local shops and services.

3. Gordon Street/ Granville Street

60 high quality private homes at 'urban' density in a block design with new amenity open space. The affordable housing target is 20%.

4. Cable Street/ Steelhouse Lane site

A mixed-use scheme for housing and employment together with new canalside access, and a 'marina'.

THE ROYAL HOSPITAL

The aims of the project regarding the old Royal Hospital site will have been greeted with a degree of scepticism.

Phil Collins, a resident of All Saints Road, has lived in the area for more than 50 years. He reflected in 2020 on what happened with the Royal Hospital.

"Tesco bought the Royal Hospital site, and then they backed out. It has been fenced off for a long time. They've stripped all the inside out right down to bare wall, put new windows in, put a new roof on it and then boarded it up. That was supposed to be the new £60M Tesco supermarket. They also bought the adjacent bus depot to stop somebody else building on it, that's all. They didn't want competition directly opposite - the old St George's Church was Sainsbury's - and they didn't want them moving into the bus depot. So, they bought it up. ASAN approached them, and they agreed for it to be used as an indoor car park, and all the money out of that went to ASAN next door."

The ongoing saga of the Royal Hospital site attracted the attention of the national newspapers. The Guardian newspaper article from 2015 provided another insight into the series of events following the closure of the Royal Hospital in 1997.

"Tesco bought the hospital site in 2000 and promised a huge regeneration scheme that would also include other shops, offices and community facilities. But they soon locked horns with Sainsbury's over another site in the city, and their plans fell into inertia. As far back as 2007, rumours begin to circulate that they would not be building the scheme after all - though at the start of 2014 the local Labour MP, Pat McFadden, received assurances everything would go ahead.

All Saints: The History, People, Places

The Royal Hospital - or what remains of it - is the main landmark in an area known as All Saints, Wolverhampton's red-light district, named after the church, that looks out onto the hospital site. For the last eight years, its vicar has been Sarah Schofield, a thoughtful and passionate emigree from Manchester, who was hurled into the Tesco story as soon as she took her current job. She talks about what Tesco has - or, rather, hasn't - done in terms of poor ethics, and 'total neglect'.

'The children who were born the year Tesco took on the site are now starting their GCSEs,' she says. 'That, to me, is a frightening fact.' Schofield went along with the idea that, on balance, Tesco's arrival would be a good thing: 'Decent jobs … and cheap, fresh vegetables.' But around four years ago, she says, she began to lose faith. 'Tesco sacked their PR company then,' she says. And I thought: 'If you've not got a PR operation, you're obviously not planning to open any time soon. But their line was always, It's about to happen. There's a line in the Anglican liturgy: The hope of glory to come. It was like that.' As time went on, she says, the mood of the All Saints neighbourhood came to be defined by the empty expanse of land at its heart.

'After a while, people lose any sense of confidence in their own power,' she says. 'You can't get people to take an interest in how to effect change, because they've seen a case study in how not to effect change. Involvement in local politics is fairly poor, you don't get residents' groups…'

Tesco's current line on Wolverhampton is that, despite its withdrawal, 'all parties are committed to bringing forward the development of the site as soon as possible and engaging with the local community throughout this process', and 'at the first available opportunity the company will update the local community on progress and the potential viable uses for the site'.

Schofield translates this crisply. 'I think it'll sit as it is, for another few years,' she says.'"

The outcome of some of these projects is covered in the final chapter, 'The Regeneration of All Saints'.

12

THE REGENERATION OF ALL SAINTS

While the aims of the 2010-2014 Local Investment Plan were admirable, they appeared on paper to focus on housing projects. It is not clear whether they addressed the ongoing impact of prostitution and kerb-crawling: an underlying problem which blighted the neighbourhood, dented its reputation and hampered its regeneration. In July 2013, one of the local ward councillors is quoted in the Express and Star: "Everyone is concerned about this [kerb-crawling], as All Saints, in particular, is a hotspot for this kind of activity… It has been going on for many years and police are doing everything they can after residents have raised fears about it."

While it would be easy to claim that All Saints has continued to drift in a downward spiral. In many respects that statement would be both undeserved and inaccurate. This chapter records many of the area's developments that signal a brighter future for All Saints.

HOUSING

A number of the improvements relating to the projects listed in the Council's Local Investment Plan for 2010-2014 are nearing completion.

THE ROYAL HOSPITAL

Sarah Schofield's prediction from 2015 proved correct and the All Saints community waited another five years for the next chapter in this tedious saga. …but it was to involve neither Tesco nor retail outlets.

In 2016, the Homes and Community Agency (HCA) bought the site from Tesco. In February 2020, Jessup, a Cannock-based company, was awarded the contract for the redevelopment of the Wolverhampton Royal Hospital site by Homes England (HE).

Plans announced in May 2021, clarify the details. It will see the main hospital building converted into a wellbeing scheme for the over-55s, made up of 38 one and two-bedroom apartments. On the land behind the hospital, a further 123 flats will be built for affordable rent and 31 for shared ownership. The planned completion date is 2024. Jessup will be working on the project in partnership with whg, a leading local housing association.

Following the outbreak of the war in Ukraine in March 2022, plans were submitted in April to convert the former porter's lodge into accommodation to house refugees. If the plans are given the go-ahead by the city council, this accommodation would be temporary for two years.

In March 2023, the Express and Star announced that the first 12 of the 192 homes to be built on the site have been completed.

WOLVERHAMPTON BUS DEPOT

Jessup and whg are also involved in a redevelopment of the former bus depot site at Cleveland Road, in front of the Royal Hospital. In December 2020, the Express and Star reported that nearly £1M had been handed to the YMCA Black Country Group Charity to help them complete the regeneration project at the old bus depot.

The project, dubbed the YMCA Cleveland Road City Gateway, will aim to transform the area. The facilities will include:

- 63 'City-living' studios/apartments for young professionals/ workers;
- 115 place Day Nursery for local families and city working families;
- community training area providing Learning and Skills programmes;
- commercial/ retail units for local services;
- YMCA Administrative HQ for YMCA operations across the Black Country.

GRANVILLE STREET/ GORDON STREET

While the scale of the new housing developments in All Saints may not satisfy everyone's expectations, a visit to Granville Street in late 2022 reveals that the landscape is changing in a positive manner. The aim in the Local Investment Plan of 2010-2014 to build high quality private housing and affordable homes in the area is being addressed.

An impressive development of four bedroom freehold town houses now occupies a new extension of Granville Street. In the 1980s, the derelict land in Gordon Street was described by an ex-resident as a "no-go area" for the children on All Saints. Now, this area is being enhanced by a smart development of town and semi-detached housing, nearing completion in September 2022.

Gordon Street, looking up towards Vicarage Road, in September 2022.

RABY STREET

In the bottom half of Raby Street, by Vicarage Road, most of the houses had been used as drug dens and brothels. Following their demolition, an impressive new housing development has been built by Keepmoat.

ASAN, and Mike Swain in particular, had been actively involved with the City Council on this project. It recognised his huge contribution to the local community by naming one of the roads, Mike Swain Drive.

THE SAINTS QUARTER

A major boost for the area has been a new housing development, the Saints Quarter. It borders Steelhouse Lane and Cable Street on part of the old Bayliss, Jones and Bayliss factory complex.

The site, which had been lying derelict for more than a decade, has been brought back to life with a housing development from Lovell Midlands. The homes are aimed at first time buyers and families. The development was not a part of the Council's 2010-2014 plan, and the scheme demonstrates a renewed confidence in the area.

The Saints Quarter will comprise a selection of 151 two-, three- and four-bedroom houses, including 89 open market and 62 affordable homes. As part of the Government Shared Ownership and Affordable Homes Programme 2016-2021, Homes England have partnered with Lovell to support the provision of the affordable housing. The Lovell website in

September 2021 revealed that all the two-, three- and four-bedroom properties had now been sold.

A member of staff from ASAN who visited the development at the time reported: "Half of the houses have already been filled. People from all over the place: London, a girl from New York here, a guy from Zimbabwe… so the people coming into the new estate are from very diverse backgrounds."

Beverley Momenabadi, Labour Councillor for Ettingshall Ward, has visited 'show homes' in these new housing developments.

"I noticed a change in the type of houses that are being built. Some of them have solar panels and electric car charging points. This will attract residents who have a commitment to the green agenda. In an area like All Saints where issues such as fly-tipping have been prevalent, this sprinkle of environmental consciousness seems like it's just what the area needs."

COMMUNITY

ALL SAINTS CHURCH

Phil and Gill Collins gratefully acknowledge the positive impact that Sarah Schofield made during her twelve years as vicar at All Saints Church.

"… they [the Diocese] did come round a couple of years back. A lot of the churches were closing. They were just seeing if it was viable to keep them open, but at the time Sarah was here. She did a lot here. She had a lot of activities going on. We used to have a craft club, knitting. Come in on a Wednesday, have a cup of tea. There was a 'knitters and natters corner'. They would have closed this down if it was just people coming in on a Sunday morning from quarter past eleven to half past twelve. It might have closed and become an Indian temple; you don't know.

As far as I know, she went on to be the chaplain at the University when she left here. Her replacement to run this church and St John's in the Square was Amanda Richards-Pike."

The area set aside for worship is now compressed into the chancel section of the original building. Many of the impressive stained-glass windows which once adorned it have disappeared, and its imposing array of solid oak pews has been replaced by modern chairs. While one celebrates the continued presence of the church, the innovations that have been introduced and the support from ASAN, there is ongoing cause for concern. The church building still faces expensive repairs. The last wedding to be celebrated there was in 2017. Gill and Phil Collins have highlighted dwindling congregations which are now in single figures. The Church Hall where two generations of All Saints pupils went to Sunday School was demolished long ago.

On 25 April 2021, the following message appeared on Facebook: "Today was vicar Amanda's last service at All Saints Church, wishing you every success in your new parish..."

A new appointment was delayed but there was brighter news in January 2023. When we contacted the Rev. Prebend David Wright, the Team Rector for the Parish of Central Wolverhampton, to enquire about Amanda's successor, Deborah Castle, Church Warden for St Peter's replied:

"All Saints is being looked after pastorally by a team from St Chad and St Mark. The priest there is Rev. Ray Gaston but services are usually led by Rev. Helen Babiy or Rev. Valerie Fairclough. The future of all churches in the Wolverhampton Deanery is under review."

However one interprets this statement, All Saints Church which once played such a central part in the life of All Saints School and its surrounding community is now just a shell, both in structure and function, of what it once was. To many in the neighbourhood, it has seemingly outlived the community it once served.

ALL SAINTS ACTION NETWORK (ASAN)

ASAN has now established a prominent role for itself in the neighbourhood. Located less than a mile from the city centre, The Workspace complex in 2021 was home to twelve organisations and enterprises promoting the benefits of 'out of city' accommodation. They have tapped into the high quality, secure space; free Wi-Fi; manned reception and extensive free parking.

Many have been tenants for five years or more. Their presence has enabled the organisation to be financially sustainable and created local employment and volunteering opportunities. The day nursery is nearly full, with residents benefitting from excellent childcare which contributes to ASAN's charitable activities.

ASAN takes pride in being a key catalyst for change in All Saints. It worked with the City Council on proposals for their Local Investment Plan, 2010-2014. The new design plans for the Community Centre, mentioned later, have been drawn up with ASAN's support. It has also helped to develop enterprises that will deliver a positive social impact. One such innovative business is 'Wood Saints', a wood recycling and re-use firm.

A 10,000 sq. ft empty industrial unit in Dixon Street has been transformed over six months into a dedicated wood depot. The building, shown above, features a wood storage area, workshop and a retail outlet that stocks ironmongery and products made from the re-used material.

Their mission is to reduce waste going to landfill and to create jobs for local people. Wood waste collected from all over the Black Country is gathered and sorted. It is reused to make quality furniture and bespoke pieces for home, businesses and community organisations: anything from tables in bars to eco-gardens in schools. On 20 March 2018, it was officially opened by local entrepreneur and TV presenter of 'The Repair Shop', Jay Blades; the Deputy Mayor of Wolverhampton, Phil Page, and thirty delegates.

Since 2016, ASAN has been working on a project to convert the former porters' lodge at the Royal Hospital building into a community café. Although the City Council is still to give the go-ahead for the plans, ASAN's record of securing grants is impressive. It is one of three organisations in the West Midlands that have recently received funding under the West Midlands Combined Authority's Green Grant Scheme. The aim of the £725K scheme is to help poorer communities improve their existing open spaces and enhance the local environment. ASAN will receive over £20,000 to transform an unused car park into a family playground which will also include a wildlife pond and habitat and bird boxes to increase biodiversity.

The contentious subject of the All Saints Community Centre was discussed earlier. A further transformation involving ASAN is hopefully in the pipeline. It has invited an architect company from Birmingham to prepare a feasibility study for re-modelling the existing Community Centre. The aim is to make more effective use of the space to convert the building into a sustainable community hub that will contribute towards the regeneration of the neighbourhood. If approved, the new layout will incorporate a café, training and community rooms on the lower floors and additional office space above. A recent enquiry revealed that the company awaits instructions to take the project further.

GROVE PRIMARY SCHOOL

The switch to an academy school has undoubtedly brought about positive outcomes. The overall effectiveness of the school was reported as 'Good' following a two day Ofsted inspection in November 2018. The key findings included praise for the headteacher, well supported by the leadership team, which "has improved the school considerably since it became an academy in 2016".

At the time of the report, it was described as a mixed school covering the age range of 3-11 with 457 pupils on its roll, significantly up on the 320 who were there during the highly critical 2015 inspection. Pupils continued to come from a wide range of ethnic backgrounds and 'only' 9% were White British. Three quarters of pupils spoke English as an additional language.

TRANSPORT: THE METRO

While All Saints is still served by a bus route along Steelhouse Lane, residents now find themselves in a favourable position for using the West Midlands Metro transport system. They can make their way to the terminus at St George's in the city centre or to The Royal stop opposite the Renault garage in Bilston Road.

The marketing material for the Saints Quarter development emphasises this point: "… its central location which is just an eight-minute walk away from the Royals metro stop service, offering regular services into Wolverhampton, Grand Central Birmingham, West Bromwich and Wednesbury".

INDUSTRY

JAMES BAKER'S BOOT FACTORY

The family business was taken over and by the early '70s the production of shoes and boots had come to an end. The factory remained open occupied by a variety of businesses. In 1995 the building was given Grade II listing. A grant for major restoration was finally obtained in 2007 and the subsequent building work has created alternative use for the property. Baker's Shoe and Boot Factory, now known as The Boot Factory, provides commercial space for about 12 units.

One business which occupied the building until recently was The LearnPlay Foundation Ltd., a creative digital media agency as well as an apprenticeship and short-course provider. It relocated from Sandwell in 2016. There were no financial incentives to set up the business in Cleveland Road but Ro Hands, its Managing Director, was attracted by "a beautiful building with its original beams and courtyard". She was also drawn by the location with its proximity to the Metro and mainline railway stations as well as the city's ring road. The business has moved in the last few months to a city centre site. A lack of parking and a dreadfully high rent for a business which is 'not for profit' with charitable aims were two considerations in making their decision. A key factor was the quality of the internet connection which proved inadequate for meeting their business demands.

Ro understands that the building's management agency has attracted new organisations to replace them. She would not necessarily recommend the factory to any business which is highly dependent on the internet. Any attempt to improve the internet's connectivity will be difficult because of the planning restrictions imposed by its listed building status. She still has great fondness for the building which she sees as ideally suited for artisan businesses with workshops creating products like jewellery and ceramics.

BARR AND GROSVENOR LTD

It is believed the existing building in Jenner Street dates to 1873, when it was occupied by Hyde and Sons, brass founders and finishers. In 1918, the company was taken over by E.P. Jenks and it took his name.

The building is now occupied by Barr and Grosvenor Ltd, a family run, Wolverhampton-based foundry machine shop. As well as manufacturing precision quality products, it is recognised as the largest weights' manufacturer in the UK.

Barr and Grosvenor Ltd is also heavily involved in a wide variety of heritage related projects across the country. These prestigious assignments include the new gates at Derby and Hereford cathedrals and a Royal Marines memorial at Plymouth. A television programme on the Quest channel in November 2021 celebrated its exceptional expertise.

LEISURE

GOWER STREET PLAYGROUND/ ADELAIDE PLAY PARK

A photo taken in 2022 of the Adelaide Play Park looking from Steelhouse Lane towards Gower Street.

The original Gower Street playground occupied a small area of land between Maxwell Road and St Joseph's School. Demolition of houses in Adelaide Street and Granville Street created space for the site to be extended out towards Steelhouse Lane.

The new playground has been named as Adelaide Play Park. In an area of dense terraced housing, the landscaped site provides an attractive open space, with playground facilities and seating for residents to relax.

SOUTHSIDE SPORTS AREA

The Southside Sports Area is managed by ASAN and occupies the site of the old St Joseph's School buildings.

Three astro turf pitches, with LED flood lighting, for 5 a side football are available as well as a large and secure car park. The pitches are claimed to offer the cheapest rates in Wolverhampton and draw in people from the All Saints neighbourhood and from around the city.

RESIDENTS' VIEWPOINT

As one would expect, opinions differ on the All Saints neighbourhood and over the last two years a small number of residents, past and present, have shared their thoughts on the last fifty or so years of changes in All Saints.

Hazel Skeldon was born in Gordon Street in 1970 and lived in the road until 1997. She recalls many happy memories of living in Gordon Street. "If it was a nice night, you would all be on your steps, even if it was just having a cup of tea. When I had my first daughter… I always would sit on the step with my daughter and she would play outside the front. We just knew everybody. All the neighbours would stop and speak to you.

The memories. I wouldn't change it for the world though. I think it makes you who you am, really. Even though I have turned out completely different to my brother and sister, I wouldn't have it any other way… no, I loved the area. You felt like you belonged… and you could sit in the street, leave your door open, and everybody just talked to everybody… but now, no.

It's just, it's just not like it was. Very rare I will walk up to All Saints. A lot of 'undesired' (drug dealers, pimps and men looking for business) still walking up and down there. There's no sense of community, at all, now. You don't know who you are living next to all the time. They're all rented houses: six-month contract, three-month… I would really like to move out of All Saints, out of Parkfields, a bit further out now, definitely. Somewhere like Tettenhall, further out that way, quieter, more fields."

Surjit Bangor is sceptical about the approach that Wolverhampton Council adopted. "To me really, we haven't actually seen that much change. I mean all we've seen is a few houses here, a few there. If they wanted to build new houses, they should have knocked down the old houses, all the old houses... we had the government grant three times to redo the houses, and if that sort of money had been spent to knock everything down, and have the new houses all together, that would have been really nice."

Despite these reservations, Surjit, like many of the older residents, has a more sympathetic view of the community.

"… it's a name, you mention All Saints, and people say: 'You don't live in All Saints, do you?!' But I've lived here for forty-five, fifty years, I don't find anything wrong with All Saints. There were lots and lots of shops and pubs. We like it in Vicarage Road, I don't think we'll move now. First it was our Mom, she never wanted to move from here. I used to get the Express and Star. There were the property pages... and, even by mistake, if I'm looking at it my Mom would say: 'You're not going to move from here, are you? You can't do this while I'm alive!' And now our kids are saying the same to us. I say, 'Chill out... I think we're happy where we are.'"

John Neave, in July 2020, recalled some of the changes he has observed in the last 80 years.

"I remember Sutherland Place, I remember poor kids there running around with no shoes on, in my time… and Portland Place… that was a very quiet place. They'd all got gas lighting. There was this little shop there that used to sell kids bottles of pop for a penny.

They knocked Portland Place down to extend the boiler house of the hospital… a very old part of Wolverhampton that was… Anyway, I was born in Gordon Street and I shall finish in Gordon Street. All my friends are here."

Beverley Momenabadi, Labour Councillor for Ettingshall Ward, passed on her thoughts in February 2021.

"Like many areas, All Saints neighbourhood has its challenges. Some of the communities within All Saints can be transient. I see a big change which is helping the area to transform into one that cements the feeling of community and achieves the Council's vision of a residential environment.

By 2030, I visualise All Saints being a forward-thinking and digitally innovative area of the city."

EPILOGUE

In 1864, Rev. Hampton recalled when "it was not really decent for a woman with any sense of propriety to walk down Steelhouse Lane", a description widely used to illustrate the teething problems of the new All Saints neighbourhood. During the intervening period, school inspectors (1954), vicars (1964,1977), church representatives (1984) and an urban planning agency (2008) amongst others have expressed grave concerns about the area, often in quite brutal terms. Elements of that notoriety still exist today. As recently as 2015, the Guardian newspaper referred to it as "Wolverhampton's red-light district".

In this book, we have identified significant signs of recovery. The redevelopment of the area in and around the old Royal Hospital site will be an outstanding example of urban regeneration. Investment elsewhere by the local authority and private organisations is producing a marked improvement in the fabric of the neighbourhood. Issues remain. The future of a major historical landmark, the Dixon's building in Cleveland Road, continues to be unresolved. Even the survival of All Saints as a parish church is under discussion.

Whether this transformation will be sustainable and achieve the Council's vision of a residential environment remains to be seen. One hopes it will and the community spirit that existed in our childhood during the 1950s will return.

Clive Holes, Derek Mills

APPENDIX

APPENDIX 1

Places of birth as listed in the 1851 Census.

- Wolverhampton and its immediate vicinity (Bilston. Sedgley, Wednesfield, Willenhall, etc): 84
- Birmingham: 8
- Shrewsbury: 1
- Shropshire villages: 35
- Staffordshire villages: 12
- Gloucestershire villages: 5
- Worcestershire villages: 2
- Distant locations (West Wales, Sheffield, Stoke): 5

BACK TO ARTICLE

APPENDIX 2

Places of birth of the All Saints sample.

Place of birth	1891	1901	1911
Wolverhampton	16	38	31
Bilston	1	0	7
Darlaston	0	1	0
Sedgley	4	0	0
West Bromwich	1	2	2
Walsall	1	0	0
Oakengates	0	0	1
Shropshire	1	0	0
Kidderminster	3	1	0
Stafford	2	0	0
Hereford	0	3	0
Worcester	0	1	0
Stoke	0	3	3
Somerset	0	2	0
unknown		(1)	
Total	29	50	44

BACK TO ARTICLE

APPENDIX 3

Employment.

Type of job	1901	1911
Heavy industries		
Mining	0	0
Iron and steel related	5	5
Construction	1	0
Light engineering/ manufacturing		
Bicycle manufacture	3	0
Automotive industry	0	2
Toolmaking	1	3
Turning	1	1
Pump making	1	1
Gas fitter	1	0
Paint and varnish making	1	2
Enamelling	2	0
Boot-making/ fitting	2	4
Other		
Warehousing/ packing	3	1
Deliveryman (milk, post)	1	2
Hospitality/ domestic	1	1

BACK TO ARTICLE

APPENDIX 4

The distribution of ethnic groups to the immediate north (e.g., Maxwell Road and beyond) and south of All Saints Road (e.g., Bowdler Road and beyond) in the Ettingshall ward of Wolverhampton.

(Data from 2011 Census)

Total No. of residents	North	358	
	South	341	
White British	North	77	21.5%
	South	174	51.0%
Polish	North	36	10.0%
	South	11	3.2%
Afro-Caribbean	North	68	19.0%
	South	20	5.9%
Indian or British Indian	North	83	23%
	South	78	22.9%
Pakistani or British Pakistani	North	7	2.0%
	South	9	2,6%
Mixed ethnic: White/ Afro-Caribbean	North	46	12.8%
	South	14	4.1%
Mixed ethnic: White/ Asian	North	3	0.8%
	South	1	0.3%

BACK TO ARTICLE

BIBLIOGRAPHY

MAPS

1750 – Isaac Taylor, map of Wolverhampton.

1775 - Yates. W.A., map of the County of Staffordshire.

1788 - Godson, Plan of the Township of Wolverhampton.

1842 - Wolverhampton Tithe map and schedule.

1850 - Bridgen, plan of the Township of Wolverhampton.

1871 - Steen & Blacket, map of Wolverhampton.

1884 - John Steen, map of Wolverhampton.

1888-91 - Ordnance Survey six inch maps of Wolverhampton and South Staffordshire, first edition.

1901 - Alan Godfrey maps, Wolverhampton (SE).

1902 - Ordnance Survey 2nd edition, 25" (Staffs) 62.10 & 62.11.

1914 - Ordnance Survey 25" edition (Staffs) 62.10 & 62.11.

1937 - Ordnance Survey 25" edition (Staffs) 62.10 & 62.11.

REFERENCES

ABCD Heritage Project: All Saints Trail.

All Saints Women's Resource Centre (1998): 'In Our Own Words'.

Baker N, 1980, Wolverhampton, The Archaeology.

Barnsby G, 1985, A History of Housing in Wolverhampton 1750 to 1975.

Brew Alec (compiler), 1999, Images of England, Ettingshall and Monmore Green.

Greenslade M W & Jenkins J G, 1967, Victoria County History of Staffordshire, Vol. II.

Harris Trevor, editor, Windrush (1948) and The Rivers of Blood (1968): Legacy and Assessment.

Mason F, 1979, The Book of Wolverhampton. The Story of an Industrial Town.

Mills M, 1993, Mapping the Past, Wolverhampton 1577-1986.

Mills & Williams, 1996, The Archive Photo Series: Wolverhampton.

Phillips Lyn, All Saints Church, 1879 -1979.

Redford A, (1964) Labour Migration in England.

Short John, Housing in Britain: The Post-war Experience.

Jon Stobart, Neil Raven, 2005: Towns, Regions and Industries: Urban and Industrial Change in the Midlands, C.1700-1840, Ch. 8:

Smith Peter, 1991, The Fall and Rise of All Saints.

Staffordshire and Stoke-on-Trent Archive Service: Staffordshire County Record Office, D1798/617/124.

Stallard Roy, Royal Hospital: Together We Cared (Video).

Upton C, 1998, History of Wolverhampton.

Walters, Jeremy, 2015, My Father's Wolverhampton 1905-1931.

Watt, Quintin (Ed), 2019, Wolverhampton's Great War 1914-1921.

White Hilary, 1998, Wolverhampton Town Centre Action Area 10: The Archaeology.

White, Hilary, with Wade, Petra, 1997, Wolverhampton Town Centre Action Plan: Archaeology Phase 1

White Hilary, 1997, Archaeology of Wolverhampton: an update.

Wolverhampton Archives and Local Studies Service

Wolverhampton Arts and Heritage Community Panel: The Blakenhall Trail.

Wolverhampton Borough Council: Report on the Declaration of the Steelhouse Lane GIA as a Housing Action Area (1975).

Wolverhampton BC: Registers of bomb damage 1940-42.

Wolverhampton Chronicle

Wolverhampton City Council, Penn Road (Graiseley) Conservation Area Appraisal.

Wolverhampton City Council, Cleveland Road Conservation Area Designation Report: Fellows Street (Blakenhall) Conservation Area, Detailed Appraisal.

Wolverhampton Express and Star.

Wolverhampton Industrial Development Association, 1936, Book of Wolverhampton.

Wolverhampton Society: Wolverhampton's Great War 1914-1921, Ed. Quintin Watt.

OTHER SOURCES

All Saints and Blakenhall Development (ABCD) Area, Detailed Historic Landscape Characterisation: https://www.scribd.com/document/17744714/All-Saints-and-Blakenhall-Wolverhapton#

A Brief Guide to All Saints Church by Martin Rispin: http://www.historywebsite.co.uk/articles/AllSaints/Church.htm

Ben Owen interview at the Imperial War Museum: https://www.iwm.org.uk/collections/item/object/80012665

Black Country Core Strategy, Appendix 2: Detailed Proposals for Regeneration Corridors and Strategic Centres (2011): http://www.wolverhampton.gov.uk/CHttpHandler.ashx?id=1493&p=0

Black Country History: http://blackcountryhistory.org

The British Newspaper Archive: http://www.britishnewspaperarchive.co.uk/

Church numbers in last 30 years: https://www.theguardian.com/commentisfree/2021/oct/26/the-guardian-view-on-the-church-of-england-the-numbers-are-not-adding-up

Cyril Kieft: http://500race.org/people/cyril-kieft/

http://500race.org/cyril-kieft-1912-2004/

Dinner for WW1 Prisoners Of War: https://www.longlongtrail.co.uk/soldiers/how-to-research-a-soldier/records-of-british-prisoners-of-war-1914-1918/

Education Act (1870): http://www.parliament.uk/about/living-heritage/transformingsociety/livinglearning/school/overview/1870educationact/

Education in England: http://www.educationengland.org.uk/documents/acts/1918-education-act.html

Express and Star Photo Archives: https://photo-archive.expressandstar.co.uk/

The Free Library: http://www.thefreelibrary.com

Grace's Guide: https://www.gracesguide.co.uk/Category:Town_-_Wolverhampton

Historic England: https://historicengland.org.uk

Hitchmough's Black Country Pubs: https://www.longpull.co.uk/downloads.html

John Barker and Cleveland House: https://landedfamilies.blogspot.com/2019/07/385-barker-of-albrighton-hall.html

John Ireland, Wolves Chairman: https://www.wolvesheroes.com/2009/08/23/ireland-a-myth-laid-to-rest/

Lost Wolverhampton: https://lostwolverhampton.co.uk/

Office for National Statistics: https://www.ukcensusdata.com/ettingshall-e00052792#sthash.BqM1GliL.LPuQGe5Z.dpbs

https://www.ukcensusdata.com/ettingshall-e00053153#sthash.sla5ulHc.2tbPXVFz.dpbs

Schools and Immigrant Numbers: http://www.educationengland.org.uk/documents/des/survey13.html

Staffordshire General and Commercial Directory 1818: http://specialcollections.le.ac.uk/cdm/ref/collection/p16445coll4/id/339965

Wolverhampton History and Heritage Society: http://www.historywebsite.co.uk/articles/ww1/war.htm

Wolverhampton Society website:
https://wolverhamptonsociety.com/

Wolverhampton City Council and Homes and Communities Agency (HCA) LOCAL INVESTMENT PLAN July 2010-2014 August 2010:

https://wolverhampton.moderngov.co.uk/documents/s15442/CC%2010.7%20Wolverhampton%20Local%20Investment%20Plan.pdf

Wolves Heroes website:
https://www.wolvesheroes.com/2020/08/29/another-sad-loss/

Wood Saints:
https://bdaily.co.uk/articles/2018/03/21/upcycling-tv-star-opens-wood-saints-in-wolverhampton

The Workhouse:
http://www.workhouses.org.uk/Wolverhampton/

YMCA 'City Gateway: https://www.ymcabc.org.uk/ymca-city-gateway/

THE AUTHORS

Derek Mills (Left), Clive Holes (Right)

After All Saints Junior School, Clive attended High Arcal Grammar School, Sedgley and then did an Honours degree in Arabic and Turkish at Cambridge University.

He spent twelve years working in the Middle East and South-East Asia on educational development projects and took time out to do a PhD in Linguistics back in Cambridge. For the last thirty years of his working life until he retired in 2014, he was an academic at various universities: Salford, Cambridge and finally, from 1997, Oxford, as Professor for the Study of the Contemporary Arab World. He was elected a Fellow of the British Academy in 2002.

Following A' levels at Wolverhampton Grammar School and an Honours degree course in Life Sciences at Liverpool University, Derek spent most of his working life as a Science/Biology teacher at schools in Leicestershire and Walsall.

While teaching in Walsall, he was awarded a Master of Education degree at Keele University.

A career change in 2002 led to work with the British Computer Society where he collaborated with disability agencies to develop accessibility guidelines and inclusive examinations for Information Technology qualifications in the UK.

ACKNOWLEDGEMENTS

The book includes recollections and photographs that several individuals have kindly shared with us. They each make a significant contribution to our knowledge of the All Saints neighbourhood. We sincerely thank the following for their involvement in this project and apologise profusely to anyone who has been overlooked.

Surjit Bangor

Robbie Bennett

Jim Barrow

Gill and Phil Collins

Ben Davis and the staff at Grove Primary School

Alan Fisher

Eric Gittins

Frank Guest Motor Repairs

Billy Howe

John Neave

Shobha Asar-Paul and the staff at All Saints Action Network

Emma Pursehouse

Jane Seabourne

Hazel Skeldon

June Tildesley (nee Kieft)

Dave Swift

Jeremy Walters

Wolverhampton Archives

Herman Williams

Clive Holes, Derek Mills

Ned Williams

All Saints: The History, People, Places

Printed in Great Britain
by Amazon

25102655R10185